Literary Agents in the Transatlantic Book Trade

By way of a case study of one of the oldest French book agencies, Agence Hoffman, this book analyzes the role played by French literary agents in the importation of US fiction and literature into France in the years following World War II. It sheds light on the material conditions of the circulation of texts across the Atlantic between 1944 and 1955, exploring the fine mechanisms of agents' negotiations which allowed texts, and ideas, to cross borders. Providing comparative insights into the history of publishing in France and in the United States in the immediate aftermath of the war, this book aims at foregrounding the role of the book agent, an all-too-often neglected intermediary in the field of book history. Grounded in archival work conducted both in France and the United States, this study is based on previously unexamined correspondence. Considering the concept of mediation as central in the field of print culture, this book addresses the dearth of scholarship on literary agents on both sides of the Atlantic, and intersects with the current scholarship on transatlantic, international, and transnational cultural and trade networks, as evidenced by the recently emerged field of sociology of translation in Europe.

Cécile Cottenet is Associate Professor in American Studies at Aix-Marseille Université, France.

Studies in Publishing History: Manuscript, Print, Digital
Edited by Ann R. Hawkins and Maura Ives

For a full list of titles in this series, please visit www.routledge.com.

Exploring the intersection of publishing history, book history, and literary and cultural studies, this series supports innovative work on the cultural significance and creative impact of printing and publishing history, including reception, distribution, and translation or adaptation into other media.

Literary Agents in the Transatlantic Book Trade

American Fiction, French Rights, and the Hoffman Agency

Cécile Cottenet

Routledge
Taylor & Francis Group

LONDON AND NEW YORK

First published 2017 by Routledge

2 Park Square, Milton Park, Abingdon, Oxfordshire OX14 4RN

52 Vanderbilt Avenue, New York, NY 10017

Routledge is an imprint of the Taylor & Francis Group, an informa business

First issued in paperback 2019

Copyright © 2017 Taylor & Francis

The right of Cécile Cottenet, (Aix Marseille Univ, LERMA, Aix-en-Provence, France) to be identified as author of this work has been asserted by her in accordance with sections 77 and 78 of the Copyright, Designs and Patents Act 1988.

Library of Congress Cataloging-in-Publication Data
CIP data has been applied for.

ISBN: 978-1-138-67859-0 (hbk)
ISBN: 978-0-367-87875-7 (pbk)

Typeset in Sabon
by codeMantra

Contents

Acknowledgments

I wish to thank my academic institution, Aix-Marseille Université, for granting me a sabbatical leave, and my research center, the LERMA (Laboratoire d'Etudes et de Recherche sur le Monde Anglophone, EA 853), for helping to fund this research. In 2014 I was awarded a Société des Anglicistes de l'Enseignement Supérieur (SAES)/ Association Française d'Etudes Américaines (AFEA) research grant from the two leading French associations of English and American studies, which contributed to the realization of this project.

I am grateful to Ann Donahue, formerly with Ashgate, for her kindness and counsel, Ann Hawkins and Maura Ives, editors of the Ashgate Studies in Publishing History series, who welcomed the project, and to the anonymous reader whose advice helped me to improve this book. The assistance of Alexandra Simmons and Nicole Eno at Taylor & Francis in the production process was invaluable. I wish to thank my editor, Elizabeth Levine, for taking on this project.

For their help in locating rights holders on both sides of the Atlantic, I am grateful to Jean Arcache, chief executive officer of Place des Editeurs, Oliver Bessard-Banquy of Université Michel de Montaigne-Bordeaux 3, Catherine Cho at Curtis Brown Ltd. (London), Lina Granada at Brandt & Hochman Literary Agents, Louise Hilton at the Margaret Herrick Library in Beverly Hills, Michèle Kastner at Editions Benoît Jacob, François Laurent at Univers Poche, Dr Paul M Pearson at the Thomas Merton Center at Bellarmine University, Steven Salpeter at Curtis Brown (New York), Gregory Schwed at Loeb & Loeb LLP, Hitesh Shah, Managing Director at Ed Victor Ltd., and Craig Tenney at Harold Ober Associates.

I thank the staff of the Firestone library at Princeton for helping me to make the most of my explorations of the papers of Charles Scribner's & Sons, Ober & Associates, Brandt & Brandt, Henry Holt, and John Day. I am indebted to Karla M. Nielsen, curator of Literature at the Butler Rare Books and Manuscript Library at Columbia University, who very kindly helped to prepare my visit to research the papers of the Society of Authors' Representatives, and offered advice and suggestions to track down right holders. I extend my sincere thanks to Adrien Hilton, formerly Processing Archivist at the Butler Rare Books and Manuscript

Library at Columbia, for her prior research into the different archival catalogues. James L. West's support in the early stages of the project ultimately led me to write this study in English, which proved slightly more ambitious than I had initially foreseen.

Conducting research in archival repositories is without a doubt one of the great pleasures of my work, and the IMEC (Institut pour la Mémoire de l'Edition Contemporaine) in Caen is definitely a superb repository for any book historian, both for the scope of its collections and its actual site. I am grateful to André Derval, head of collections, for allowing me to explore the Hoffman archive, and to archivist Elisa Martos for her infinite patience in perusing the incomplete catalogue for this archive.

To my colleague and friend Ruth Menzies, many thanks are due for her early editing of the chapters, her—once again—painstaking revision of my commas and dashes. I warmly thank Madeleine C. Hage for her close reading of an early version of the text, and extend my gratitude to Francesca Genesio for her help with the last chapter. Through their assessment of this work, Hélène le Dantec-Lowry, André Kaenel, Anne Olivier-Mellios, Françoise Palleau-Papin, and Jean-Yves Mollier brought an enlightening Franco-American and interdisciplinary perspective that extends across literature, history, and cultural studies. I am especially indebted to Claire Parfait for her erudite suggestions and her revisions; her enthusiasm certainly helped me through the long months of writing.

Last, but certainly not least, I most sincerely wish to thank Georges Hoffman for sharing some of his family's history, and allowing me to conduct research into his father's papers.

Permissions

Many thanks are due to all those persons who graciously authorized me to reproduce extracts from previously unpublished correspondence.

The letters of Michel Hoffman and of Jenny Bradley are reproduced with permission of Georges Hoffman, Director of Agence Hoffman.

The letters of Marcel Duhamel are reproduced with permission of M. and Mme Jean-Pierre Briois.

The letters of Dionys Mascolo are reproduced with permission of Mme Solange Mascolo. Solange Mascolo.

The letters of Robert Esménard are reproduced with permission of Francis Esménard, President of Editions Albin Michel.

The letters of Harold Ober to Nancy Hale are reproduced with permission of Harold Ober Associates Incorporated.

The letters of Sven Nielsen are reproduced with permission of Jean Arcache, President of Place des Editeurs.

The letters of Raymond Chandler are reproduced with permission of Ed Victor Ltd.

The letters of Naomi Burton Stone are reproduced with permission of Ms. Susanna Kendall.

The letters of Sonia K. Chapter are reproduced with permission of Curtis Brown Group Ltd, London, on behalf of Sonia Chapter. Copyright © Sonia Chapter 1945.

Introduction

Jean-Paul Sartre's celebration of American literature and authors in his well-known 1946 *Atlantic Monthly* article has become staple, almost banal, evidence of the Americanization of French literature, and to some extent, of the Americanization of French culture. Nearly two years after the end of the war, the future Nobel laureate, and France's most prominent intellectual and cultural gatekeeper, exclaimed in grandiloquent fashion,

> At once, for thousands of young intellectuals, the American novel took its place, together with jazz and the movies, among the best of the importations from the United States. America became for us the country of Faulkner and Dos Passos, just as it had already been the home of Louis Armstrong, King Vidor, the Blues. The large frescoes of Vidor joined with the passion and violence of *The Sound and the Fury* and *Sanctuary* to compose for us the face of the United States—a face tragic, cruel, and sublime.[1]

What Sartre attempted to show Americans was that French readers' taste for an American literature that generally did not appeal to the larger US public had developed even before World War II, foreshadowing the "American tidal wave which, after the Liberation, was to break upon intellectual France," in the words of translator-cum-scout Maurice-Edgar Coindreau.[2] "The face of the United States" for the French certainly partook of what Claire Bruyère has called "*le prestige de l'étranger.*" Spanning the French literary scene between the 18th and the 20th century, Bruyère has shown how this *prestige* or image induces among writers and publishers different strategies, from rejection to imitation and adaptation, on the part of writers, to translation, on the part of publishers.[3]

Sartre's conclusions tell only part of the story, focusing as they do on the literary dimension of transatlantic cultural currents—the reception of American *literature*, as distinct from fiction, by French *literary* writers and students. In 1948, Howard C. Rice, then director of the US Information Library in Paris, supplemented these views, chiefly couched in terms of taste, with a more material and perhaps trivial account, when he wrote,

> The phrase "*traduit de l'américain*," now generally used, has a definite commercial value to the bookseller. Every publisher dreams of landing another bestseller as profitable as "Gone with the Wind." Publicity frequently uses bait phrases like "this book has sold over two million copies in America . . ."[4]

Rice was hinting at the existence of the transatlantic commerce of books, and the lucrative appeal of French translations from American English. As of 1948 the very distinction between American English and British English in the *Index Translationum,* international bibliographies of translations compiled by the United Nations Educational, Scientific, and Cultural Organization (UNESCO), is indicative of the growing importance of the phenomenon in France and elsewhere. Already by 1946, translations from English—both British and American—made up more than half the total number of translations published in France.

Taste, therefore, was not the only factor in the development of a transatlantic Franco-American book trade. Howard Rice suggested three categories of middlemen and tastemakers who participated in the importation of US fiction and literature into France in the postwar period, namely translators, booksellers, and publishers. They certainly facilitated the crossing of borders—linguistic and cultural—to bring US titles into the hands of French readers, thereby allowing access to a culture that both fascinated the French public and frightened many intellectuals who feared the advent of mass culture. Looking deeper into the workings of these transatlantic crossings, we may distinguish a fourth category of middlemen whose names seem vowed to oblivion: the book agent.

Ever since the 1890s, literary agents have played an increasingly important part in the shaping of the domestic US book trade. As Mary Ann Gillies has shown in her 2007 groundbreaking study of the rise of agents in Britain, literary agents developed conjointly as a result of the multiplication and diversification of book rights which came to characterize the development of an Anglo-American book market. As for the international book trade, it would not have developed as it did in the post–World War II era had it not been for agents working on different continents. Regarding the transatlantic Franco-American book trade, I contend that it rested upon several factors, including the work of pioneering agents such as Michel Hoffman, who in 1934 established what is now the oldest literary agency operating in France. After successively escaping Bolshevism, and the Nazi regime, St-Petersburg-born Hoffman settled in Paris and began to negotiate French rights, especially to Russian and German playwrights and novelists, before becoming one of the leading agents in charge of foreign rights for American and British authors. Acting as co-agent, as most French agents still do, Hoffman mediated between American and British agents, and French publishers; occasionally between American and French publishers. Although reciprocal exchanges were also carried out through these channels, the exporting of American rights to French texts falls outside the scope of this essay, and would warrant a study of its own.

Although not the first historically—this position was then occupied by the Franco-American William A. Bradley agency founded in 1919—the Agence Hoffman was one of the earliest operations, and possibly the first or second largest French literary agency after the Second World War in terms of negotiated titles. In this respect, Hoffman's network-building, negotiating, and business practices may be taken as representative of the very few other French agencies of the period. Building on this case study, this book aims to shed light on the material conditions of the circulation of texts across the Atlantic between the United States and France in the years 1944–1955. It examines the minute mechanics and fine details of the negotiations for French rights conducted by one of the most prominent French co-agents. Looking into routes seldom observed from the transatlantic perspective, which has tended to focus on the English-speaking cultural area and market, I attempt to reinstate agents in their role as mediators in the circulation of texts, but also to rehabilitate them within a print culture scholarship that has so far neglected this specific figure.

The terms "agent" and its corollaries, "co-" and "sub-agent" require definition. Agents can be "unofficial" facilitators, writers, critics, or translators, who, as a friendly service, or sometimes in exchange for a commission, strive to place an author's manuscript with an editor or a publisher, sometimes going as far as offering banking services, in the form of loans . . . as genuine book agents will sometimes extend to authors. Examples of such literary friendships verging on agenting abound in both French and American literary history. As for the official literary profession of agent, it was defined in the mid-1940s in a pamphlet issued by the New York Society of Authors' Representatives. This professional society had been founded in 1928 in New York City, where agents were largely concentrated, to harmonize and improve the practices of the profession through a code of ethics, and "stamp out and overcome pernicious practices."[5] The agent was herein defined as "an author's business representative. He is responsible for all business and many other matters relative to the writer's total literary output."[6] However broad it might be—supplemented in the pamphlet by a list of specific functions performed by agents—this definition nevertheless sums up the common characteristics of the profession. Describing his work in 1965, agent James Oliver Brown wrote,

> The literary agent performs a complex and varied function, which can't be too well defined . . . I'm a business manager-adviser,

coordinator, protector of rights, exploiter of all rights to all writings of the writers I represent, such rights including book, magazine, dramatic, motion picture, radio, television, recording, translation. My important function as an agent is bringing in money for the writer, getting the most money possible in the interests of the writer, from every possible source.[7]

Agents are brokers, as well as legal counsellors. The term "agency" should be understood as referring to structured, established offices, be they single-manned or operating with a large staff. In fact, in an attempt to help distinguish the "legitimate agents" from the "pseudo-agent," in 1949 the Society of Authors' Representatives modified its by-laws and stipulated that membership could be only solicited by agents who could give "satisfactory evidence of the ability to give the full services of a literary agent," and had been established for at least three years.

In France, there are few agents, as understood in the Anglo-American sense of authors' representatives, and even fewer were working in the 1940s and 1950s. As we shall see in the course of this study, the very specificities of French publishing partly explain why the profession never fully developed, although agencies acting as authors' representatives could be found in Paris as early as the 1920s. To state things simply, a French publishing contract automatically grants the publisher secondary rights to the work, contrary to American contracts that distinguish between the different types of rights, leaving the author at liberty to retain secondary rights and ultimately entrust them to an agent. Consequently, the first French agents—and the majority of those still operating today—were co-agents or sub-agents, working as local connections for a foreign party, and not as individual representatives of authors. While some agents use the two terms interchangeably,[8] we might distinguish between co-agents, connections working officially as representatives of foreign agencies, and sub-agents, who work as connections for foreign publishers or authors.[9] Although Michel Hoffman sometimes acted as subagent for American publishers or in some rare instances for US authors, his activities were largely those of co-agent; still, following the French usage, the terms "agent" and "co-agent" will be used alternatively in the following chapters.

As demonstrated by Cold War scholars, the post—World War II period is of particular significance for transatlantic Franco-American cultural exchanges. Before examining the material conditions of the circulation of texts—and of rights, as agents trade in intangible book rights—we need to look at the historical circumstances that affected the material conditions of publishing more generally. Although this study spans some thirty years between the 1930s and the mid-1950s, and delves into the origins of the two biggest French book agencies, its focus is on the years between 1944 and 1955, a period opening at a time when most publishing activities were resuming in France, and ending, symbolically, with the implementation of the Universal Copyright Convention, signaling American publishers' determination to further widen their foreign markets. Contrary to French publishing, Hoffman's activities were brought to a standstill during the war, as he joined the French army and then the Résistance, and resumed in the summer of 1944. In the history of French publishing, 1955 also marks the end of the purges led by the publishing and literary world against those imprints and publishers who were tainted by suspicion of collaborating with the German enemy.[10] In fact, this period offers a fascinating insight into the reorganization and modernization of French publishing, and the growing enthusiasm for US fiction and literature, or the "flooding" of the French market as this phenomenon was being decried by those fearing the taint of mass culture.

Cold War and Cultural Diplomacy scholars have explored this period from a political and ideological perspective; and literary and cultural studies have often noted the rise and influence of American culture on French artists and writers, from Jazz to the importation of the hard-boiled noir detective in fiction and cinema. Still the viewpoint on these cultural transfers has often either reinforced the notion of "cultural imperialism," or served to denounce the "coca-colonization" of Europe, sometimes referring to standard anti-American clichés. I contend that a story of the period remains to be told from the perspective of publishing history, relying on a comparative history of publishing on both sides of the Atlantic. Such a comparison is all the more essential as the 1950s is a period of intensified modernization of publishing in both countries, as exemplified by the first conglomerates, the rise of mass and trade paperbacks, of emblematic series, and for France, of the first book clubs.[11] As Evan Brier suggests, the literary agent is as much a product as a sign of this ongoing modernization—actually going back to the turn of the 20th century for France, and the last quarter of the 19th century in the United States.[12] One of the questions raised here is precisely the extent to which French co-agents contributed to this modernization, and to the reconstruction of publishing after the crisis of World War II which had left the publishing sector in a state of confusion.[13] Not unlike the United States, France had suffered from harsh restrictions and shortages of raw material, especially paper, and publishing activity had to a large extent slowed down during the war, with many small firms actually disappearing by the mid-1940s. Other serious consequences of the German occupation include censorship, of Jewish authors and of any anti-German literature, but also of US and English-language works, and the rampant mistrust in the literary and publishing sphere toward those writers and publishers who might have collaborated with the enemy. The dark years of occupation and French collaboration, as well as the violence of the purges among writers and publishers starting in 1944 have been well documented by Pascal Fouché, Jean-Yves Mollier, Anne Simonin, or more recently by Gisèle Sapiro in *La guerre des écrivains, 1941–1953*.[14] In 2008 Martine Poulain revealed that a form of passive collaboration had also been a most common practice among librarians, not least at the head of the Bibliothèque nationale.[15] Her eye-opening work also underlines, as Noë Richter had already suggested, that French men and women, far from turning away from books and reading, most ardently patronized public libraries during the war.[16] Books, if not *the* book, were then a preoccupation in France during the war, and at the heart of many a conflict. More or less directly, the French "thirst" for American fiction banned by censorship at the hands both of the Germans and of the democratically elected Vichy regime, combined with the slow recovery of French publishing, confirmed American publishers' view that the French market was worth looking into, as they gradually extended their activity on the international scene, forgoing their traditional hesitations. As Beth Luey notes,

> U.S. book publishers had participated in international trade from their beginnings, first as importers of English books, but not until the twentieth century did they become full, and eventually dominant, participants in the world book trade. World War II hastened this process.[17]

Indeed, the war itself had served as catalyst for this new internationalization, as US book exports had for the first time exceeded imports during the conflict.[18] Therefore, the volume of texts, books, and rights exported to France was unprecedented, as compared with the pre-war period.

The choice of 1955 as the end point of this analysis is not merely a historical convenience. As I have suggested, an institutional account of publishing in the 1950s presents major changes in publishing, which ushered forth a new era on both sides of the ocean. On the international level, and on a symbolic one, a step was taken toward the adoption of common principles of international copyright law, which would culminate in the eventual signing of the Berne Convention by the United States in 1989, with the ratification in 1955 of Universal Copyright Convention (1952) by the United States. As Joseph Dubin, Chairman of the Committee on Copyright Law Revision wrote at the time,

> The Universal Copyright Convention . . . is a landmark in the field of copyright law. It creates no new law of copyright, but in harmonizing existing national systems, on a simplified reciprocal national treatment basis . . . [i]t represents a contract, through a plan of copyright, between groups of countries until then radically opposed to one another.[19]

Although the Universal Copyright Convention is generally seen as a vast concession to the United States who were still refusing to join Berne, partly because of its reluctance to adopt the concept of moral rights, it did help to ease things on the international publishing scene, as the United States did eventually waive the infamous manufacturing clause and the required registration for foreign works in the United States. At least, it could help in presenting the United States as a committed actor in the internationalization of the book, and not merely as an obstacle.

Transnationalism and Sociology of Translation

"Transnational literary space," *Weltmarket*, world literature(s), geographies of the book and its mapping, literary networks . . . the recent proliferation of interdisciplinary scholarship using transnationalism and networks as operative concepts in cultural and literary studies attests to the increasing focus on the international circulation of cultural and literary products, and on the ways in which they traverse, or even break open, boundaries.[20] In parallel, the renewed interest in translation and the emerging European field of sociology of translation, and the cultural turn in translation studies, also reflects the emphasis on the potentialities of a trans-border perspective on literary history.

"Transnational" has become a buzzword in academia, sometimes all-too conveniently encompassing what is not exactly transnational. The focus here on the circulation of texts and books between the United States and France, the movement across national, cultural, economic, and financial boundaries, seems to warrant the name "transnational history," yet the distinctions between "transnational," "global," "international," or simply "comparative" history remain hazy.[21] An early practitioner of international history, American historian Akira Iriye outlines some of the clearest distinctions between international and transnational history today:

> International history deals with relations among nations as sovereign entities . . . . Transnational history, in contrast, focuses on cross-national connections, whether through individuals, non-national identities, and non-state actors . . . . The globe is seen as being made up of these communities that establish connections with one another quite apart from interstate relations. International and transnational phenomena may sometimes overlap, but often they come into conflict.[22]

In this perspective, then, this study aims to explain the processes of such cross-national connections through an individual, non-state actor. Still, the nation-state is here maintained as a category of analysis, as I attempt to demonstrate the interconnection between two national narratives of print culture, partly basing my explorations on a comparative approach.

To the transatlantic dimension is here added the parameter of translation, which becomes a cultural and legal issue. True, books in English also circulated in France, as the case of Henry Miller—published in English in Paris—famously attests; yet these are not the focus of this essay. In this regard my position regarding the emerging field of sociology of translation should be clarified, as it has provided entry points to this analysis.

Pascale Casanova's *La République mondiale des lettres* (1999), translated into *The World Republic of Letters* (Harvard University Press, 2004) may be seen as a first foray into the field. Largely applying Pierre Bourdieu's sociology of culture, Casanova examined the consecrating power of translation into French—and translators—upon several works labelled as exemplary of World Literature.[23] Positing that literature has always been a global phenomenon, Casanova offered a new perspective on literature, as opposed to the national histories of literature, basing her analysis on the idea that the history and economy of literature is the history of the struggles for literature as a stake, struggles that actually make world literature. Claiming that Paris has always been the "Greenwich meridian" of literature and regarding the City of Lights as "a universal homeland exempt from all professions of patriotism, a kingdom of literature set up in opposition to the ordinary laws of state, a transnational realm whose sole imperatives are those of art and literature,"[24] Casanova clearly focused on the sole autonomous pole of literature, defined by Bourdieu as escaping economic and political constraints. This in turn might explain why Casanova concentrates almost exclusively on translators and men of letters—Valéry Larbaud or Maurice-Edgar Coindreau—and shuns the economic dimension of literary exchanges, all the while resorting to a commercial metaphor to refer to the cultural mediators, "polyglot, cosmopolitan figures of the world of letters," acting as "foreign exchange brokers, responsible for exporting from one territory to another texts whose literary value they determine by virtue of this very activity."[25] However, in a 2002 article, Casanova did claim that the role of translators will not be fully understood as long as they are not re-inserted into a larger network of mediators and consecrators, including literary agents.[26] This book therefore undertakes to shed light on this specific mediator in the transnational field of publishing, the "foreign text broker," to take up Casanova's metaphor. Moreover, its focus is not merely on the autonomous literary pole, as it takes into consideration the transatlantic transfers of literature, mid-list novels, and pulp fiction, which made up the bulk of Michel Hoffman's French rights contracts.

The influence of Bourdieu's sociology of culture is openly acknowledged, and in fact embraced, by the founders of the sociology of translation.[27] It could be surmised that perhaps the centrality of power relations in this form of sociology, the emphasis on the autonomous pole in the field of cultural production—as well as in the transnational field of cultural exchanges—has so far hindered the in-depth study of literary agents, viewed only as economic mediators and therefore confined within the heteronomous pole.[28] Again, proponents of a bourdieusian sociology of translation such as Gisèle Sapiro and Johann Heilbron, like Casanova, do acknowledge the role of agents in the circulation of translations:

> A sociological approach to translation must therefore take into account several aspects of the conditions of transnational circulation of cultural goods: firstly, the structure of the field of international cultural exchanges; secondly, the type of constraints—political and economic—that influence these exchanges; and thirdly, the agents of intermediation and the processes of importing and receiving in the recipient country. (my emphasis)[29]

Still, so far few proponents of this emerging field have chosen to concentrate on literary agents, choosing rather to lay emphasis on cultural mediators—translators, scholars, critics.[30] Gisèle Sapiro's distinction of three categories of mediators mirrors the nature of the constraints weighing upon the transnational field of translation or publication: she differentiates between the political (translation institutes . . .), the cultural (translators, scholars, or critics), and the economic (publishers and book agents) mediators.[31] Yet Heilbron and Sapiro consider the economic approach as inherently reductive, as it would "consider translated books as commodities," thus occulting the "specificity of cultural goods as well as the modalities specific to their production and marketing."[32] Nevertheless if the transnational field of cultural production cannot be plainly assimilated to the field of international economic exchanges, each having its own internal structure, the dual nature of books as cultural goods and commercial commodities makes it all the more essential for a sociology of translation to connect with the study both of the book market and of international relations. The flows of translations must not only be quantitatively assessed, as they are in this strand of sociology, but should also be considered within the framework of intensified international exchanges, under the effect of globalization. The mechanics of negotiations of book rights must be viewed within the specific field of transatlantic publishing, which presupposes a comparative approach and the consideration of political/ideological and economic/financial constraints.

Print Culture: A Dearth of Scholarship on Agents

In the midst of the current academic enthusiasm for all things global and transnational, it is perhaps not surprising that in 2013 the Society for the History of Authorship, Reading and Publishing (SHARP) chose to hold its annual international conference on "Geographies of the Book." As early as 1958, Lucien Febvre and Henri-Jean Martin's seminal *L'apparition du livre* had pointed the way toward such "geographies" of the book in the modern period, mapping the diffusion of printing in Europe in the modern period, and underlining how the circulation of books was organized first in relation to the general economic and cultural conditions of each country, but also depended on infrastructure and communication networks.[33] Taking their cue from Martin and Febvre several historians have since then focused on the circulation of books and texts, not only from author to reader, but also across political boundaries and nation-states, as illustrated by the works of Robert Darnton and James Raven over the past three decades. In his 1993 essay "Selling Books Across Europe, c. 1450–1800: An Overview," James Raven was already laying out a program for an international history of print, a history of European networks through which circulated both the written word, and ideas:

> Commerce in books, the mechanics of cultural transaction, underpins the ways in which frontiers for the written and printed word, vernacular or otherwise, were both created and breached. It defines communication networks that spread over early modern Europe, either as channels of confrontation or else as a lace of like minds, linking pulpits, lecterns, courts, churches, schoolrooms, libraries and parlours.[34]

In 1999 American book historian Michael Winship called for a shift away from national book histories to a transnational or international focus.[35] By 2008, as demonstrated by Leslie Howsam's historiographical essay, the international turn in print culture had become a reality, as attested by her exploration of the works of Richard Sher, James Raven, or Meredith McGill.[36] GIS (Geographic Information System) technology and state-of-the-art database technology are now being commonly used to map trade routes across Europe, and around the world.[37] Still, most transatlantic studies concentrate on an English-speaking zone, seldom taking into account the issue of translation. Moreover, however attractive maps and routes might be, as in the case of Franco Moretti's challenge to traditional literary history and literary studies, *Graphs, Maps, Trees*, the processes of circulation are not always examined in detail.

Strangely enough, amid the growing interest for international circulation of texts and books, the figure of the book agent has until now received little attention from scholars of print culture. The last volume of the major reference work *Histoire de l'édition française, Le livre concurrencé, 1900–1950*, published in 1986, paved the way for incoming studies on the role of intermediaries participating in the diffusion and circulation of books as commodities, envisaged in a long line going from book-peddlers to modern distribution, as suggested by Alain-Marie Bassy in his conclusion to the volume.[38] In 2008 Sabine Juratic, reflecting on some of the "gray areas" of book history scholarship, also pointed to the role of intermediaries in the commerce of books.[39]

Several interconnected reasons may account for the dearth of scholarship on French agents, both in France and abroad: the very small number of agents, hence the relative scarcity of archival material[40]; the risk of being criticized for a material, economic approach to literature in a country where publishers continue to uphold a 19th century *gentleman publisher* ideal—viewing themselves as cultural guardians performing their role out of a sense of love and duty both to literature and authors, thereby downplaying the business side of their trade[41]; the relative contempt in which book agents are still held by publishers, and possibly by most literary professions, on the French side of the Atlantic. As we have suggested, the very nature of French publishing contracts—the publisher being granted the whole set of rights to a work—partly explains why the profession has never fully developed, although agencies could be found in Paris as early as the 1920s.[42] The opinion on agents held by French publishers, quite reminiscent of US publishers' outcries as expressed in the early part of the 20th century, testifies to the unfavorable context in which agencies were hard put to thrive. Antoine Gallimard's recent reaction to US agent Andrew Wylie's attempted "hostile takeover" of French classic authors is a very good example of French publishers' continued mistrust, and evokes the assumption, expressed around 1906, that the agent is merely a "leech on the author, sucking blood entirely out of proportion to this latter service."[43] Besides a few articles in the trade and mainstream press, French scholarship on this issue remains limited to only a few unpublished academic dissertations.[44]

In the United States and Britain, where the profession was born, developed, and codified,[45] recent scholarship testifies to the importance of these intermediaries. Surprisingly no full-length study was published between James Hepburn's seminal *The Author's Empty Purse & The Rise of the Literary Agent* (1968) and Mary Ann Gillies's *The Professional Literary Agent in Britain, 1880–1920* (2008), but one does find expanded accounts such as James L. West's chapter on agents in *American Authors and the Literary Marketplace Since 1900* (1998) or the passing remarks in Ronald Weber's *Hired Pens* (1997). Still the literature on agents is fragmentary and not always reliable; Gillies has noted that this literature falls mainly into three complementary categories, namely agents' memoirs and accounts,[46] studies of publishing houses or individual authors touching upon author/publisher/agent relations, and more general treatment of several authors[47]; to which might be added some published author/agent correspondences.[48] On co-agents or sub-agents, there remains much to be written.

Approach

My approach is grounded in history and print culture, although it does combine elements from the sociology of culture and of translation. The case study of the Hoffman agency between 1934 and 1955 allows me to reintroduce the figure of the agent into Robert Darnton's model of a communication circuit, as a figure envisioned as both an intermediary and a mediator. Darnton's circuit, presented in his 1982 article "What Is the History of Books?," aimed to provide a model through which to view and understand the "life cycle" of books, "the way books come into being and spread through society,"[49] from author to publisher to printer to bookseller to shipper to reader. He suggested how the production and distribution of the book are affected and influenced by intellectual, political, and economic conjunctures. Interestingly, in his 2007 reassessment of his own model, Darnton underlined the importance of literary agents whose early, 18th century traces he had found in the archives of the Société Typographique de Neuchâtel, pointing out how agents, one aspect of publishing history, were, as far as he could tell, still not quite "assimilated . . . in the history of books."[50]

Bruno Latour's refined definitions of the terms "intermediary" and "mediator" are pertinent here inasmuch as I propose to observe Hoffman within a professional network extending in its most simple dimension between Paris and New York, via London. In *Reassembling the Social: An Introduction to Actor-Network-Theory* (2005), Latour specified how an intermediary differs from a mediator to the extent that the former does not effect transformations, but connects between two poles or groups, whereas mediators generate transformations as they "transform, translate, distort, and modify the meaning or the elements they are supposed to carry."[51] For the moment we may venture that co-agents act as intermediaries when they act as bankers—the focus of the last chapter—while in all matters of negotiations they become mediators compelled to translate, transform, and sometimes modify the elements, or input, they carry. As we shall see, the ability to act as mediator/translator/pedagogue was especially important in an age when publishers and agents on each side of the Atlantic viewed their practices differently, not even taking into consideration the linguistic dimension of these business exchanges. In line with Jordan and Patten's (1995) insistence that mediation was to become a principle figuring in "any new paradigm of publishing history," I believe that the role of "mediating agencies" interposed between author and publisher, or between publisher and publisher, and the question of how these "altered the nature, pace, and results of publishing," are questions no less valid for the 20th century than they are for the 19th century.[52]

Considering book agents as mediators and/or as intermediaries necessarily raises a series of questions, starting with the obvious: What did they mediate? Between whom? How did they mediate? Answering the question of what was mediated requires a distinction between "tangibles" and "intangibles": co-agents essentially trade in rights—here French volume rights—but are also led to circulate the actual material texts and books, as they are invariably asked by publishers to provide examination copies. Finally, agents represent rights holders and act as their fiduciaries, entitled to collect and transfer monies received from these negotiations. As we shall see, this was a not inconsiderable source of problems in the immediate aftermath of the war.

"How" is possibly the central issue in this book, pertaining not only to the means and strategies of mediation, but also the conditions in which such mediations could take place. In fact, this study attempts to take apart the "black box," to clarify the fine mechanisms and workings of the agency. Which competences did Hoffman develop to build up his business and satisfy his partners? What professional networks helped him to start and consolidate his business? What obstacles and difficulties were left to overcome? How, in other terms, did Hoffman participate in the processes and networks that allowed American texts of fiction to cross borders, and in several cases, to become ultimately part and parcel of a French literary corpus? I contend that through the circulation of texts—and of books—agents participate widely in the circulation of ideas and of cultures, in this way moving beyond the scope of mere commercial mediators. In effect, through his contacts with both the US and the French publishing world, Hoffman perhaps contributed to the transmission of a professional business culture, which imperceptibly made its way into French practices, just as French publishing was slowly moving into a modern era, as underlined in volume IV of *Histoire de l'édition française*.

This study is not one of the reception of American fiction in France, but rather, it analyzes the historical, material, and financial conditions and context of negotiations of French rights, that ultimately enabled the realization of cultural transfers—as is particularly eloquent in the case of adaptation of US hardboiled fiction through its publication in various French publishers' series such as "*Série noire*" and "*Un Mystère.*" In other words, I hope to demonstrate *how* exchanges were conducted. Consequently, I have not chosen a quantitative approach, which can be as reductive as a merely economic approach. It should be noted that sources remain unreliable. The *Index Translationum*, a compilation of national bibliographies providing the titles and numbers of books translated in different countries, was begun under the aegis of the Society of Nations in 1932, interrupted in 1940, and was continued by UNESCO in 1948. It would appear to be the best source for a quantitative approach, yet several elements make it difficult to use this source[53]: the distinction between "American English" is not mentioned before 1948, and when it is, several errors in the attribution of the author's origins can be found. Second, annual statistics are difficult to compile, as publishers did not always have the time to list their publications accurately, and several rectifications had to be made each year to include titles published the previous year. A comparison with statistics taken from the *Bibliographie de la France* reveals disparities that cannot easily be accounted for.[54] Going beyond a mere quantitative approach also allows a glance at unsuccessful, yet eloquent, negotiations for rights.

Finally, the very matter of sources partly explains the scope of this study: Although it is based on extensive archival work, the nature of the archive proved a challenge to the writing of an exhaustive narrative, as the Hoffman archive has not yet been fully inventoried at the *Institut pour la mémoire de l'édition contemporaine* (IMEC) in Caen, and parts of it remained inaccessible at the time of writing.[55] For the biographical details on Michel Hoffman, I am in large part indebted to Georges Hoffman, his youngest son, who agreed to an interview.

Organization of the Book

The book is composed of five chapters, opening with a contextualizing analysis of what can be called the "first globalization" of the book trade, going back to the middle of the 19th century, and spanning the years between the adoption of the Berne Convention in 1886, and the 1930s. Indeed, understanding the beginnings of the Hoffman agency requires an exposition of both the French and American publishing scenes in the early decades of the 20th century, and an account of the French taste for American books prior to the Second World War. As Hoffman's activities were brought to a standstill during the conflict, the second chapter reflects on the immediate aftermath of the war, highlighting both the changes it wrought on French publishing—on material, psychological, and political levels—and the transformations of American publishers' outlook on foreign markets. Indeed, in the first few years following World War II, US publishers and agents literally scrambled for foreign rights, spurred by wartime experiments such as the Overseas and Transatlantic Editions. In the complex ideological and economic situation of French publishing characteristic of the *libération* period, Hoffman and fellow co-agents regularly put their diplomatic skills to the test: while they were asked to find the most adequate matches among French publishers who were not all untainted by the suspicion of collaboration with the German enemy, they also had to contend with disastrous material conditions, and strive to reassure their transatlantic partners by clarifying situations left pending since before the conflict. As publishing both in France and the United States recovered, and as the Cold War began, the transatlantic book trade became of particular interest to US diplomacy which saw books as effective instruments of propaganda (Chapter 3). Indeed, due to the strong Communist influence during and after the Liberation, France represented a particular challenge for US cultural diplomats. This chapter examines how, in a context of increased cultural exchanges between 1946 and 1955, Hoffman developed his professional networks, striving to fulfill his partners' expectations in terms of information gathering and matchmaking, all the while sustaining pressure and facing new forms of competition. Matchmaking and negotiations are the focus of Chapter 4. Which titles and genres did Hoffman negotiate? Which French publishers were most interested in US fiction? What financial terms were offered, and to what extent did French rights contracts differ from US domestic contracts? Looking closely at contracts and offers, I propose to show how a set of factors—pressure on the part of American agencies, French taste and demand, international demand, and the "bestselling effect"—combined to either facilitate or complexify agents' activities. Ultimately, this chapter emphasizes the role of co-agents in the delicate negotiation of advances, royalty scales, and in the supervision of the quality and faithfulness of translations. As the concluding chapter demonstrates, sticking points often slowed or stalled negotiations; because agents are not only diplomats of sorts, but also brokers and fiduciaries, money remained a central issue both during negotiations and after the contract had been signed. Chapter 5 highlights how money proved both a lubricant and a cause of frictions: Delay in the remittance of statements and of payment was a recurrent source of complaint among US agents and publishers. Ultimately French publishers' idiosyncrasies, combined with the difficult economic situation and the country's choice of monetary policies, contributed to the transatlantic divide which Hoffman strove to bridge.

Notes

1 Jean-Paul Sartre, "American Novelists in French Eyes," *Atlantic Monthly* 78, no. 2 (August 1946): 114.
2 Maurice-Edgar Coindreau, "William Faulkner in France," *Yale French Studies* no. 10, "French American Literary Relationships" (1952): 85.
3 Claire Bruyère, "Du prestige de l'étranger en littérature," *Cahiers Charles V, "Le livre et l'édition dans le monde anglophone"*, ed. Marie-Françoise Cachin, Claire Parfait, 32 (December 2002), 195–219.
4 Howard Crosby Rice, "Seeing Ourselves as the French See Us," *The French Review* 21, no. 6 (May 1948): 438.
5 Certificate of Incorporation of the Incorporated Society of Authors' Representatives, May 3, 1928. Society of Authors' Representatives Records, 1939–1991—MS #1173—BOX 1MS COLL SAR—Folder By-laws IV.
6 Society of Authors Representatives, undated [1946?] pamphlet, SAR MS#1173, Box 1.
7 James Oliver Brown, "Literary Agents," *The Writer* (July 1967): 15–17.
8 Paul R. Reynolds, "veteran" American agent and son of Paul Revere Reynolds who founded his agency in 1893, used the term "subagent" in reference to co-agents collaborating with American agents. See Paul R. Reynolds, "Should Every Writer Have an Agent?" *Saturday Review* (January 9, 1965): 75.

9 See the French Center for Publishing Professionals' newsletter, *La lettre de l'asfored,* 5, October-November 2006, online. http://www.asfored.org/newsletter.php?nl=35.

10 On the collaboration of writers and publishers, and on the purges see Pascal Fouché's two-volume *L'Edition française sous l'Occupation, 1940–1944* (Paris: Bibliothèque de Littérature française contemporaine de l'Université Paris 7, 1987); Pascal Fouché, ed., *L'Edition française depuis 1945* (Paris: Editions du Cercle de la librairie, 1998), Jean-Yves Mollier, "L'édition française dans la tourmente de la Seconde Guerre mondiale," *Vingtième Siècle. Revue d'histoire* 4, no. 112 (2011): 127–138 and Mollier, *Édition, presse et pouvoir en France au XXe siècle* (Paris : Fayard, 2008), as well as Gisèle Sapiro, *La guerre des écrivains, 1940–1953* (Paris: Fayard, 1999). For a larger perspective on the purges, see also Herbert Lottman, *The Purge: The Purification of the French Collaborators after World War II* (New York: William Morrow, 1986), Bénédicte Vergez-Chaignon, *Histoire de l'épuration* (Paris: Larousse, 2010), Albrecht Betz, Stefan Martens, *Les Intellectuels et l'Occupation: 1940–1944* (Paris: Editions Autrement, 2004), Marc-Olivier Baruch, ed., *Une poignée de misérables: l'épuration de la société française après la Seconde Guerre mondiale* (Paris: Fayard, 2003).

11 For an overview of the modernization of publishing in the early 1950s, see Henri-Jean Martin, Roger Chartier, and Jean-Pierre Vivet, ed., *Histoire de l'édition française, Tome IV: Le livre concurrencé, 1900–1950* (Paris: Promodis, 1986).

12 Evan Brier, *Novel Marketplace: Mass Culture, the Book Trade, and Postwar American Fiction* (Philadelphia: University of Pennsylvania Press, 2009), 23 and following.

13 See Martin, Chartier, and Vivet, ed., *Histoire de l'édition française, Tome IV,* John Tebbel, *A History of Book Publishing in the United States, Vol IV: The Great Change, 1940–1980* (New York: R.R. Bowker, 1981), and Beth Luey, "The Organization of the Book Publishing Industry," in *A History of the Book in America, vol 5: The Enduring Book, Print Culture in Postwar America,* ed. David Paul Nord, Joan Shelley Rubin, and Michael Schudson (Chapel Hill: University of North Carolina Press, 2009), 29–54.

14 See Anne Simonin, *Les Editions de Minuit, 1942–1955: le devoir d'insoumission* (Paris: IMEC Editions, 1994).

15 Martine Poulain, *Livres pillés, lectures surveillées. Une histoire des bibliothèques françaises sous l'Occupation* (Paris: Gallimard, 2008).

16 Noë Richter, "La lecture publique de 1940 à 1945," in *La vie Culturelle sous Vichy,* edited by Jean-Pierre Rioux, (Paris: Editions Complexe, 1990), 117–135.

17 Luey, "The Organization of the Book Publishing Industry," 30.

18 Ibid., 31.

19 Joseph S. Dubin, "The Universal Copyright Convention," *University of California Law Review* 42 (1954): 89.

20 See Miles Ogborn, and Charles W.J. Withers, *Geographies of the Book* (London: Ashgate, 2010), Robert Fraser and Mary Hammond, ed., *Books without Borders* (Basingstoke: Palgrave Macmillan, 2008), Franco Moretti, *Atlas of the European Novel, 1800–1900* (New York: Verso, 1998), and *Graphs, Maps, Trees* (New York: Verso, 2005), Gisèle Sapiro, Moretti and sociologists of translation Heilbron draw on Immanuel Wallerstein's concept of World Systems developed in the 1970s. For a critique of Moretti and Casanova's conceptions of World Literature, see Pier Paolo Frassinelli and David Watson, "World Literature: A Receding Horizon," in *"Traversing*

Transnationalism; The Horizons of Literary and Cultural Studies, TEX-TXET," ed. Pier Paolo Frassinelli, Ronit Frenkel, and David Watson, *Studies in Comparative Literature* 62 (Amsterdam, New York: Rodopi, 2011), 191–208.

21 For an enlightening international discussion on transnational history, see Christopher A. Bayly, Sven Beckert, Matthew Connelly, Isabel Hofmeyr, Wendy Kozol, and Patricia Seed, "AHR Conversation: on Transnational History," *The American Historical Review*, 111: 5 (December 2006): 1441–1464.

22 Akira Iriye, *Global and Transnational History: The Past, Present, and Future* (Basingstoke: Palgrave Macmillan, 2013), 19.

23 *The World Republic of Letters* is largely based on Casanova's doctoral dissertation in sociology, "L'espace littéraire international" (1997), under the supervision of Pierre Bourdieu.

24 Pascale Casanova, *The World Republic of Letters* (Cambridge, Mass.: Harvard University Press, 2004), 29.

25 Ibid., 21.

26 Pascale Casanova, "Consécration et accumulation de capital littéraire," *Actes de la recherche en sciences sociales*, 144 (September 2002): 17.

27 On the influence of Bourdieu on the "social turn" in translation studies, see Rainier Grutman, " Le virage social dans les études sur la traduction : une rupture sur fond de continuité," in *Carrefours de la sociocritique,* ed. Anthony Glinoer, *Texte*, no. 45–46 (2009): 135–152.

28 Bourdieu's field theory has come under the fire of criticism, if not literal attacks, in the past decade or so. For an overview of some of these critics, see Anthony Glinoer, "De quelques critiques récentes adressées à la science des œuvres de Pierre Bourdieu," COnTEXTES (November 6, 2011), http:// contextes.revues.org/4881. On the excessive focus on the literary field and its limitations, including the potential "entrapment" of the author, see Bernard Lahire, *Franz Kafka. Eléments pour une théorie de la création littéraire* (Paris: La Découverte, 2010).

29 Johann Heilbron and Gisèle Sapiro, "Outline for a sociology of translation. Current issues and future prospects," in *Constructing a Sociology of Translation*, ed. Michaela Wolf and Alexandra Fukari (Amsterdam: John Benjamins Publishing Company, 2007), 95. This essay provides a view of the leading sociologists in this field.

30 Two notable exceptions are Laurent Jeanpierre, who builds on Casanova's conception of Paris as the Greenwich meridian of World Literature and shows the importance of French scholars stationed abroad, as well as the role of translators such as Maurice-Edgar Coindreau, Valéry Larbaud, Victor Jolas in the interwar years; and Giorgio Alberti, in his portrait of book agent Erich Linder, cultural and economic mediator in Italy. See Laurent Jeanpierre, "'Modernisme' américain et espace littéraire français : réseaux et raisons d'un rendez-vous différé," in *L'espace culturel transnational*, ed. Anna Boschetti (Paris: Nouveau monde éditions, 2010), 385–426, and Giorgio Alberti "L'agent littéraire Erich Linder: création, définition et légitimation d'une nouvelle profession dans l'édition italienne après la deuxième guerre mondiale," in *L'espace culturel transnational*, ed. Anna Boschetti, 469–482.

31 Gisèle Sapiro, "Introduction," *Les contradictions de la globalisation éditoriale*, ed. Gisèle Sapiro (Paris: nouveau monde éditions, 2009), 20.

32 Heilbron and Sapiro, "Outline for a sociology of translation," 94.

33 Lucien Febvre, Henri-Jean Martin, *L'apparition du livre* (1958; repr., Paris: Albin Michel, 1999). See also Sabine Juratic, "Commerce et marchés du livre,

vus de Paris, à l'époque moderne," in *50 ans d'histoire du livre: 1958–2008,* ed. Dominique Varry (Lyon: Presses de l'ENSSIB, 2014), 44–61. This collective volume is a tribute to Henri-Jean Martin and outlines his legacy.

34 James Raven, "Selling Books Across Europe, c. 1450–1800: An Overview," *Publishing History* 34 (January 1, 1993): 2.

35 See Michael Winship, "The Transatlantic Book Trade and Anglo-American Culture in the Nineteenth Century," in *Reciprocal Influences; Literary Production, Distribution and Consumption in America*, ed. Steven Kind and Susan S. Williams (Columbus: Ohio State University Press, 1999), 98–122.

36 Leslie Howsam, "What Is the Historiography of Books? Recent Studies in Authorship, Publishing, and Reading in Modern Britain and North America," *The Historical Journal* 51, no. 4 (December 2008): 1089–1101. Howsam comments specifically on Richard Sher's, *The Enlightenment & the Book: Scottish Authors & Their Publishers in Eighteenth-Century Britain, Ireland, & America*, James Raven, *London Booksellers and American Customers: Transatlantic Literary Community and the Charleston Library Society, 1748–1811*, and Meredith McGill, *American Literature and the Culture of Reprinting, 1834–1853.*

37 See the "French Book Trade in Enlightenment Europe" project under the supervision of Simon Burrows and Mark Curran, publicly launched in 2012. It maps the trade of the Société Typographique de Neuchâtel between 1769 and 1794 and tracks the movement of about 4,000 titles across Europe.

38 Alain-Marie Bassy, "Conclusion," in *L'Histoire de l'édition française, Tome IV, 575.* The role of these intermediaries can certainly be conceived as one of the "lacuna" that Roger Chartier and Henri-Jean Martin signaled for future historians to fill; see Roger Chartier, Henri-Jean Martin, "Introduction," *L'Histoire de l'édition française, Tome IV, 8.*

39 Juratic, "Commerce et marchés du livre, vus de Paris, à l'époque moderne," 60.

40 See Pierre Astier, "La France est l'un des derniers pays au monde où il n'y a pas (ou en tout cas très peu) d'agents littéraires," "Portraits d'écrivains (5). Dix questions à l'éditeur et agent littéraire Pierre Astier," June 16, 2006, Congopage [blog], http://www.congopage.com/Portraits-d-ecrivains-5-Dix (accessed May 20, 2014); personal interview with Georges Hoffman, 2014.

41 For a better understanding of the figure of the gentleman-publisher, see Susan Coultrap-McQuin, *Doing Literary Business; American Woman Writers in the Nineteenth Century* (Chapel Hill: University of North Carolina Press, 1990).

42 Voir Marcel Berger, "Souvenirs d'une agence littéraire (1918–1922)," *Toute l'édition*, No 248 (November 3, 1934): 2.

43 Anonymous [Albert Curtis Brown], "'The Commercialism of Literature' and the Literary Agent," *The Bookman* (October 1906) 134.

44 See for example Jennifer Sandler, "Les agents littéraires en France," Mémoire de DEA, Histoire socio-culturelle, under the supervision of Jean-Yves Mollier (Université de Versailles-St Quentin en Yvelines, 2001).

45 David Finkelstein and Alistair McCleery wrote in *An Introduction to Book History* (London: Routledge, 2002) that "The rise of the professional literary agent from the late nineteenth century onward has been described in detail in several works" (95); yet they seem to summon mainly Hepburn (1968) and an early article by Mary Ann Gillies (1993). I thus beg to differ, and maintain that, at least for the "consolidation" phase of the profession, as opposed to the "rise", little is to be found.

46 See Curtis Brown, "Bargaining with Writers," *Harper's Monthly Magazine,* 171 (1935: June/November): 26–35; his memoirs, *Contacts* (New York and London: Harper & Brothers, 1935), and Paul Reynolds, Jr, *The Middle Man*

(New York: William Morrow & Co, 1971), Helen Strauss, *A Talent for Luck, An Autobiography* (New York: Random House, 1979).

47 Hugh Ford, *Published in Paris; L'édition américaine et anglaise à Paris 1920–1939* (1975; repr., Paris: IMEC Editions, 1996) reveals the role played by William A. Bradley in the publication of modernist giants Gertrude Stein and Henry Miller. For reference to British agents, see Peter D. McDonald, *British Literary Culture and Publishing Practice, 1880–1914* (Cambridge: Cambridge University Press, 1997) and David Finkelstein, *The House of Blackwood: Author-Publisher Relations in the Victorian Era* (University Park: Pennsylvania State University Press, 2002).

48 See for example Florian J. Shasky and Susan F. Riggs, ed., *Letters to Elizabeth: A Selection of Letters from John Steinbeck to Elizabeth Otis* (San Francisco: Book Club of California, 1978); or Richard S. Kennedy, ed., *Beyond Love and Loyalty; The Letters of Thomas Wolfe and Elizabeth Nowell* (Chapel Hill and London: University of North Carolina Press, 1983).

49 Robert Darnton, "What Is the History of Books?" in *The Book History Reader*, edited by David Finkelstein, Alistair McCleery (London: Routledge, 2002), 10.

50 Robert Darnton, "What Is the History of Books? Revisited," *Modern Intellectual History* 4:3 (2007): 498–500.

51 Bruno Latour, *Reassembling the Social: An Introduction to Actor-Network-Theory* (Oxford: Oxford University Press, 2005), 38.

52 John O. Jordan and Robert L. Patten, ed., [1995] *Literature in the Marketplace: Nineteenth-Century British Publishing & Reading Practices* (Cambridge: Cambridge University Press, 2003), 12.

53 For an analysis of the problems posed by the *Index translationum* as a source for the study of translations, see Gisèle Sapiro, ed., *Translatio. Le marché de la traduction en France à l'heure de la mondialisation* (Paris: CNRS Editions, 2008).

54 See Jean-Yves Mollier, "Paris capitale éditoriale des mondes étrangers," *Le Paris des étrangers depuis 1945*, ed. Antoine Marès and Pierre Milza (Paris: Publications de la Sorbonne, 1994), 373–394. The statistics presented by Mollier for the number of translations into French, taken from the *Bibliographie de la France,* do not quite tally with the figures of the *Index translationum.*

55 As much of a blessing as this may be for historians who dream of treading (almost) virgin territory, the confusion of a partly organized archive proved daunting. To my regret, a large part of the archive remained inaccessible, in spite of the gracious help of archivists in Caen.

1   Mediators in the Pre-War Transatlantic Market

When Michel Hoffman opened his Paris agency in 1934, the circulation of, and the trade in books between the United States and France were not new. In fact, as several signs attest, an "early globalization" of the book trade had begun developing around the middle of the 19th century: besides the active role of Parisian publishers and booksellers in the distribution of American books in English, advances in copyright law, the implementation of bilateral treaties, and international pressures for the adoption of the Berne Convention (1886), are evidence of cross-Atlantic currents of literature.

Internationalization of the Book Trade

The involvement of the United States in the international book trade throughout the 19th century has been demonstrated, not least by Michael Winship, who, as early as 1999, was calling book historians to shift their focus from the national to the international.[1] Although early book exchanges occurred, primarily between the United States and Britain, evidence of relations with France was also found in customs statistics; still, these were predominantly related to imports from France rather than exports from the United States. Yet cultural and literary transfers between the United States and France predate the Berne Convention, and there is ample evidence of the transfer of serialized fiction between the two countries in the press in the early 1800s—be it the publication of Victor Hugo or Zola in the United States, or that of James Fenimore Cooper or Harriet Beecher Stowe in the French press. As early as the 1780s, English-language books were sold, and also published, in France, by Théophile Barrois, and later on at the Librairie des étrangers. The role played by Galignani—with its bookstore, lending library, newspaper (1814–1895), and publishing activities—is now well established. Nevertheless the vast majority of English-language books published and/or sold in Paris remain those by British authors throughout the 19th century.[2] In the 1930s, the Albatross Modern Continental Library, launched in 1932, was instrumental in introducing US modern and contemporary authors to France, through its selection of titles in English.

Although mostly read by native speakers of English, its high-quality reputation soon made it the ultimate taste-maker for French readers alike. Also established in the 1930s, the English-born, Paris-based publisher Jack Kahane, followed by his son Maurice Girodias during and after the war, also contributed to a large extent to the printing, publishing, and distribution of books in English in the aftermath of World War I. The role of father and son in the dissemination of some of American literature's greatest works, including of course Henry Miller, cannot be overlooked.

The professionalization of the book trade in several countries, the development of international organizations, and the evolutions of international copyright legislation are both evidence of, and transformative forces within the international publishing field and internationalization of the book trade. While internationalization of the art market is generally viewed as a post–World War II phenomenon, the globalization of the book trade started in the first half of the 19th century. The development of American branches for British publishers, and British branches for American imprints, is attested in the 1830s by Saunders & Otley's New York branch in the 1830s, and Wiley and Putnam's pioneering opening of a London branch.[3] The heated debate on "piracy" of British but also French translations in the United States between the 1840s and the end of the 19th century provides other evidence of a transatlantic, mostly Anglo-American trade, as emphasized by Michael Winship. The very notion of "piracy" is debatable, for in the absence of actual international or bilateral copyright agreement, cheap reprinting cannot technically be called as such.[4] It is a well-known fact that prior to the passing of an international copyright act in 1891, many American and British publishers—at least the "best," or rather, those with the most capital—acted according to a set of extralegal rules known as "courtesy of trade," and regularly remunerated authors abroad. Jeffrey Groves explains that this "mutually beneficial agreement between respectable houses" hinged on two principles: whoever bought the rights or advance sheets would thus announce his right to publish to other competitors; whoever published an author was authorized tacitly, "by association," to publish the full works of that author.[5] In 1959 Wallace Putnam Bishop, basing his analysis on several US publishers' cost books and correspondence, demonstrated that many British authors did in fact receive payment from the other side of the Atlantic, although this certainly never amounted to what they would have earned under genuine international copyright legislation. Such was the case for Anthony Trollope, who was paid by Harper & Brothers in spite of their reputation as "harpies" in publishing, Charles Reader, Wilkie Collins, George Eliot, Thomas Hardy, Victor Hugo—who received £750 for *Ninety-three* from Harper & Bros.—or Dickens himself, whom Lea & Carey of Philadelphia had even paid for *The Pickwick Papers* without solicitation.[6] Not only do these facts partly contradict the most vocal lamentations of Charles Dickens,

Thomas Carlyle, or the defenders of Walter Scott—supposedly ruined by American publishing crooks and held up as a symbol of publishers' transatlantic wrongdoings to call for international copyright—they also attest to the organization of a transatlantic trade even before international legislation had been adopted.

The process of the internationalization of the trade in texts and rights is also reflected as early as the mid-19th century by first, the creation of professional organizations of publishers in several countries, including in France that of the Cercle de la Librairie in 1847, or in Switzerland, the Société suisse des libraires et éditeurs in 1849. In 1896 the International Publishers Congress (*Congrès International des Editeurs*), ancestor of the International Publishers Association, convened for the first time for the purpose of proposing measures to protect Berne, in order to rethink, and harmonize their profession, all the while reflecting growing preoccupation with internationalization and the risks entailed.

As for debates and concerns over international copyright standards, expressed as early as the 1830s in the United States, they found the most adequate of settings in the International Literary and Artistic Association presided by none other than Victor Hugo, who was the driving force in the success of the 1886 Berne Convention. As Thomas Loué suggests, the emergence of such vital, and highly organized, professional associations in the last quarter of the 19th century is not surprising, when we consider the parallel developments of publishing in Western countries as exemplary of a transitional phase, spanning the 1880s to the 1930s/1940s, when on the one hand capitalism was taking over, and publishing swiftly incorporating, and on the other, a first "globalization" movement can be traced.[7]

The debates over, and the evolution of international copyright are naturally correlated with the development of an international trade, and hence, of literary agents. The advances in international copyright legislation in the late 19th and turn of the 20th century no doubt both promoted and reflected the development of international book markets.[8] American book manufacturers' reluctance to engage in international multilateralism in terms of copyright, and to join the Berne Convention—which it only ratified over a century after it had first been declared, in 1989—as well as the heated debates among American publishers, authors, and printers between 1837 and 1891, have been well documented.[9] The contest revolved essentially around books in English, and centered on the relations between the United States and England. Although McGill's refined considerations fall outside the scope of this study, her insistence that these debates be viewed in the larger political framework of the American foundational principles, as well as the context of the times, is particularly enlightening. She demonstrates how the fight against international copyright was the reflection of fundamental and original American fears of excessive governmental consolidation.[10] One may distinguish several periods in the debate, going back to the 1830s and 1840s. Examining the context of these decades, Ezra Geenspan has shown that the growth of the domestic and international book trade, and the professionalization of the literary profession combined with the commercialization of books were all factors that fostered the idea that international protection of authors was necessary.[11] Greenspan indicates that the debate was not clearcut, but rather, "a many-sided, many-handed contest between competing interests to determine the definition of the territory on which literary professionalism was to take place in modern America."[12] For the sake of clarifying this complex entanglement, the following explanation may be apt to oversimplify.

Certainly the growing sense of unrestricted reprinting and piracy on both sides of the Atlantic was the spark that lit the debates. Dickens most famously put his case several times, deploring the unjust exploitation of his works at the hands of unscrupulous American publishers, and the well-worn tale of Walter Scott dying bankrupt as a result of such practices circulated widely. According to Bishop, the acts of so-called piracy grew to such an extent in the 1870s and 1880s with the proliferation of cheap libraries that American reprint publishers themselves found they had run out of "publishable" material and were ready to embrace international copyright.[13] In favor of such an act on the American side of the Atlantic, one finds primarily publishers, Putnam among the first, and authors, who felt that they would stand to benefit from such a protection, which would shield them from competition from British books and perhaps allow them to make a living with their pen. Other arguments in favor of international copyright suggested that the waves of cheap reprints of British books had not only delayed the development of a genuine American literature, but that such literature perverted American taste, as it did not carry the Republican values of the nation. In an 1886 letter to the American Copyright League,[14] Philadelphia printer Roger Sherman summed up some of the main arguments against international copyright legislation, by and large reflecting the ideas held by book manufacturers and trade organizations who did not support the American Copyright Association's dedication as it attempted—and failed—to pass a bill eight times between 1868 and 1885. It is striking to note, with McGill, that the terms of the debate were partly couched in the terms of a defense of democracy, as Sherman contended that the interests of a few (some mere 200 people) were being defended against those of 55 million, who in fact benefited greatly from a cheap literature that had no doubt contributed to the intellectual development of the nation. More to the point, Sherman insisted that such an act would in fact benefit only publishers, and threatened to "yield" the US market to British printers and manufacturers. This was the cornerstone that would ultimately lead to the insertion of the manufacturing clause in the 1891 Chace Act, to mollify and protect book manufacturers.

In effect, the passing in 1891 of the international copyright Act or Chace Act in the United States soon proved very different from the extraordinary breakthrough that had been expected on both sides of the Atlantic, although it did go some way toward setting the international standards of rights protection. It is also highly symbolic of the "globalization" of the market for intellectual property.

This Act would only be applicable to works by foreign authors provided their countries of origin could prove reciprocal protection of American literary works, or were members of an international association; the principle of reciprocity was proclaimed by the Chief of the Executive, and the very first country to ask for, and to be granted, this "bilateral agreement" was France.[15] The introduction of the principle of reciprocity, as argued by Horace Ball in 1944, was indicative of the United States' publishers' ulterior purpose, which was "to negotiate or bargain for equal treatment in those countries for American authors."[16]

One of the important conditions, and restrictions, of the Chace Act was the stipulation of national treatment: in order for foreign works to be copyrighted in the United States, foreign authors would have to conform to the same requirements as US citizens, namely the affixation of copyright notice, registration, deposit, and renewal of copyright[17] just as US authors and publishers were to conform to French requirements of *dépôt légal* (copyright deposit), which would ultimately be lifted in France in 1925. Aside from the pettiness of the tax for registering copyright, set at $1 for foreigners, and at half a dollar for US nationals, foreign works were also required to be registered on or before the date of their publication anywhere else in the world, which proved virtually impossible for French authors. Such requirements did not exist for foreign non-national authors in France, and potentially represented obstacles to the spread of French translations in America.

The 1909 revision of the US Copyright Act did not put an end to such formalities. As a matter of fact, it persisted in setting formalities for copyright protection in the United States. The other infamous impediment to international free trade in intellectual property was the so-called Manufacturing clause, or article 3, of the 1891 Act, which required that foreign works be typeset in the United States in order to be protected in the United States. In effect, this concession to the powerful US typesetters was meant to protect the American market from a British "invasion," and was not a deterrent for French works. The importation of books in languages other than English, typeset and manufactured elsewhere, was not prohibited under this article. It could, however, prove problematic for books printed and published in English in Paris. One could argue that the Chace Act, while it protected foreign authors, failed— intentionally—to protect foreign publishers, so that domestic publishing and printing might be favored.

Although it might be conceived as a sign that the US book market was indeed opening, one legitimate question regarding the 1891 Act is whether it in fact had an impact on the US/French book market, perhaps helping to make it more "fluid." By putting an end to, or at least thinning out, the flow of pirated editions of French works observed in the 1870s and 1880s, the Chace Act resulted by the same token in a decrease in the circulation of French literature in the United States, which had appeared in cheap editions, but technically not illegally, on account of the absence of international copyright.[18]

The Chace Act had another, indirect consequence, which was to foster the protection of US authors and of the domestic market. As James L. West has remarked, "Publishers in the United States were encouraged by the Chace Act to cultivate their own territories and resources, and to publish books by their own scientists, historians, philosophers, and fiction-writers."[19] As noted by Michael Winship, high import tariffs in the late 19th century had already done much toward the protection of the domestic market.[20] For a great many years the United States would thus continue to cultivate its authors and domestic market.

The field of international trade of texts and books thus remained far from level, and in fact, was quite asymmetrical. Yet the trade between the United States and France did flourish as of the 1930s, as France pushed for a universal protection of literary and artistic property.

As Eva Hemmungs Wirten and Joseph Dubin noted some 50 years apart, France was certainly one of the key players in the advent of the Berne Convention, and one of the leaders championing the rights of authors and intellectual property. It was also "the undisputed ruler of the bilateral universe,"[21] having concluded some twenty treaties "for reciprocal protection of authors' rights" between 1852 and 1862.[22] For Dubin, the French decree of March 28, 1852, could be "hailed as the broadest recognition of literary and artistic property."[23] As early as the mid-19th century, this decree already protected works published in foreign countries, without any prerequisite of reciprocity of protection, provided simply the works were indeed protected in their country of origin. France was indeed the first country—and one of the largest exporters of copyrights, with England, at the time—to extend protection to works of foreign authors without requiring reciprocal protection. It also allowed foreign publishers to collect monies in France, thereby facilitating the book trade.[24] The only limitation was that works by foreign authors would be protected under the terms of their own country; thus the US duration of copyright would be retained for US works protected in France.

It is by now well established that, although not a signatory member, the United States was able to benefit from Berne through a "back door," namely through the copyrighting of works simultaneously in the United States and in a member country—very often Canada—in order to secure protection in all the member countries, including France. Thus were

American works given a form of protection. In addition to this, US authors were granted protection under either the 1852 decree or the 1891 bilateral agreement. As a matter of fact, the question of which legislation was to apply for the protection of foreign authors in France remained a tricky one until the passing on March 11, 1957, of the *loi sur la propriété littéraire et artistique*, which compiled all the jurisprudence between 1793 and 1957.[25] In 1933, the *Droit d'auteur* bulletin was still debating whether the French assurance of protection given to the United States, and the presidential proclamation, actually constituted a bilateral treaty, and tended to think that the 1852 decree still applied. This entailed the absence of full assimilation of foreign nationals. On the other hand, the US Copyright Office seems to have regarded the 1891 proclamation as an actual bilateral treaty, similar to other such treaties treaties that assured reciprocity of protection for American authors, to counterbalance the continuing self-exclusion from Berne.

In all cases, even the 1891 bilateral "treaty" and the back door to Berne only protected works in English. Protection of the translation of a work under *droit d'auteur*—and subsequently, in the author's own country—was to be secured by the French publisher, or the authors themselves. This was made very explicit in most foreign rights contracts drafted by either US agents or publishers requesting that foreign publishers do their utmost to prevent the translations to "vest in the public domain," by affixing copyright notice to the copies circulated in other countries. Although the United States did not join Berne before 1989, it is interesting to note that one of the first rights to be expressly included as a minimum requirement in the 1886 Convention was the right of translation. As Hemmungs Wirten notes, the fact that this was achieved largely through the agency of the French says something about the way the French have considered translation at least since the late 19th century. The commonly stated divergence is that under the doctrine of copyright, translations are considered as "derivative works," while under the doctrine of droit d'auteur, translation is assimilated to a right of reproduction, and thus it is the author's exclusive right. Venuti also points out that the right of derives in part from moral rights in one's work, which should be construed as the author's "right to object to a distorted treatment of the work which may damage the author's reputation."[26] There should consequently follow from the existence of droit moral in the French droit d'auteur, the point that translation cannot be dissociated from the initial right of publication of a work.

Besides this legal evidence of a deep concern with the internationalization of the book trade, and the nations' will to overcome obstacles to the circulation of ideas, the increasing number of books translated throughout the world, as shown in the *Index Translationum* beginning in 1932, further demonstrates the effects of a pre–World War II "cultural globalization."

Books in Translation

In 1932 the League of Nations began compiling lists of books translated throughout the world, soon followed by general statistics, known as the *Index Translationum*. Such a bibliographic instrument was then considered as contributing to the fair sharing of knowledge, one of the preconditions for world peace, the League of Nation's ultimate goal, and was in fact the only successful project among the League's other endeavors.[27] The compilations were interrupted between 1940 and 1948, and published after the war by United Nations Educational, Scientific, and Cultural Organization (UNESCO). The very fact that a non-governmental, transnational organization would painstakingly compile these lists is evidence of the growing phenomenon of translation and of the intensification of exchanges through and of books throughout the world. However, the *Index Translationum* is problematic, and indeed, not entirely reliable, for several reasons: first, the lists are compiled from national bibliographies that do not all agree on the definition of what constitutes a book (a number of pages, a binding . . .); second, for several years, books that were not published early enough were subsequently included in the following year's lists, or even two years later, which can be most confusing for annual counting. Moreover, categories shifted after the war: while "arts and literature" comprised a category of its own before 1940, after 1946 "arts" and "literature" make up two distinct categories. Ultimately, regarding French statistics, the mention of the original language from which books were translated poses another problem: before 1940, English and "American English" are not distinct, presumably because the bibliographic conventions and contractual discourse did not feature the label "*traduit de l'américain*" before 1945. The dissociation of English and American, as of 1948, in the *Index Translationum* does not preclude a number of errors in the compilations: predictably for the times, Boris Vian's *J'irai cracher sur vos tombes*, published under the pseudonym of Vernon Sullivan, features under the category "*traduit de l'américain*," as Vian had intended.

Taking into account these methodological considerations, it is difficult to make any general and valid assessment regarding the period between 1932 and 1955: The sheer total number of translations published in the world rose in this period by a factor of seven and one half (from 3,208 in 1932 to 24,275 in 1955); yet if we consider the mechanical ratio of translations per country—albeit an absurd variable—we note a drop from 534 translations per country in 1932, to 476 in 1955, the number of countries providing information having increased from 6 to 51. This increase in the number of countries submitting figures from their national bibliographies of translated titles is perhaps most indicative of the importance, symbolically and quantitatively, of translation in the world.

Concerning the United States and France, we should comment upon the discrepancy in the quantity of translations—for all categories—listed between 1932 and 1938: on average, France translated twice as much as the United States. It is difficult to assess the volume of books imported and exported in translation: although we have average estimates of the proportion of books, in translation or not, exported by the United States, Germany, and Great Britain, these do not distinguish translations. Nevertheless the available figures do suggest that the United States was not a key player in the exportation of books and translations before World War II: the proportion of foreign book sales before 1940 averaged 3% to 5% of the total US book production, against approximately a third for Germany, Great Britain, and France.[28] As I shall try to show, the war ultimately transformed this situation, leading US publishers to actively seek out foreign book markets. As David Nimmer wrote, "Even as late as World War II, the United States remained a net importer of copyrighted goods. Since then, however, it has gradually become the principal copyright exporter in the world."[29]

We might argue that the combined lack of language skills on both sides of the Atlantic with an overall ignorance of foreign business practices, as can be surmised from the professional correspondence of the mid-1940s, account in part for the "traditional diffidence" of foreign publishers toward foreign rights markets prior to World War II.[30] Prohibitive prices, and the cost of translation, were potentially additional obstacles, as some US publishers seemed to believe that French publishers were definitely cutting them a rough deal, holding on as they did to the idea of the general richness of America.

The cosmopolitanism of the new and innovative generation of US publishers who had emerged in the 1910s and 1920s, many of them Jewish, and the influence of émigré European publishers in the 1930s—especially German and Eastern European—is well documented.[31] Certainly, both culturally and through networks of close ties with Europe, émigré men and women paved the way for a swift internationalization of the book and rights trade in the post–World War II era. The cosmopolitanism of the Knopfes needs no retelling, and has certainly become part and parcel of the publisher's "legend". As Alfred Knopf recalled in 1948,

> . . . I suspect that before the summer of 1914 few American publishers ever visited the Continent in search of books; when one left London it was to go on holiday. Certainly when in 1921 my wife and I first went to Germany, Denmark, Sweden, and Norway (as well as France), we found that very few if any American publishers had been there before us.[32]

Still, John Tebbel somewhat qualifies this statement, recalling and specifying that "Knopf was hardly the first publisher to go abroad in search of authors (the practice was as old as modern publishing), but he went to places nearly all the others had never thought worthwhile . . . ."[33]

Just as he reaped contracts for European writers—after initially buying sheets outright from British publishers—Knopf was also able to multiply translation contracts for his American authors. Other influent editors, such as Doubleday's Harold S. Latham beginning in 1929, took regular trips to Europe, while other houses relied on scouts to probe the European market, either on a regular basis, as Horace Liveright and Ezra Pound's relations attest, or from time to time.[34] In the 1930s publisher Robert Haas was provided suggestions of French titles—almost all published by Gallimard—by a host of official agents, such as Denyse Clairouin, and unofficial scouts, including André Maurois, or Jacques Porel and Caresse Crosby. The latter was the wife of American expatriate Harry Crosby, with whom she had founded, in Paris, the Black Sun Press, an English-language imprint, which published Kay Boyle, D.H. Lawrence, and James Joyce.[35]

Ultimately, the relations with French literary agencies are further evidence that American publishers were not estranged from the French literary scene, as attested by the Bradleys' relationships, (both business and personal) with the Knopfes, Ben Huebsch of Viking Press, or Cass Canfield of Harper & Brothers.[36]

Seeking to correct a number of erroneous statistics on translations, in 2011 the French historian Blaise Wilfert looked into an as yet relatively neglected bibliography in *La Bibliographie de la France*. For the period 1900–1925, he found that among the forty-four most republished foreign authors in France (i.e., with at least three translated editions), only five were American, lost in a list of mostly British and Russian writers including Dickens—heading the list with fifty-one re-editions—Shakespeare, H.G. Wells, Walter Scott, Conan Doyle, Tolstoy, Dostoievsky, Gorky, or Turgenieff.[37] To be more specific, out of these five, only four were authors of fiction: Edgar Allan Poe, Harriet Beecher Stowe, James Fenimore Cooper, and Mark Twain. Cooper's complete works, in French, were published and re-published eight times between the 1820s and 1870s, by eight different imprints. The gigantic success of Stowe's worldwide bestseller, which presumably inaugurated the beginnings of US cultural exportations, is attested to, if only by the number of translations of *Uncle Tom's Cabin* published in France between 1852 and 1853, no fewer than eleven, which is highlighted by Claire Parfait as an unprecedented phenomenon in 19th-century French publishing.[38] Interestingly, the dialect in both *Uncle Tom's Cabin* and *The Adventures of Huckleberry Finn* did not deter 19th-century French translators, who in fact paid no heed to the differences between "Englishes."[39] The fate of Twain's *Tom Sawyer* is particularly interesting and eloquent of its "internationalization," as its translation into French in the last decades of the 19th century—from a British version—caused it to shift from general literature to children's literature.[40] As Ronald Jenn has demonstrated, Twain's novels seem to have been viewed as quintessentially American. As for Edgar Allan Poe, he had not yet been superseded by Hemingway and Steinbeck in the American Pantheon of US literature since his introduction in France by Charles Baudelaire; indeed, to quote British scholar Marcus Cunliffe's famous quip, the French would come to claim him as their very own "Edgarpo"—much in the way that Faulkner and Hemingway's fames were initially largely attributed to their French reception.[41] Ultimately, Cooper's works would continue to feature among the world's most translated works of all times at least until the mid-1950s, mostly packaged in France as children's adventure literature, sharing the spotlight with, again, Hemingway.[42] In spite of the great number of translations from these authors, to whom we might add Herman Melville, in France, American literature until World War I was relegated to the margins of literature, often published as children's books and/or adapted for children.

As French literary scholar and translator Marc Chénetier remarks, American literature truly and progressively became visible between the two world wars. While scholarly and critical acclaim would soon no longer be limited to the 19th-century Poe-Stowe-Cooper-Twain quartet, "general," non-scholarly readers were exposed to US fiction, comprising 19th-century "classics," modern and modernist writers, as well as a wider range of popular and bestselling fiction. The story of American expatriates in Paris in the 1920s and 1930s and the fascinating networks of the Lost Generation need not be told again, except perhaps to underscore the development of a restricted field for US publishing, in Paris, and the all-too-often neglected role played by William and Jenny Bradley, not only as literary agents but also as hosts of their salon on the Ile Saint-Louis close to Notre Dame. William Bradley briefly served as Gertrude Stein's agent in the United States, and was largely responsible for the American publication of the *Autobiography of Alice B. Toklas* by Harcourt, Brace; more to the point, he also negotiated the contracts for English-language publication in Paris of Charles Henri Ford and Parker Tyler's *The Young and Evil* and Henry Miller's much less confidential, but just as cult, *Tropic of Cancer* with Jack Kahane at Obelisk Press.

Thus as Poe and Stowe slowly faded into the background, in the 1920s translated works of Upton Sinclair, Willa Cather, Sherwood Anderson, and John Dos Passos paved the way for Hemingway, Erskine Caldwell, and Faulkner in the 1930s. Although slightly less prominently celebrated by French scholars of the 1940s, they rubbed elbows in French catalogues and reviews with Theodore Dreiser, Frank Norris, while Van Vechten and Langston Hughes timidly approached with *Spider Boy* (Albin Michel) and *Not Without Laughter* (Editions Rieder). Ultimately, bestsellers, popular or not, were issued by French publishers, once again

illustrating a developing globalization and the emergence of world literature: Cooper was joined by Jack London, scooped by Hachette, whose
yearly multiple publications—five in 1931, four in 1936—demonstrate
his popularity; Sinclair Lewis, the 1930 laureate of the Nobel prize
whose books regularly graced the lists of US bestsellers throughout the
1920s and 1930s, was among the favorites, with as many as twelve different French publishers contracting for his works between 1929 and
1938. Other bestselling fiction jostled with American realism and mod-
ernism in French catalogues, among them the works of James Branch
Cabell (Jurgen, published by Fayard), Fanny Hurst, and Zane Grey, under
the imprint of Tallandier. This brief exposé, suggesting who was being
or was about to be "popularized" in the 1920s and 1930s, validates a
common claim. Implied in Pascale Casanova's conception of Paris as the
"Greenwich Meridian of Literature" is the idea, articulated earlier by
French scholar, critic and translator Marc Chénetier, that the critical,
literary reputations of several US modern authors were indeed launched
by the French: Examples include Faulkner, who was transformed "from
a regional hick writer into a novelist of Nobel stature under the influence
of Maurice-Edgar Coindreau's translation," or Hemingway, Gertrude
Stein, and Henry Miller earning a critical reputation in the United States
by way of "the quality of French critical assessments."[43]

This overview, although incomplete, also suggests that French readers
were already being exposed, as they increasingly would after 1944, to
segments of US lowbrow/popular fiction; after all, French publishers'
selections of titles to be translated were not only guided by distinguished
and highly literary scholars and translators such as Coindreau, André
Maurois or Jean Giono, but also hinged upon very pragmatic business
considerations, namely the sales potential of individual works and
authors. The French scholarly emphasis on US "literature" or, to borrow
from a more recent US classification, "upmarket fiction" has to some
extent concealed part of the 20th-century story of cultural mediation
in the book trade between the United States and France. Certainly the
dominant position of Gallimard within the French publishing field partly
accounts for this situation.

The story of US literature in France between the 1930s and the mid-
1960s often blurs with that of possibly the most prestigious publisher,
and there is no denying the part played by Gallimard in bringing to
French readers, in translation, Faulkner's *Sanctuary* (1933), Hemingway's
Farewell to Arms (1931), Sherwood Anderson's *Winesburg, Ohio* (1927),
Dos Passos' *Manhattan Transfer* (1928), or Erskine Caldwell's *God's
Little Acre* (1936). As will be demonstrated, Coindreau's role as scout for
these texts is well established, and the publisher also benefitted from a
small number of men on its staff—Raymond Queneau, Maurice Sachs—
who were sufficiently proficient in English to read literature in the
original text. Indeed, Gallimard had started developing an international

publishing policy as early as the interwar period: with 368 translations out of 2,200 titles published in 1936, it could rightfully claim that "From the beginning, les Editions de la NRF have considered it their role to apprise the French public of the most characteristic examples of all foreign literatures."[44] By that time, over half the number of foreign titles in Gallimard's catalogue were translations from the English language, with 19% translated from American English.

Nevertheless, a closer look at the interwar period between 1920 and 1939 brings to light a host of publishers who actively participated in the importation of US fiction and literature: from the oldest and largest, established before the mid-19th century—Hachette, established in 1826, Firmin-Didot, with roots in 18th-century printing and typography, Librairie Garnier Frères, Boivin et Cie, who had taken over the business of Librairie Furne and published Mencken's *Prejudices* in 1929—or Stock, whose origins date back to the early 18th century; to younger yet well-established houses such as Fayard, established around the mid-19th century, Flammarion (founded 1875), Albin Michel, Tallandier, Payot, Emile-Paul Frères, all established around 1900. Still more recent publishers such as Editions Bourrelier (1931) or Nouvelles Editions Latines (1928) headed by Fernand Sorlot, whose translation of Fannie Hurst's *Back Street* (1933) was a bestseller, shifted their gaze to the Atlantic.[45] It should be noted that several among these publishers produced series, specialized either in children's literature—Flammarion, Hachette, Fayard—popular literature, or foreign literature, which were perfect outlets for the works of Cooper, London, or Zane Grey. Hachette's re-editions of Jack London in their series "*Les meilleurs romans étrangers*", starting in 1931, after they had bought off all his French rights from Crès, was a fantastic boon for the publisher; Stock's tradition in translation was consolidated when it acquired the rights owned by translator Albert Savine to the "*Bibliothèque cosmopolite*" founded in 1896. In the 1920s, this library was continued under the name "*Cabinet cosmopolite*" by Maurice Delamain and Jacques Boutelleau aka Chardonne in the 1920s, and published Fitzgerald's *Tender Is the Night*, and Pearl Buck's *East Wind, West Wind*.[46] Without a doubt, these publishers, along with other cultural and economic mediators, helped to shape the French field of translation in the 1920s and 1930s.

The examination of texts translated from American English into French in the 1920s and 1930s provides an overview of the French perception of American literature and fiction. French literary tastes shifted from the 19th-century Poe-Stowe-Cooper-Twain "quartet" to modern American writers—William Faulkner, John Dos Passos, Sherwood Anderson, Ernest Hemingway. Yet publishers were not alone in shaping, or re-shaping, French literary appetites; in fact, French co-agents were part of a larger network of mediators and middlemen, which included magazine editors, translators, and scouts.

Mediators and Mediation

A "Who's Who" of French literary and cultural mediators who contributed to making American literature visible to the French in the 1930s would probably open with literary scholar-Princeton professor-translator-cum-literary-agent Edgar-Maurice Coindreau, regional novelist Jean Giono, novelist and translator André Maurois, translators and critics Bernard Faÿ, Eugene Jolas and Victor Llona, the poet Philippe Soupault, Charles Cestre, who was the first Chair of American Literature and History at the Sorbonne from 1927 to 1941, and "king of publishing" Gaston Gallimard. Laurent Jeanpierre's in-depth analysis of the pre-war networks of importers of American modern literature, which holds that this literature was only beginning to emerge visibly in that period, is a convincing attempt at a sociology of cultural mediators, in a Bourdieusian framework. Taking as premise the idea that the importation of cultural goods—here, literature—depends on the positions of the mediators in the field of reception, he demonstrates how there emerged in the pre-war period new types of mediators, who had acquired a new form of cultural capital. More specifically, their mastery of English—far from generalized in France at this time—and cosmopolitanism led them to embrace new aesthetics, and turn more resolutely to modern literature, as opposed to a set of former mediators who held on to more conventional views, which pushed them to promote realist US writers. In this way, already consecrated French author-mediators—such as Giono, Maurois, Drieu la Rochelle, or Kessel—prefaced "realist" writers such as Melville, Hemingway, or Steinbeck, while Malraux introduced Faulkner, and the surrealist Soupault translated Sherwood Anderson, E.E. Cummings, or William Carlos Williams.

Furthermore, Jeanpierre underscores the role played by little modernist reviews: the networks of little reviews, whose editorial boards were often Euro-American and whose members moved from one magazine and one Atlantic shore to the other, were definitely transatlantic. In particular, Jeanpierre points out *Transition*, a review created in 1927 by Eugène Jolas. Publisher Jack Kahane's description in his "memoirs" provides insights into its role:

> Transition was conceived . . . as a means of making known, to such of the public as were interested, the manifold prevalent experiments in the renovation of art forms, much needed and long overdue . . . .
> With many of its theories I am in complete disagreement, but no one can deny the services it has performed, and the extent to which it helped in the establishment of Gertrude Stein's own reputation for one, and James Joyce's for another, as well as having been an encouragement and an inspiration to numerous young writers, whose names but for its existence would probably never have been known.[47]

The fact that Jolas had been born in the United States and lived much of his life in Alsace made him a perfect mediator and intermediary for US literature in France. The list of authors featured in the 27 issues of *Transition*, published between April 1927 and February 1933, would become a publisher's dream—part of Joyce's *Finnegan's Wake*, Gertrude Stein, Hart Crane, Allen Tate, Kay Boyle, William Carlos Williams, or André Breton . . . Nevertheless, the readership for such reviews remained confidential, restricted to those French and American readers who patronized the rue de l'Odéon and its prize institution, Adrienne Monnier and Sylvia Beach's bookshop, Shakespeare and Company, which was also the primary distributor of such little magazines.

Presumably more widely distributed were Victor Llona's translations. Llona, who lived alternately in Paris and in the United States, was one of those rare individuals whose linguistic skills enabled him to translate not only from English but also from Russian into French. Working as Cather's translator for Payot (1924) and Editions du Sagittaire (1925), he also produced the first French translation of *The Great Gatsby* for Kra (1927) and translated and adapted Sherwood Anderson, and Edna Ferber's *Showboat* for Fayard (1931). The 1931 anthology of American texts he edited in French for Denoël—the firm had just been established the year before with the help of an American associate, Bernard Steele—is a compendium of the Franco-American nexus who would contribute so much to the good fortune, and to the mythologizing, of American literature in France: on the American side stood Sherwood Anderson, Louis Bromfield, James Branch Cabell, John Dos Passos, Dreiser, Hemingway, Sinclair Lewis, Ludwig Lewisohn, Jack London, Upton Sinclair, Gertrude Stein, and Glenway Wescott; on the French side of translators and prefacers, were Bernard Faÿ, Régis Michaud, André Maurois, and Maurice-Edgar Coindreau.

The latter are perfect examples of the emergence of a new type of cultural and literary mediator, according to Jeanpierre, scholars and professors whose connections with the United States often came in the form of professorships: Faÿ taught at Columbia and at the University of Iowa, as well as in the Collège de France before his exclusion in 1944 on the grounds of his collaboration with the Vichy régime[48]; Maurois lectured in several universities during his first visit to the United States in 1927, then again in 1930–1931, before his wartime "expatriation" from 1940 to 1946. As for Coindreau, initially trained as a Spanish-language professor, he occupied a position in the French department at Princeton University from 1922 to 1961. The role of Coindreau as translator and "scout"—for Gallimard—is such that in 1948, Sartre famously proclaimed that American literature was, for him, "Coindreau literature," thus suggesting the importance for the French who did not read English, of his excellent translations. In fact Jeanpierre highlights how a third network of cultural mediators emerged within French wartime expatriate circles, supplementing the two networks, one academic and the other *avant-garde*, formed before the war.

This attempt at a sociology of cultural mediators distinguishes the mediators in terms of their functions—translators, prefacers, critics— and strives to identify their positions in the "transnational field" of translation. Jeanpierre reminds us that "the international circulation of texts is" "the result of various operations" at the hands of a "multitude" of actors, such operations shaping a "transnational field" that does not exist empirically, that is, an intermediary space wherein the struggle for acquisition of cultural or symbolic capital is waged between importers of increasingly cosmopolitan status after the war.[49] Influenced, like many French sociologists, by Bourdieu, Jeanpierre alludes to book agents, but sets them apart from the cultural intermediaries who, as in Pascale Casanova's *World Republic of Letters*, are his focus. Indeed, French sociologists classify book agents as commercial intermediaries.[50] Be that as it may, I contend that literary agents actually competed with the great *cosmopolitains* of the 1930s and helped to shape the transnational field of translation.

Viewed from a sociological angle, the field of translation is structured according to three lines or logics: economic, political, and cultural. French sociologist Gisèle Sapiro, who has studied in great detail the con- temporary French field of international translation, acknowledges the preexistence of international exchanges even before the globalization of the book market in the 1960s. While I agree that the cultural and the economic cannot be superimposed or collapsed, I would argue that the book agent—and indeed, book publishers as well—are not *only* com- mercial intermediaries or mediators, inasmuch as the consequences of their actions are cultural. As Mary Ann Gillies demonstrates, if early literary agents helped to transform literary culture between the 1880s and 1920s, they continued to do so in the following decades.[51] By way of selecting, negotiating, transferring, and promoting books to French publishers, agents and co-agents participated in taste-making, and indeed, shaped the culture that was imported from the United States to France. Furthermore, I doubt that 20th-century French publishers would consider themselves as commercial intermediaries, and would much rather prefer to be called "gentlemen of letters," in spite of—or precisely because of—the 19th-century echoes of the term. Conversely, translators do not always act merely as "cultural mediators," as there is evidence that they sometimes serve as commercial middlemen, perform- ing functions very similar to those of book agents, and in fact, in some cases, acting in conjunction *with* agents. Archival evidence shows that in the 1930s, several translators were entrusted by agents with books to "place" with French publishers.

At the turn of the 20th century, the advent of a transatlantic publishing field was made possible thanks to, and was indeed structured by, a host of middlemen moving from American publishers to French editors, publishers and authors, and back to the other side of the Atlantic. In her dissertation on editor and agent Theodore Stanton, focusing on the placing of material in newspapers, Shelley Selina Beal outlines several categories of such middlemen who were already operating in the 1890s, providing a glossary of nine "types": editors; impresarios, theatrical and lecture bureaus; literary agents; manuscript readers; news agencies; newspaper syndicates; publishers' representatives and scouts; story bureaus, brokers, and critics; translators, and writers' associations.[52] I would here like to clarify the definitions and missions of three of these categories who come into play in the transfer of books across the Atlantic.

Beal defines "scouts" as "[i]mportant precursors of other professional middlemen, especially literary agents."[53] While scouts can indeed be viewed as precursors, they also continued to work alongside literary agents—and still do. They act as publishers' representatives, on a salaried or on a commission basis; their role is to spot new talent and recommend authors to be translated or published. As already noted, Ezra Pound scouted for flamboyant US publisher Horace Liveright, and is famous for introducing T.S. Eliot who published *The Waste Land* under the Boni & Liveright imprint; Maurice-Edgar Coindreau certainly acted as scout for Gallimard before the war, benefitting from a fantastic vantage point at Princeton and in Virginia. From scout, Coindreau virtually became Gallimard's agent: by 1945 the French publisher was actually sending him lists of American authors whose French rights they had not been able to acquire, asking if he could possibly help to obtain them.[54]

In his *Chronicles of Barabbas*, published in 1935, US publisher George H. Doran attributed the slow development of agents in America to the very presence and efficiency of publishers' scouts:

> In the United States the literary agent is not quite as all-powerful as in England and for two reasons. The London literary agent extends his activities to cover America. Another reason is that American publishers are much more enterprising in their scout work, that is, men and women from the publishing houses are ever on the alert making direct contacts with authors.[55]

If scouts to a certain extent preceded book agents, they differ from the latter in that they did not all have the same competence or leverage to actually negotiate the acquisition of foreign rights. Scouts—even to this day—might be employed solely to watch foreign markets and report on titles they find potentially interesting. The second, central difference is that scouts are employed by one publisher, and paid a fixed salary, no matter how many titles they actually bring to their employer, and are expected to give their personal opinion on the books, be it laudatory or not.

Agents

Mary Ann Gillies has shown how the emergence and rise of book agents developed in connection with, and in fact helped shape, the debate on literary property, as questions of copyright and international protection were coming ever increasingly to the fore. For British publisher and former agent Michael Joseph, writing in 1925, it was clear that "agents have sprung into being mainly as a result of the development of foreign and other new rights, and of conditions which called for the protection of authors' interests generally."[56] Ten years later, remarking on the changes brought to publishing, Albert Curtis Brown, founder of the eponymous agency, invoked familiar arguments to claim both the need for, and the undeniable presence of agents:

> Successful literary properties now command so many widely varied markets, and such intricate contracts, that the happy owner of such properties would be quite mad to spend the time to muddle through with marketing them himself, knowing nothing of the daily-changing tides and eddies; and the good, kind, old-fashioned publisher who used to take over all of his authors' rights and re-sell at 50 per cent commission such as were outside his province, knows now that he cannot spare the time to look after all these new-found rights for his successful author. That can be done only by someone who has mass-machinery for it, which it no longer pays any one publisher to maintain, except at a commission no author nowadays is disposed to give.[57]

By 1950, the standard Simon & Schuster agreement listed some 22 different rights, ranging from primary rights (trade edition rights, book club, textbook rights . . .) to secondary rights (dramatic, motion picture, radio. . . .). But in the 1880s and 1890s, many authors in Britain continued to sell their copyrights outright, not realizing—or more to the point, not being advised by publishers to consider—the value of distinct, subsidiary rights. The "inventor" of literary agenting, A.P. Watt, had been instrumental, in accord with the British Society of Authors, in advising authors to retain their "outside" or secondary rights, foreseeing the great value of copyrights; by the 1910s authors' complete "ownership" of secondary rights was clearly becoming a standard feature for British and American authors. As for the role of international copyright legislation in the relations between the United States and England, in 1895 it was put forth rather bluntly by Scottish man of letters and founding editor of *The Bookman,* William Robertson Nicoll,

> Another impulse to the literary agency was the Copyright Act with America. Authors who contrived to transact business with their own

publishers at home found themselves utterly confused and baffled when they had to deal with America. They did not know where to take their wares, they could not tell what terms would be reasonable, and, above all, they could not enforce payment. The English literary world still remembers well an American gentleman who made many purchases in this country. He paid very little in advance, as a rule, but his royalties were calculated on the most liberal scale. The result was, as a rule, bitter disappointment . . . . Here the literary agent has proved invaluable, and it is difficult to see how his aid can be dispensed with.[58]

Nicoll went on to remark on the absence of such agencies in the United States by 1895. Indeed, agenting in the United States developed later and at a different pace. While Gillies asserts that by 1914 J.B. Pinker and Albert Curtis Brown had already refined the Watt agenting template in Britain, and that agents "had thoroughly insinuated themselves into the fabric of publishing and literary culture, and in the process so had contributed to a wholesale change in it,"[59] observers of the American publishing scene would have found that difficult to claim, even as late as the 1920s.

Nicoll was thus hard put to name the first American agency, opened three years before by Paul Revere Reynolds. True, as noted by Shelley Beal, Reynolds' early activities remained limited to the representation of British interests, starting with publishers—he had begun as Cassell's representative and scout in New York, before becoming co-agent for the Watt, Pinker, and Curtis Brown agencies of London.[60] Like A.P. Watt who wavered in his early loyalties to authors, it seems that the first US agents functioned primarily as agents' and publishers' representatives, or placed mainly serials on the magazine market; only by the 1920s would they start handling all of an author's literary properties and help build and promote their public image, as J.B. Pinker had done when representing Joseph Conrad. In fact, US and British agents continued to work in close collaboration until World War II.

American publisher Robert Sterling Yard provides a curious explanation for the early American agents' rather limited activities in the transatlantic trade, restricted namely to the placing of British authors' manuscripts in American outlets: in 1913, invoking the US authors' greater business acumen, he concluded that these authors had rather handle their publishing arrangements directly with US publishers, which, to all accounts, British authors could not do, being geographically and physically removed from the American market, and hence their requiring a middleman.[61] At the heart of his argument, however, was not so much his praise of authors, but rather that of US publishers: in short, their honesty and close relations with authors provided ample guarantees against the intrusion of agents. Contrary to many detractors of agents, Sterling Yard was shrewd enough not to play on the publisher's image as "gentleman of letters," fully realizing that the rise of agents was a business matter.

> Consider the author the producing department of a joint business of which the publisher is the selling department, each helping the other for the common benefit and dividing the profits and losses of succeeding ventures covering a series of years on a basis fair to both, and you have the most effective moneymaking possible in publishing. Americans, with their superior business keenness, are quick to see this, which accounts for the superior effectiveness and satisfaction of American publishing relations and the small place the literary agent occupies in them.[62]

By 1938, US literary agents had become "fixtures" in the US publishing world, a status their British counterparts had already reached by the 1910s. In 1912, *The Writers' and Artists' Yearbook* listed sixteen British agents, two "leading" American agencies, Reynolds and Wiener, and no "continental" agency; by 1933, the list featured fourteen US agents, sixteen by 1939. On the other hand the 1927 edition of *Who's Who in Literature?* listed twenty-two American agents. In any case, by 1928, the number of New York book agents with solid business ethics was sufficiently substantial to warrant the incorporation of the New York Society of Authors' Representatives. In 1939, according to the *Yearbook*, leaders included Brandt & Brandt, Curtis Brown, Jacques Chambrun, Carol Hill, Paul Reynolds & Son, Ann Watkins, and Willis Kingsley Wing; only one operated outside of New York City.

Acceptance was slow in coming, with publishers often deploring the meddling of agents in their "friendly" and "harmonious" relation with the author, and logically resenting the middleman when it came to business. In fact, agents' reputations continued to be an object of concern to the agents themselves: in 1928, the Society of Authors' Representatives was organized in order to "stamp out and overcome pernicious practices of authors' representatives" which damaged the image of the serious agent and possibly, to establish a code of business ethics—which would only come about in 1939.[63] Still, by 1935 agents were no longer viewed as the "leeches" and "cankers," destroying the "harmonious relationship between author and publisher."[64] By that time, Albert Curtis Brown could write in his memoirs that "The old days of suspicion and huckstering have mostly vanished as between experienced buyers, and experienced sellers representing the authors."[65] As indeed, in his *Chronicles of Barabbas* (1935), American publisher George H. Doran wrote,

> I have had large dealings with literary agents, and if I had my publishing life to live over again, I would choose, except in isolated instances, to deal with authors through a reputable agent rather

than with the authors direct . . . . An agent, through his knowledge of general publishing conditions and practice, is often able to explain satisfactorily some point in question. Again it is a convenience to a publisher to be able to confer with literary agents and ascertain quickly what books and authors are open for negotiation. On the whole, I feel that the literary agent has been a constructive force in modern publishing.[66]

This assessment gives a partial view of the advantages, gradually recognized by authors and publishers alike, provided by an agent: to the author, legal advice, clarification of contractual points, and in the case of author's agents, reading and editing of manuscripts; to publishers, knowledge of availability of rights. The use of agents in negotiating contracts for American authors outside the domestic market, however, had been acknowledged from early on, even by those who, like Henry Holt in 1905, famously expressed their contempt for the agent, "the parent of most serious abuses . . . a very serious detriment to literature and a leech on the author, sucking blood entirely out of proportion to his later services."[67] This was the very function US agents seem to have performed for some time before taking up the handling of an author's complete works. Of agents' international operations, Holt wrote:

> He has found great uses,—great relatively to the little industries of literature—and great powers. The uses are in finding publishers for new authors, especially authors living away from the literary centres—often steering them away from sharks. [. . . .] Moreover, the agent can be very useful in arranging the business of a few authors popular enough to be published in both serial and book form in England, the United States, Canada, and Australia, and sometimes—occasionally through translations—in other places.[68]

Agents in France

As most American agents had done primarily when establishing their business, French book agents in the 1920s and 1930s acted mostly—and indeed, to this day—as publishers' and agents' agents transacting in foreign rights, named subagents for the first category and co-agents for the second one.[69] Indeed, even today French book trade professionals conclude that there are no literary agents, in the Anglo-American sense of the term (i.e., representatives of authors), in France. The majority of French agencies, concentrated in Paris, work primarily as co-agents for foreign agencies and, what is more, there exists only a handful of agencies in France. This is generally explained, by the very men and women who have chosen this line of work, by the fact that publishing contracts in France do not separate primary rights from secondary or outside rights, and indeed, an author will relinquish, or entrust, the different rights to his work to his publisher, undermining the need for an agent whose role is, precisely, to market these rights as best he can.[70] Georges Hoffman's depiction of this age-old tradition consolidates the image of paternalist publishers, not unlike that of the American gentlemen of letters and gentlemen publishers of the 19th century. In 2014, Antoine Gallimard, head of and heir to possibly the most prestigious French literary house, argued that one of the reasons for the exceptional French situation in regard to agents—i.e., the lack thereof—was the "very privileged relation between publisher and author,"[71] the very relation whom agents were repeatedly accused of breaking . . . This strikes an uncanny echo with the words of renowned editor and publisher Walter Hines Page in his famous "Confession," published in . . . 1905! For Page, the "peculiarly close friendship" between publisher and author was

> . . . . the reason, too, why the "author's agents" seldom succeed in raising the hopes of unsuccessful writers. As soon as a writer and a publisher have come into a personal relation that is naturally profitable and pleasant, a "go-between" has no place. There is no legitimate function for him.[72]

But let us come back to earlier times in France. Although we find traces of early agencies established in the late 1910s, such as the short-lived Agence Littéraire Française begun in 1918, by 1936 the account of a British survey of book agents in the trade magazine *Toute l'édition* noted that this was a "profession still seldom found in our country."[73] As in Britain and the United States before, one of the greatest fears was the absence of any specific requirements for entry into the profession, and of ethics among agents: in 1935 the French trade magazine *Toute l'édition* had reported on the trend of "gangster" middlemen operating in the United States, passing as agents and swindling authors, thereby giving the profession a bad name across the Atlantic.[74] In 1928 *The Writers' and Artists' Year-Book* opened its "literary agents" section with these cautionary words,

> Owing to complaints of the methods of some literary agents it has been deemed advisable, in the interests of writers, to cut the usual details of the terms upon which business is negotiated. Anyone needing the services of an agent is likely to make a more careful choice if preliminary investigation is a forced necessity. MSS. should not be forwarded before preliminaries are arranged.

The agent section of *The Writers' and Artists' Yearbook* seems to confirm the notion that by the second half of the 1930s, French agents remained few in number: for 1939, only one "continental" agency was listed, Mideuropean Literary Service in Budapest. By 1950, one French agency was listed among the seven continental ones. This by no means reflects the reality of the situation in France, as we shall see, but it is eloquent inasmuch as—*The Yearbook* being a British publication aimed at an English-speaking public—it reveals some indifference on the part of British and American publishers and possibly authors toward literary representation on the European continent. On the other hand, these figures might also be accounted for by the fact that most US publishers and agencies continued to work through British agents for representation in France and elsewhere in Europe, and thus felt no need to list other middlemen, whose cut would increase the cost of the transactions. Be that as it may, at least as many as nine agents or agencies operated in France in the 1930s, including the William A. Bradley agency, established in 1918, the Bureau Littéraire International, headed by Marguerite Scialtiel, the Bureau Littéraire Denyse Clairouin, and the Hoffman Agency, all trading in the buying and selling of foreign rights, working either as subagents or co-agents. Other, less prominent agencies included Storkama, Agence Littéraire Internationale, headed by Deszo Schwartz, Agence Littéraire française, or Agence Littéraire franco-britannique-américaine.

The William A. Bradley Agency

Chronologically, the Bradley agency preceded all other French agencies trading in international rights. The history of the Hoffman agency is tied on several levels with that of William A. Bradley and his wife Jenny, if only because in the late 1970s or early 1980s Jenny Bradley, who was about to retire with no heir, asked the Hoffman agency to take up her business.[75] In addition, be it by way of books sent by mistake from the United States to one or the other, or through their joint efforts to organize the profession in the late 1940s, the paths of Hoffman and Bradley repeatedly crossed. Their correspondence reflects both competition and the acknowledgement of their respective positions as the leading French agents after the Second World War. Unlike most French agencies which, to this day, only work as co-agents, the Bradleys initially represented several American authors as well.

The Bradley agency was started in France in 1923 by New Englander William A. Bradley and his French wife, Jenny Serruys Bradley. The two had met during the war, when William was serving in France and Jenny was helping to run a program which allowed American soldiers to spend time in French homes on their leaves of absence. William Bradley, a graduate of Columbia University, was also a translator of French works, and had acquired editorial skills, as well as possible contacts in the literary and publishing world, writing reviews for *The New York Times* and working for several other magazines and newspapers. Working as a scout for Harcourt, Brace and Company provided him with further opportunities to develop his own networks.

In the 1920s and early 1930s, the Bradleys played an important role in the publication of modernist writers; scattered throughout the scarce secondary literature on the Bradleys are several anecdotes suggesting their close relationship with many in these circles, and some tales have taken on the tinge of legend. In his biography of Ford Madox Ford, Max Saunders provides personal insights into the characters of William and Jenny Bradley: as seen by Stella Bowen, Jenny was a great and witty conversationalist, while William was perceived as "an extremely cultivated and sensitive person with a kind of whimsical gaiety that could create the party spirit at any dinner-table where he sat."[76] Jenny is reported to have lent money and a table to Joyce, upon which the self-celebrated artist may have written part of *Ulysses*; her relations with Joyce do not end there, as she was godmother to Ford Madox Ford's daughter Julie, and Joyce was to act as godfather.[77] Becoming—however briefly—Gertrude Stein's agent through Madox Ford, William A. Bradley achieved the wonderful feat of publishing her *Autobiography of Alice B. Toklas* as well as *The Making of Americans* in the United States with Harcourt, Brace. He was also responsible for securing a contract for Henry Miller's *Tropic of Cancer* with Jack Kahane's Olympia Press.[78] The Bradleys' close relation with Alfred and Blanche Knopf—as indeed they acted as representatives of the publishers in the early 1930s, as well as of Ben Huebsch's Viking Press—led them to negotiate French rights to Carl Van Vechten, Langston Hughes' *Not Without Laughter*, and Willa Cather. Through other agents and American publishers, they were able to close deals with Gallimard for *God's Little Acre* and *Tobacco Road* when Erskine Caldwell was still represented by agent Maxim Lieber and introduced to the French by Maurice-Edgar Coindreau. Other Gallimard authors they met through personal acquaintances: Faulkner had met William Bradley in New Haven as early as 1918, while Hemingway was introduced to them by Ford Madox Ford and Stella Bowen. Dos Passos and Sinclair Lewis further featured on their roster of literary luminaries.

The Bradleys also acted as agents for French authors prior to and after the war, many of whom were published in France by Gallimard—Henry de Montherlant, Jean Giono, Jean Giraudoux, André Gide, and most famously Jean-Paul Sartre, Simone de Beauvoir, and Albert Camus, who was published by Knopf; others included cultural mediators and writers Régis Michaud, who had taught in the Romance Languages departments of several American universities and wrote a series of scholarly works and anthologies on American literature, and Paul Morand, author and diplomat, close to the *Nouvelle Revue Française*, who would ask Bradley to provide him with good American short stories for the new "Renaissance de la nouvelle" series he would edit for Gallimard.[79]

In addition to working as publishers' agents and scouts, the Bradleys worked as co-agents, especially for Marion Saunders in New York with whom they had a mutual agreement. According to agent Georges Borchardt who worked for Saunders after the war, her representation of Bradley earned her the handling of almost all of the big French authors' properties in the United States. Indeed, Jenny Bradley, in return for bringing Gallimard the major American authors of the 1930s, had obtained the French publisher's approval to represent their authors across the Atlantic as an informal *quid pro quo*.[80] The daughter of a British Foreign officer, Saunders had travelled extensively throughout Europe, and according to Borchardt, spoke several foreign languages, including French; indeed, she also translated several books. It was through Saunders that the Bradley agency secured a very important and potentially lucrative contract, the French rights to Margaret Mitchell's *Gone with the Wind*, which was published by Gallimard in 1939, just before the Germans declared censorship of all translations from English. As has now been uncovered, Saunders had obtained Mitchell's authorization to handle the foreign rights to the novel under false pretenses, as she had not been authorized to do so by Mitchell's publisher. In 1943, she admitted failing to remit some $28,000 in royalties earned since 1938. After Saunders had been fired by Mitchell, Jenny Bradley was finally hired to handle her rights in France, and was able to recover the royalties owed Mitchell, a large proportion of which seemed to have been confiscated by the Germans during the occupation.[81] Although Saunders did not close shop following this unfortunate mishap, this "swindle" of sorts was facilitated by the international scope of the transaction: it was especially difficult for American authors to ascertain the truth about foreign publishers' statements and indeed even to receive the money owed them, if they could not rely on a trustworthy agent to represent their foreign rights. In similar fashion, agent Madeleine Boyd had been discharged by Thomas Wolfe in 1932 when she failed to remit a royalty advance from the German publisher of *Look Homeward, Angel*.[82] These two anecdotes emphasize the need for serious agents to handle the foreign business of American authors in the complex international book market.

The Hoffman Agency

Second on the timeline, then, was the Hoffman agency, which came about as the result of connections between Michel Hoffman and the London agency A.M. Heath. Hoffman was born in 1906 in Saint Petersburg, into a well-to-do Jewish family of the great bourgeoisie. His father, chief engineer for Siemens, had supervised the first electric installations in Saint Petersburg and other great works such as the trans-Siberian railroad line. He was ultimately to die in the Soviet prisons, branded as quintessentially bourgeois. Following the 1917 Russian revolution, in the mid-1920s Michel Hoffman fled into exile and spent nearly a decade in Berlin, where he finished his LLD, writing a doctoral thesis on the German agrarian economy.[83] In 1933, he founded a literary newspaper, *Das Echo der Zeit*, wherein he edited Russian émigré writers who, like him, had fled the regime. In Berlin, he presumably became acquainted with several Russian emigré writers, such as Evgueni Zamiatin, an early Bolshevik who had left the party, or Ivan Bunin, future Nobel Prize in Literature and the first Russian writer to be awarded this prize. He also grew close to German writers Erich Kaestner, author of the bestselling children's book *Emil and the Detectives* (1929) and anti-Nazi Bruno Frank.[84] That same year, informed by his janitor of an impending *Sturmabteilung* raid, Hoffman was able to escape to London, presumably the most logical haven, as he had been educated partly in English and was almost bilingual. He spent a few months there, penniless and without any job prospects, until he encountered someone from the respectable A.M. Heath agency, established in 1919. The agency then wished to expand their activities outside England and asked Hoffman if he would represent them on the continent, to which he eventually— reluctantly, according to his eldest son—agreed. Consequently, he relocated to Paris in the course of 1934.[85]

In addition to the representation of Heath, Hoffman built up his business representing German and Russian writers in exile. The "Agence littéraire et dramatique internationale," headed by Michel Hoffman and Zachary Kagansky, was opened in 1934; by October of that year, Kagansky seems to have disappeared from the picture, as his name is no longer to be found on the agency's letterhead, and by 1936 the agency had been renamed "Agence littéraire et dramatique Hoffman." Hoffman may have met Kagansky in Berlin, where the latter had worked both as a translator for several Russian playwrights, including Alexei Tolstoy, and as a business agent.[86] Given the lack of biographical information as well as archives from the early period of the Hoffman agency, these mere letterheads leave us with a series of questions: How could Hoffman, who arrived in Paris as the result of a second exile with virtually no money in his pocket, open a literary agency, in such a short span of time? And how did he develop his business prior to the war?

As Robertson Nicoll already mentioned in 1895, very little economic capital is in fact necessary for this form of venture, since "there are no losses, the expenses of conducting an office are very small."[87] One may very well conduct business from one's own apartment, as indeed many agents started out doing. Furthermore, no formal training or degree were required, as the trade journal *Toute l'édition* remarked in 1936 on the English situation, "The root of all evil is that anyone today can call themselves a literary agent. No special condition is required to practice this profession."[88] The absence of any kind of pre-requisite could prove, in certain cases, highly dangerous for authors and publishers and explains the need for the establishment by the Society of Authors' of a code of ethics on the other side of the Atlantic in the 1940s. As we have seen with the careers of several agents, many took to this business after working as assistant editors, either in publishing or on the staff of newspapers and magazines, or working as publishers' scouts. Hoffman in fact combined a set of competences, or cultural capital, that may well have made up for the lack of economic capital: his son recalls that next to Russian, English was practically a second mother-tongue, one he had acquired through a private English-speaking tutor, which was quite common among families of his class. His years in Berlin had provided him with an opportunity to master the German language perfectly, acquire editing skills, and complete his LLD. His thorough legal background certainly helped in understanding the intricate international copyright issues to be found in foreign rights contracts. Hoffman's other great asset was his acquaintance in Berlin, the second Russian Mecca after Paris in the 1920s, with a network of Russian playwrights, translators, and people from the German world of theater, which allowed him to build the agency on the representation of Alexei Tolstoy, the estates of Gorky or Leonid Nikolaievitch Andreieff. It is safe to assume that Hoffman was introduced to this world by Sachari Kagansky and Bernard Rubinstein, former head of the publishing imprint J. Ladyschnikow Verlag in Berlin and translator. Hoffman joined forces with Rubinstein and helped manage the representation of Ladyshnikow's authors in Paris, which included Leonid Andreieff, Leo Tolstoi, Yiddish author Asch Scholem, as well as Maxim Gorky.[89] In turn, he was brought into contact with another Russian agent working in London, Baronness Marie von Budberg, who negotiated the translation of these authors into English.[90] As specified by Shelley Beal, the rights to dramatic performances continued to be controlled by the Société des Auteurs et Compositeurs Dramatiques, and Hoffman's "dramatic" activities seem to have been restricted to the negotiation of translation rights, adaptation rights for screenplays and radio scripts[91]; in some cases, managers of Russian literary estates would take advantage of his location in Paris to ask him to take out a membership to the Société des Auteurs et Compositeurs Dramatiques, thereby ensuring that they would actually get paid for performances in France.

I have found no material evidence of contacts between Hoffman and the wide circle of Russian émigrés in Paris, aristocrats and bourgeois alike. As Catherine Gousseff has shown, Russians had begun emigrating in the 1880s, after early anti-Semitic acts, followed by further waves in 1905, then more massively in the 1920s, with France, Poland, and Germany the first destinations or transit-places. This anti-bolshevik emigration was diverse, but the vast majority of narratives have extolled the role played by the elites, at the expense of the presence of *émigrés* hailing from lower classes. Gousseff has remarked on the relatively small number of Jewish Russians in France, observing however that they were "well represented among the intelligentsia," acting as "intermediaries between (. . .) culturally and politically distinct communities."[92] Coming from the great bourgeoisie, Hoffman may have benefitted from the very tight Parisian intellectual and artistic networks of Russians who developed a strong solidarity with immigrants in the 1920s, and provided newcomers with several resources and professional outlets: as Marc Raeff notes, as of 1925, Paris, following Berlin, became the focus of Russian publishing in exile[93]; artists and writers could earn a living from translating, writing articles and reviews, or copyediting in one of the Russian-language newspapers . . . It is most likely that Hoffman, Kagansky, and Rubinstein found a French public already familiar with things Russian, after the experience of a "Russian vogue" in the 1920s, extending from the Diaghilev ballet, Russian cinema, and the Russian cabarets of Pigalle.[94] After the war, Hoffman's nationality quite possibly helped him to ingratiate himself with Moscow-born Elsa Triolet, companion of the French poet Louis Aragon. In spite of Triolet's aversion to agents, after the Goncourt Prize had been awarded her in 1944 for *Le premier accroc coûte 200 francs*, Hoffman succeeded in securing her representation for a brief period of time, acting in collaboration with Curtis Brown in London.

Aside from representing Russian writers' properties, the Agence Littéraire et Dramatique Hoffman had already made connections with A.M. Heath in London in the 1930s, which presumably brought Hoffman to work in collaboration with Brandt & Brandt, whose European co-agent was Heath. In turn, he was able to obtain contracts for several American Brandt & Brandt clients, including John Dos Passos—*Journeys Between Wars* (1938)—Marjorie Kinnan Rawlings, whose bestseller *The Yearling* he sold to Albin Michel before the war, Bessie Breuer, Ethel Vance and James Gould Cozzens, whose *S.S. San Pedro*, contracted for by Gallimard in 1934, was ultimately published in . . . 1950! Other contracts were in fact obtained through collaborations with the Bradley agency.

Although such collaborative work brought in new contracts, Hoffman does not seem to have encouraged cooperation with other French agents, as this entailed a further sharing of commissions. The customary commission for an author's representation, as set by A.P. Watt and usually followed to this day by agents around the world, is 10%; however, agents negotiating foreign rights usually ask for 20%, a rate justified by the fact that US agents will generally market such rights through co-agents with whom they share this commission.[95] The less scrupulous agents, who did not intend to lose out on their commission, sometimes increased rates: as Elizabeth Nowell explained in a letter to Thomas Wolfe, his former agent, Madeleine Boyd, had charged him 30% so that she would earn 10%, give 10% to Brandt & Brandt who handled foreign rights, and 10% to the foreign agent.[96] This, however, was quite exceptional and unorthodox, especially as it amounted almost to the commission taken by publishers for the same service, which was precisely one of the arguments in favor of agents. Indeed, in his 1906 reply to Henry Holt's attacks, Albert Curtis Brown claimed that it was not rare for British publishers to charge 25% to 30% to place British material in US magazines, a standard practice continued at least until the early 1960s.[97] The standard 15% or 20% commission for foreign rights was, and is still, split between the US agent and, in our case, the French co-agent; if two co-agents came into play, in addition to the US agent, the commission was split three ways.[98] The contracts for which a French co-agent had to split a commission with a French fellow agent, a British representative and the US agency were indeed not the most lucrative ones. This is presumably what prompted William A. Bradley to stray from the A.P. Watt agenting template, to charge US publishers a 20% commission even for direct publisher/publisher negotiations. As we shall see in the following chapters, Michel Hoffman and Jenny Bradley would continue to vie for transatlantic clients in the post-war period, by and by adapting to the rules of international agenting.

While agents in the 1920s and 1930s could hope to thrive with the development of an international book market and the French enthusiasm for American fiction which had not abated since the 19th century, they also faced competition on the part of other middlemen. Contrary to scouts, who received a fixed salary, Bradley and Hoffman depended on the actual sale of rights for their livelihood; relying on diversified linguistic competences, and on international networks, they were part of an emerging profession that was inherently tied to others in the book trade. The good health of their agencies depended on that of publishing on both sides of the Atlantic.

Notes

1 Michael Winship, "The Transatlantic Book Trade and Anglo-American Culture in the Nineteenth Century," 98–122.
2 See Diana Cooper-Richet, "La librairie étrangère à Paris au XIXe siècle. Un milieu perméable aux innovations et aux transferts," *Actes de la recherche en sciences sociales. Édition, Éditeurs (1)* 126–127 (March 1999): 60–69.
3 Eza Greenspan, *George Palmer Putnam, Representative American Publisher* (Philadelphia: Pennsylvania State University Press, 2000).
4 See Wallace Putnam Bishop, *The Struggle for International Copyright in the United States*, Ph.D. diss., Boston University, 1959: "Piracy was looked upon as being unethical by the best publishers, but it was not illegal until 1891" (21).
5 Jeffrey Groves, "Courtesy of the Trade," in *A History of the Book in America, Volume 3, The Industrial Book, 1840–1880*, ed. Scott E. Casper et al. (Chapel Hill: University of North Carolina Press, 2007), 140.
6 Bishop, *The Struggle for International Copyright in the United States*, passim. For more complete data, see Bishop's tables pp. 57–64.

7 Thomas Loué, "Le Congrès international des éditeurs 1896–1938—Autour d'une forme de sociabilité professionnelle internationale," in *Les Mutations du livre et de l'édition dans le monde du XVIII° siècle à l'an 2000*, ed. Jacques Michon and Jean-Yves Mollier (Quebec, Paris: Presses de l'Université de Laval/L'Harmattan, 2001), 531–543. This transitional period between the 1880s and 1940s is also suggested by the choice of period for the fourth volume of *A History of the Book in America*.

8 As Meredith McGill has shown, the debate on the internationalization of print was already vibrant in Jacksonian America. Meredith McGill, *American Literature and the Culture of Reprinting, 1834–1853* (Philadelphia: University of Pennsylvania Press, 2007).

9 For the evolution and the debate on international copyright in the United States see Meredith McGill, "Copyright," in *A History of the Book in America, vol. 3, The Industrial Book, 1840–1880*, ed. Scott E. Casper (Chapel Hill: University of North Carolina Press, 2007), 158–178 and Ezra Greenspan, *George Palmer Putnam, Representative American Publisher*. For recent developments in copyright studies, see Paul Goldstein, *International Copyright: Principles, Laws, and Practice* (Oxford: Oxford University Press, 2001), Ronan Deazley, Martin Kretschmer, and Lionel Bently, *Privilege and Property: Essays on the History of Copyright* (Cambridge: Open Book Publishers, 2010), Peter Jaszi and Martha Woodmansee, "Copyright in Transition," in *A History of the Book in America, vol. 4, Print in Motion: The Expansion of Publishing and Reading in the United States, 1880–1940*, ed. Carl F. Kaestle and Janice Radway (Chapel Hill: University of North Carolina Press, 2009), 90–101; Edward Samuels, *The Illustrated Story of Copyright* (New York: Thomas Dunne Books, St Martin's Griffin, 2002), James L. West, III, "The Expansion of the National Book Trade System," in *A History of the Book in America, vol. 4, Print in Motion* (Chapel Hill: University of North Carolina Press, 2009), 78–89; and "The Chace Act and Anglo-American Literary Relations," *Studies in Bibliography* 45 (1992): 303–311. See also Shelley Selina Beal, "Theodore Stanton: An American Editor, Syndicator, and Literary Agent in Paris, 1880–1920," Doctoral thesis (University of Toronto, Department of French Studies/Collaborative Program in Book History and Print Culture, 2009), passim, and Gillies, *The Professional Literary Agent in Britain, 1880–1920*.

10 McGill, *American Literature and the Culture of Reprinting*, 81–83.

11 See Greenspan, *George Palmer Putnam*, 87–89.

12 Ibid., 89.

13 Bishop, *The Struggle for International Copyright in the United States*, 37–39.

14 See Bishop, *The Struggle for International Copyright in the United States*, 152.

15 "L'Adoption de la nouvelle loi concernant la protection des droits d'auteur aux Etats-unis," *Le Droit d'auteur* [Le Droit d'auteur: revue du bureau de l'Union Internationale pour la Protection des Œuvres Littéraires et Artistiques], 4, no. 3 (March 15, 1891): 25–36. The Proclamation was signed by President Harrison on July 1, 1891.

16 Horace Ball, quoted in Jaszi and Woodmansee, "Copyright in Transition," 95.

17 Goldstein, *International Copyright*, 18.

18 See Beal, "Theodore Stanton."

19 West, "The Chace Act and Anglo-American Literary Relations," 310.

20 Winship, "The Transatlantic Book Trade and Anglo-American Culture in the Nineteenth Century."

21 Eva Hemmungs Wirten, "A Diplomatic *Salto Morale*: Translation Trouble in Berne, 1884–1886," *Book History* 14 (2011), 90.

22 Joseph S. Dubin, "The Universal Copyright Convention," *University of California Law Review* 42 (1954): 93.

23 Hemmungs Wirten links the French "generosity" with its actual linguistic and literary domination: "Extending the right of national treatment to foreign authors without asking anything in return was the kind of quintessential gesture of cultural supremacy that secured the French a leading role in the development toward Berne" ("A Diplomatic *Salto* Morale," 90). Nicolas Bouché however reminds us that the 1852 decree was intended as a defensive measure (*un texte répressif*, 482) against the importation of foreign pirated editions. Nicolas Bouché, *Le principe de territorialité de la propriété intellectuelle* (Paris: L'Harmattan, 2002).

24 Goldstein, *International Copyright*, 17.

25 The *droit d'auteur*, which should be distinguished from the doctrine of copyright on several grounds, one of which is the incorporation in the 19th century of *droit moral*, was regulated very much on the basis of the laws of January 1791 passed during the Revolution. Very few revisions were enacted throughout the 20th century, until 1957. The 1957 Act has since been abrogated with the passing of a new law in 1992.

26 Lawrence Venuti, *The Scandals of Translation, Towards an Ethics of Difference* (London: Routledge, 1998), 52.

27 See Pamela Spence Richards, *Scientific Information in Wartime; The Allied-German Rivalry, 1939–1945* (Westport, Ct.: Greenwood Press, 1994), 8.

28 See Malcolm Johnson, "The Foreign Distribution of American Publications," *Library Quarterly* 24, no. 1 (1954): 114–123 and Luey, "The Organization of the Book Publishing Industry," 29–54.

29 David Nimmer, "Nation, Duration, Violation, Harmonization: an International Copyright Proposal for the United States," *Law and Contemporary Problems* 55, no. 2 (1992): 214.

30 John B. Hench, *Books as Weapons: Propaganda, Publishing, and the Battle for Global Markets in the Era of World War II* (Cornell: Cornell University Press, 2010), 180.

31 See for instance George Hutchinson, *The Harlem Renaissance in Black and White* (Cambridge, Mass.: Belknap Press, 1996), West, "The Expansion of the National Book Trade System," and John A. Tebbel, *The Golden Age between Two Wars, 1920–1940* (New York: R.R. Bowker, 1981) and Hench, *Books as Weapons*, 11–18.

32 Quoted in Gerald Gross, ed., *Publishers on Publishing* (London: Secker & Warburg, 1962), 355. Berlin-born, French-educated New York agent Georges Borchardt holds a rather distinct view of Blanche Knopf, of whom he said that although a very gracious woman, "[she] was [also] fluent in French but knew very little about literature" (interview, 2).

33 Tebbel, *The Golden Age Between Two Wars*, 115.

34 See Tom Dardis's 1995 biography-cum-publishing story of Horace Liveright, *Firebrand* (New York: Random House, 1995).

35 (Robert Haas?), draft notes, mss, dated May 18, 1932—Random House Records, 1925–1999, MS 1048: Box 122—Correspondence— 1925–1945.

36 BRH; inventory of Knopf Papers, Harry Ransom Center.

37 Blaise Wilfert-Portal, "La place de la littérature étrangère dans le champ littéraire français autour de 1900," *Histoire & mesure* XXIII, no. 2 (December 1, 2011). http://histoiremesure.revues.org/3613.

38 Claire Parfait, "Un succès américain en France: *La Case de l'Oncle Tom*," *E-rea* 7, no. 2 (2010). doi:10.4000/erea.981.

39 Jean-Marc Gouanvic, "Panorama de la traduction-importation de la littérature américaine en France (1820–1960)," *Genèses de Textes—Textgenesen Volume 3: Event or Incident/Evénement ou Incident: On the Role of Translation in the Dynamics of Cultural Exchange/Du rôle des traductions dans les processus d'échanges culturels* (Bern: Peter Lang, 2010), 161.

40 Ronald Jenn, "From American Frontier to European Borders," *Book History* 9 (2006): 235–254.

41 On Cunliffe's quip and these issues, see Marc Chénetier, "American Literature in France; Pleasures in Perspective," in *As Others Read Us: International Perspectives on American Literature*, ed. Huck Gutman (Amherst: University of Massachusetts Press, 1991), 79–95.

42 See Cercle de la Librairie, statistiques Index Translationum—1953, 1954, 1955 (IMEC).

43 Chénetier, "American Literature in France; Pleasures in Perspective," 82.

44 See Gisèle Sapiro, "À l'international," in *Gallimard, un siècle d'édition, 1911–2011*, ed. Alban Cerisier and Pascal Fouché (Paris: BNF/Gallimard, 2011), 136. Editions de la Nouvelle Revue Française was the name of Gallimard until 1919.

45 Sorlot published the first French pirated translation of Hitler's *Mein Kampf* in 1934, with the purpose of denouncing the rise of National Socialism in Germany. The publisher, avowedly right-wing, was sentenced to "national indignity" (*indignité nationale*) and forbidden to work as publisher, but was rehabilitated in 1948 and recovered his publishing house, which is still operating today. Paradoxically, Sorlot had also published Franz Boas' *Race and Racism*, which had been banned by the German censors.

46 Jacques Boutelleau aka Chardonne would be jailed after the war for collaborating with the enemy. Albert Savine played an important part in the translation and importation of foreign literatures in France in the second half of the 19th century. In 1884, Savine published the first-ever French translation from the Spanish of Jacinto Verdaguer's *La Atlantida*. As of 1886, at the head of La Nouvelle Librairie parisienne, he published the first French translations of Tolstoy, Wilde, and Ibsen.

47 Jack Kahane, *Memoirs of a Booklegger* (Newmarket, ON.: The Obolus Press, 2010), 181–182.

48 On Bernard Faÿ's collaboration with the German enemy during the war, anti-masonic writings and downfall, see Poulain, *Livres pillés, lectures surveillées*, passim.

49 Jeanpierre, "'Modernisme' américain et espace littéraire français: réseaux et raisons d'un rendez-vous différé," 388.

50 French sociologist Gisèle Sapiro, in *Les contradictions de la globalisation éditoriale* (Paris: Nouveau Monde éditions, 2009), identifies and classifies publishers and book agents as "economic intermediaries," while "cultural mediators/ intermediaries" encompass translators, writers, critics and scholars (20).

51 Gillies, *The Professional Literary Agent in Britain, 1880–1920*, 6.

52 Beal, "Theodore Stanton," 10–13.

53 Ibid., 12.

54 Maurice-Edgar Coindreau, *Mémoires d'un traducteur, entretiens avec Christian Giudicelli* (1974; repr., Paris: Gallimard, 1992), iii.

55 George H. Doran, repr. in Gross, ed., *Publishers on Publishing*, 201.

56 Michael Joseph, repr., in Gross, ed., *Publishers on Publishing*, 38. Joseph had worked for the Curtis Brown agency before founding his own London publishing house in 1935 . . . which might explain why he would have good things to say about agents.

57 Curtis Brown, *Contacts*, 282.

58 William Robertson Nicoll, "The Literary Agent," *The Bookman* (May 1895): 249–250.
59 Gillies, *The Professional Literary Agent in Britain, 1880–1920*, 6.
60 Beal, "Theodore Stanton," 95–96.
61 See Robert Sterling Yard, repr., in Gross, ed., *Publishers on Publishing*, 80.
62 Ibid.
63 "Certificate of Incorporation of the Incorporated Society of Authors' Representatives," SAR MS 1173, Box 1. The SAR received several queries from authors about member and non-member agents, indicative of fraudulous practices.
64 See ONE [Albert Curtis Brown], "'The Commercialism of Literature' and the Literary Agent," *The Bookman* (October 1906): 134; Michael Joseph, "The Literary Agent," *The Bookman* (September 1925): 34. The title of Curtis Brown's essay was apparently slightly modified from its original publication in *Fortnightly Review* of August 1, 1906, as quoted by Mary Ann Gillies.
65 Curtis Brown, *Contacts*, 281–282.
66 George H. Doran, quoted in Gross, ed., *Publishers on Publishing*, 202.
67 Henry Holt, "The Commercialization of Literature," *Atlantic Monthly* 96, no. 5 (Nov. 1905): 583. Epitomizing the common arguments brandished by publishers and agents in favor of and against literary agents, the debate over the "commercialization of literature" between Henry Holt and Albert Curtis Brown is well-known. Curtis Brown, "'The Commercialism of Literature' and the Literary Agent."
68 Holt, "The Commercialization of Literature," 580.
69 See Georges Hoffman, "agent littéraire" in Pascal Fouché, ed., *Dictionnaire encyclopédique du livre*, vol. 1 (Paris: Cercle de la Librairie, 2002), 39–40: "The main activity of French literary agencies is the representation of foreign works whose rights they handle through agreements of exclusive representation" (my translation, 40). On the distinction between sub-agents and co-agents, see La lettre de l'asford, no. 5, October-November 2006, http://www.asfored.org/newsletter.php?nl=35.
70 "Portraits d'écrivains (5). Dix questions à l'éditeur et agent littéraire Pierre Astier"; Georges Hoffman, personal interview, February 2014.
71 In this interview printed in the French mainstream cultural magazine *Le Nouvel Observateur*, Gallimard was asked to respond to the declarations of US agent Andrew "the Jackal" Wylie. Gallimard's deplorations recall a bygone era in US publishing: responding to the common and recurrent criticisms preferred by authors and agents against the lack of promotion on the part of publishers, he defended his profession, defining it as a "craft" (*métier d'artisan*) and assuring the interviewer that a publisher is always and completely "behind each and every book." "Antoine Gallimard: 'Nos auteurs ne sont pas si mal payés!'" April 10, 2014, http://bibliobs.nouvelobs.com/actualites/20140417.OBS4319/agents-litteraires-le-coup-de-gueule-de-gallimard.html.
72 Walter Hines Page, *A Publisher's Confession* (1905; repr., Garden City and New York: Doubleday, Page & Company, 1923), 54.
73 "A still uncommon profession in our country." See the reminiscences of an early book agent who had endeavored to represent authors, Marcel Berger, "Souvenirs d'une agence littéraire (1918–1922)," *Toute l'édition*, no. 248 (November 3, 1934): 2. The review of the survey of London agents is to be found in E. Buisson, "Ce que fut, ce qu'est, ce que doit être l'agent littéraire," *Toute l'édition*, no. 319 (April 11, 1936): 7.

74 See Paul Trédant, "Gangsters de l'édition—leur activité aux Etats-Unis," *Toute l'édition*, no. 264 (February 23, 1935): 4.

75 This explains why a rather large part of the Bradley archive has remained within the Hoffman archive at IMEC in France, while another part was sold to the Harry Ransom Center for the Humanities at The University of Texas. This archive is complementary to the Hoffman archive, as it sheds light on several aspects of the transatlantic book trade between the 1920s and 1970s.

76 Max Saunders, *Ford Madox Ford: A Dual Life: Volume II: The After-War World* (1996; repr., Oxford: Oxford University Press, 2012), 161.

77 Ibid., 331.

78 William Bradley's efforts for Stein's sake are described in Ford, *Published in Paris. L'édition américaine et anglaise à Paris 1920–1939.*

79 Between 1907 and 1929, Régis Michaud worked as assistant professor and professor at Princeton, Smith, the University of California, and the University of Illinois; as such, he embodies, like Coindreau and Faÿ, the new type of cultural mediator highlighted by Jeanpierre. W.A. Bradley represented Michaud directly, and their correspondence eloquently reveals the sometimes difficult author/agent relationship, as Michaud proved very demanding and repeatedly asked for advances from publishers. Paul Morand, writer and diplomat, published a series of "Paris Letters" in *The Dial* between 1923 and 1929.

80 Borchardt claims that after the war Gallimard authorized Jenny Bradley to represent their catalogue, in return for the Bradleys' bringing them the major US authors of the 1930s and 1940s. See Interview of Georges Borchardt by Jolgie Ferrari-Adler, September/October 2009, http://www.pw.org/content/agents_editors_qampa_agent_georges_borchardt.

81 See Ellen F. Brown and John Wiley, *Margaret Mitchell's Gone with the Wind: A Bestseller's Odyssey from Atlanta to Hollywood* (Plymouth: Taylor Trade, 2011), 243.

82 See Kennedy, ed. *Beyond Love and Loyalty; The Letters of Thomas Wolfe and Elizabeth Nowell*, 23.

83 There are no secondary sources on Hoffman; I am grateful to his son Georges Hoffman for providing me with the following biographical data, inevitably fragmentary. Georges Hoffman, Personal interview, February 16, 2014.

84 Thomas Dietzel, Hans-Otto Hügel, *Zeitschriften 1880–1945: Ein Repertorium, Volume 1* (Munchen, New York, Paris: Saur, 1988). According to this register, only two issues of the *Echo der Zeit* were published. Interestingly, Hoffman's name is here spelled with two "n"s.

85 See Jennifer Sandler, interview with Boris Hoffman, in Sandler, "Les agents littéraires en France," vol. 2, Master's Thesis, Histoire socio-culturelle, dir. Jean-Yves Mollier (Université de Versailles-St Quentin en Yvelines, 2001), Appendix, pp. 1–24.

86 Information on Kagansky is fragmentary. He may have been at the head of a Russian-language imprint in Berlin, Izdatel'stvo Z. Kaganskogo. He is also presented as a scoundrel, who pirated Boulgakov's play *Zoika's apartment*. See August 30, 1933, letter from Nicolas Boulgakov to his brother Mihail Boulgakov, quoted in Marie-Christine Autant-Mathieu, "Une rencontre manquée: Boulgakov aux Vieux-Colombier," *Les Cahiers de la Comédie Française* no. 18 (1996): 109–124. Judging from several bibliographies and auction catalogues, it seems that after his career as book agent in both Berlin and Paris, he eventually fled to Casablanca where he opened his own imprint.

87 Nicoll, "The Literary Agent," 250.

88 Buisson, "Ce que fut, ce qu'est, ce que doit être l'agent littéraire," 7 (my translation).
89 Bernhard Rubinstein was deported and died during the war.
90 Hoffman seems to have remained on friendly terms with von Budberg, as evidenced by post-war correspondence. Marie Von Budberg, or Moura Budberg, was the mistress of Maxim Gorki and H.G. Wells, and a supposed Soviet agent.
91 Beal, "Theodore Stanton," 62–63.
92 Catherine Gousseff, *L'Exil russe, la fabrique du réfugié apatride* (Paris: CNRS Editions, 2008), 12.
93 Marc Raeff, *Russia Abroad. A Cultural History of the Russian Emigration, 1919–1939* (Oxford, New York: Oxford University Press, 1990), 77.
94 Gousseff, *L'Exil russe, la fabrique du réfugié apatride,* 151–152.
95 This practice certainly became standard after the war: see Reynolds, "Should Every Writer Have an Agent?," 69–70; 75–76. James Oliver Brown, "Literary Agents," *The Writer* (July 1967): 15–17.
96 See Elizabeth Nowell to Thomas Wolfe, November 2, 1935, "Of course, old lady [Madeleine] Boyd charged you about 30%: 10% for her, 10% for Brandt and Brandt to whom she gave the foreign rights, and 10% to the foreign agent to whom Brandt entrusted the actual sale" (Kennedy, ed. *Beyond Love and Loyalty,* 31).
97 See The Authors Guild, "Your Book Contract—A Guide for the Use of Members of the Authors' Guild in the Negotiation of Contracts with Book Publishers" (1961), which cites the 1947 Random House standard contract highlighting a 25% cut for the publisher, perceived by the Guild as "an excessive fee for the agency function" (32).
98 See Jenny Bradley to Michel Hoffman, June 6, 1945: "I know not what your arrangement was with Curtis Brown. As for me, I have always worked with them—and all other agents—on the basis of an equal threeway split when I went through their representative" (BRH.BRA.C03B04D05).

2 New Beginnings: 1944–1946

The Second World War certainly disrupted publishing in France, as well as in the United States. In France, men and women did not experience the war in exactly the same ways: following the death of her husband in 1939, Jenny Bradley resumed the agency's activity, and continued to work during the conflict; as for Michel Hoffman, he had enlisted in the French army. Following his demobilization after the June and July debacle, he spent most of the later years of the war in the South, where he eventually met his wife. There is evidence that he joined the Résistance, where he met French writer Joseph Kessel, also of Jewish Russian origins. Resuming his activity in 1944, he returned to Paris after it had been liberated in August of that year, and soon took stock of the morally disastrous situation of French publishing. The war had wrought many changes, material, psychological, and political, on French publishing, but it also modified the outlook of US publishers on international markets. Whereas they had not been particularly pre-occupied with these markets before, wartime experiments such as the Council on Books in Wartime, and the creation of the American Book Publishers' Bureau opened the eyes of US publishers to new lucrative potentialities abroad.

French Publishing and the War

French publishers, like those in the United States, had suffered from wartime censorship and severe shortages of ink and paper. However, whereas in the United States these restrictions had been imposed by the democratically elected government, in France they were implemented by the enemy, aided by the Vichy regime which had chosen full collabora-tion with the Germans. In effect, French wartime censorship had begun as early as 1939, and several publishers, loath to provoke the discon-tent of the Germans, had promptly presented their own lists of books to ban, leading French book historian Jean-Yves Mollier to emphasize their traditional and historical submissiveness.[1] The most general lack of resistance by librarians further illustrates this situation among the keep-ers of books.[2] German censorship, at first carried out by two separate entities, was particularly strict, accompanied by the aryanization of Jewish publishing houses by the *Propagandastaffel*,[3] which consisted in the replacement of former founding administrators and publishers by non-Jewish personnel.[4] Between 1940 and 1943, four lists of banned and prohibited books were issued, and officials from the Vichy administration promptly collaborated with the occupants, issuing their own lists of recommended and banned titles. The Bernhard list (1940) resulted in one of the most spectacular raids, with 700,000 volumes confiscated from libraries and bookstores.[5] As early as July 1941, the *Syndicat des Editeurs* (French Publishers' Association) issued a circular letter informing publishers that by order of the German *Propaganda Abteilung*,[6] any publication or re-edition of a British or American work published after 1870 was prohibited.[7] French publishers certainly could not believe the official line that this was intended as a paper-saving measure. In subsequent lists of books to be banned from publishers, bookstores, and libraries, British and American works featured prominently, alongside Russian works, and titles by Jewish authors. Most librarians did not resist these orders, many simply taking out the call slips from the catalogues so that the "incriminated" books might not be checked out. Still, a survey of publishers published in the fall of 1941 demonstrated the popularity and demand for big English-language novels, emphasizing as examples the excellent sales figures for Giono's translation-adaptation of *Moby Dick*—reprinted three times in the second semester of 1941— or for Fannie Hurst's *Back Street*.[8] Martine Poulain has demonstrated that these measures certainly did not deter French men and women from reading books; on the contrary many public libraries saw an increase in the number of readers, who found escape in the classics still left on the shelves.[9] Another form of censorship by the Vichy administration was conducted during the war by way of the Commission for the supervision of paper, created in April 1942, to which manuscripts had to be sent prior to publication and which issued individual authorizations to publishers. Among the five members of this commission we find Bernard Faÿ, administrator of the Bibliothèque nationale, translator and former friend of Gertrude Stein.[10] Still the final decision regarding the distribution of printing paper rested with the Germans.

In the aftermath of the war, the creation of various "reparations" committees, meant to assess the degree of collaboration by publishing houses, fostered suspicion among writers and publishers. This, in addition to the emergence of a new generation of young *intellectuels,* men and women of the Résistance who had acquired a new form of "moral capital" and a new vision of the world, would radically change publishing.[11]

While the French publishing scene was grappling to reconstruct itself, American publishing seems to have got back on its feet rapidly, and publishers were quick to rise to new occasions. One such opportunity was the conquest or consolidation of new, international markets. As Beth Luey notes,

> World War II interrupted and then transformed the American book publishing industry. When the war ended, however, fundamental changes had begun in the industry that led to expansion of the domestic and international markets, shifts in the importance of various sectors of the industry, new methods of capitalization to fund expansion, and an increasing tension between consolidation and cultural diversification . . . . By 1945 the United States had taken its place as a world power, and U.S. publishing began to take its place in the international market.[12]

In view of these changes, as the French thirst for English-language novels continued to grow and the majority of American publishers remained generally ignorant about the situation overseas, French agents definitely had a new and important part to play. In the last two chaotic and exciting years of the war, the Hoffman agency played its card and joined in the reconstruction of French publishing by way of importing US fiction and literature. In the process, it sowed the seeds of the future development of its transatlantic business. Quoting Robertson Nicoll's depiction of A.P. Watt as a "diplomatist," Mary Ann Gillies has emphasized how trust was, and is, the "basis of an agent's job."[13] Between 1944 and 1946, Hoffman gradually earned the trust of his French and transatlantic partners by performing diplomatic missions of sorts. The following pages will focus on his ability to gather information and his competence as matchmaker, as American publishing was getting ready to swoop down on the French rights market.[14]

The War and Recovery of US Publishing—The Scramble for Foreign Rights

For John B. Hench the consequences of the war on publishing in America were extraordinarily positive:

> The entry of the United States into the Second World War had a great impact on the nation's book-publishing industry. The war brought the trade fully out of the doldrums of the Great Depression. During wartime, book reading assumed a greater importance among the public than it had previously. Having done so well financially during the war, publishers wished to maintain that prosperity after the conflict was over.[15]

If book historian John Tebbel is also to be believed, American publishing briskly recovered from the war. The impact of the Great Depression was not as dramatic as one would have expected and indeed in 1939 the structure of the book trade was relatively unchanged, with sales figures remaining quite good. Since the United States entered the war later than France, the first years of the conflict were actually favorable to US publishing in several ways: books about the war sold well, as illustrated by the fantastic sales of Alice Duer Miller's poem *The White Cliffs*, journalist William L. Shirer's *Berlin Diaries* or the selection of Churchill's *Blood, Sweat and Tears* by the Book-of-the-Month Club; in fact, the 1940 book production figures were the highest in 25 years, and publishers even took advantage of the European slump: that year Penguin Books announced that it would start printing its pocket-size paperbacks in the United States.[16] Trouble really began in 1942, as book prices and production gradually came under government control via the War Production Board, and paper, ink, and other restrictions affected the trade, with houses losing staff to the draft. Bookmaking material became scarce, and wastepaper saving campaigns became part and parcel of the war effort. Paradoxically, this had a positive effect on book production, leading publishers to make smaller and lighter books, opening the way for the huge popularity of pocket-sized books. Such volumes, already marketed with great success by Avon with their Pocket-Size Books in 1941, were made increasingly familiar to US soldiers with the Armed Service editions during the war. In 1944, although 15% less paper was used, US book manufacturers produced more books than in any previous year.[17] As Beth Luey underlines, although paperbacks were not a technological innovation of the post-war era—in 1939 Pocket Books had been launched with considerable funding and backing from Simon & Schuster, and the US branch of Penguin Books opened that same year—they did constitute a marketing and selling innovation.[18] Trade paperbacks would take considerable shares of the widened domestic and international markets after 1945.

In spite of continued shortages of various bookmaking materials, as early as 1944 American publishing was already rising above adversity, as the demand for books exceeded production capacities. In spite of a drop in titles, nearly half a billion dollars' worth of books were produced, representing nearly twice the volume of 1939, and business took off after the revocation in August 1945 of some 300 individual orders and schedules that had made up the restrictions planned by the War Production Board.[19] As Tebbel writes,

> In the immediate aftermath of the war, it was obvious during the first year of peace, 1946, that the anxieties and restrictions of the past were about to yield with a speed people had not quite anticipated to an entirely new era, the dimensions of which no one at the

time foresaw. There was a general feeling that a boom would begin, after a decent interval of cleaning up and preparation. Few, however, could have believed what lay ahead.[20]

What lay ahead, in addition to the growth of the domestic market, thanks to the rise of paperbacks, book clubs, and new bookselling outlets, was the expansion of international markets and the improvement of marketing techniques. The scramble for foreign rights began as the conflict was still raging. By the end of 1943, the attention of the 68 members of the Book Publishers Bureau[21] was called to the post-war prospects. These were outlined by the Publishers' Association of Great Britain in an article on the "Sale of Foreign Book Rights" in *The London Bookseller* cautioning British publishers "to retain control wherever they can over continental translation rights because it is probable that those rights may prove to be of considerable value after the war."[22] Such a warning was heeded by American publishers, and 1943 reports by the Book Publishers Bureau attest to the ongoing debate on the question of joining the Berne Convention. While the Bureau argued against entering, still the focus was clearly on international matters, as suggested by the number of "publisher-ambassadors" sent abroad during the war to gauge potential markets, including Curtice Hitchcock in England and Holt's then Vice-President, William Sloane, in China.

Several wartime factors and events may account for the change in US publishers' outlook on foreign book markets: the decline of British publishing and book distribution as occasioned by the war; the presence in America of foreign publishers in exile; the success of wartime experiments in international marketing and distributing; and Cold War ideology, which saw a move from propaganda to cultural diplomacy. As the Cold War got underway, a definite shift was evidenced by the transformation of the notion, coined by publisher W.W. Norton and publicized by Roosevelt, that books are "weapons in the war of ideas," to a conception of books abroad as "ambassadors of good will and information," as quoted in a United States International Book Association (USIBA) pamphlet.[23]

James L. West and John Tebbel have noted how the arrival of European *émigré* publishers infused US publishing with a new international flavor. Kurt Enoch, Kurt Wolff, and Jacques Schiffrin are among the most notable examples. Enoch perfectly epitomizes international publishing, and is now renowned as the vanguard of the post-war trade paperback revolution, with Ian Ballantine and Victor Weybright: German-born, with a prior experience in publishing in Germany, his credentials as an international publisher were earned through the co-founding of the French-based Albatross Modern Continental Library, a series of English-language paperbacks, with John Holroyd

Reece and Max Christian Wegner. This series, intended to rival the hugely successful Tauchnitz editions, was supposedly launched under the tutelage of Albert Curtis Brown, who claims to have introduced Reece and Wegner, and in return obtained a substantial share of the business.[24] Albatross and Tauchnitz ultimately joined forces, assigning distribution to Albatross.

Enoch's excellent market sense would again flourish in New York, where he had arrived penniless in October 1940. Introduced by British publisher and founder of Penguin Books (1935) Allen Lane, he soon collaborated with Ballantine at the US Penguin branch. When Ballantine left in 1945 to found the popular paperback imprint Bantam Books, Enoch was left to manage the Penguin branch in America. Ultimately, in 1948 he would cooperate with Victor Weybright at the head of New American Library, a Penguin branch. New American Library differed from Bantam in that it not only published relatively cheap reprints of classics, but also included high-quality works in its catalogue.

Although Jacques Schiffrin is not as frequently mentioned as the founders of Pantheon Books, Kurt and Helen Wolff, his trajectory is nevertheless particularly interesting for this study, as it also partly illustrates the turmoils of French publishing during the war. Schiffrin represents a perfect example of a Franco-American transatlantic intermediary. Born in 1892 in Baku and educated in Saint Petersburg, as was Hoffman, he was the acclaimed creator of the French Pléiade series, initially founded as an independent imprint intended for the publication of Russian classics in translation, which was sold to Gallimard in 1936. In the summer of 1940, following German orders, Gallimard informed Schiffrin that he was being let go, as his name was among the first on the blacklist of "overly prominent" Jews established by German ambassador to France Otto Abetz.[25] With the help of Varian Fry and the "Emergency Rescue Committee" in Marseille, after several unsuccessful attempts, Schiffrin and his family were finally able to escape to New York. There he again set out to establish an imprint of French underground texts geared toward French readers exiled in the United States; its catalogue included such classic underground works as Vercors' *Le Silence de la mer* and Joseph Kessel's *L'Armée des ombres*. In 1944, he began to work with the Wolffs, who were in the process of creating Pantheon Books, and edited a series of French texts, including Camus' *L'Etranger* in 1946.

These are but a few examples of émigré publishers who contributed to the progressive internationalization of American publishing during the war and early peacetime. Other experiments attest to the opening of US publishing to new shores. Among such experiments was the joint organization of trade publishers and government, coming together to promote US books abroad, especially on the European continent.[26] The wartime coalition between the Office of War Information and book publishers grouped under the Council on Books in Wartime (CBW) is well documented in John B. Hench's 2010 *Books as Weapons*. The Council, founded in early 1942 and composed mostly of members of the Book Publishers Bureau, allied with the Office of War Information (OWI), found in the war and in the government's efforts:

> an opportunity to solve the linked, lingering problems of profitability and professional identity, and to solve them not only for the duration of the war, but for the long term, for what one observer called 'the smart man's peace' that lay beyond wartime.[27]

As Hench states, the list of individual members in the coalition clearly reflected the best of contemporary US trade publishing, and represented many, if not most, of the publishing giants of the century.[28] With only one publisher from the most recent circle of New York Jewish publishers, Harold Guinzburg, then President of The Viking Press, the rostrum included Harold Edward H. Dodd (Dodd, Mead), Cass Canfield of Harper & Brothers, Archibald G. Ogden (Bobbs-Merrill), John Farrar, and Trevor Hill of Doubleday, Doran, most of whom made up informal Ivy League old boys' circles.[29]

The OWI was free to use the publishers' facilities to print, publish, and distribute books that helped the war effort, which on the one hand amounted to propaganda and, on the other, was a means of ostentatiously exonerating publishers from all accusations of commercialism. Congress soon put an end to the coalition's domestic strategy based on lists of "imperative books" for American readers, yet it did not obstruct their international endeavors, resulting most famously in the publication and distribution of the Overseas Edition series, planned in 1944 and executed in 1945. In addition to these, a smaller series, Transatlantic Editions, was published and distributed from England, under the supervision of Guinzburg, stationed there with the OWI.[30] These books were intended as post-liberation propaganda, to fill the gap in European countries until local publishing facilities recovered. Thus were US publishers made aware that this "priming of the pump" secured them with an advantage in the race toward new international markets.[31]

Because of the nature of the CBW/ OWI coalition, and perhaps because US publishers truly believed that their books would spread the good word, the tinge of propaganda is ever-present in their discourse, often blending with commercialism, as can be seen even in this private outcry by Blanche Knopf:

> France . . . is hungry for books from England and America, particularly America. There is a terrific cry for books for translation and in the English language. We here cannot conceive how a country like France with no free literature, no free reading for five years, what it

means for them to get books again. The most important thing is to make it possible for the French to get our point of view both politically and culturally.[32]

Again it should be stressed that in spite of German and French censorship, the French had not stopped reading during the war, nor had they completely interrupted other cultural practices.[33] In order to stave off criticisms of overt propaganda such as exuded by the previous statement, the books selected for translation into French, Italian, German, and Dutch were chosen among publishers' lists of American books already in print. According to Hench, the selection of mostly non-fiction works reflected middle-brow taste: many of the best modernist writers, who might have been considered too close to the far left of the political spectrum—Sinclair Lewis, Theodore Dreiser . . .—were excluded, and a certain "disinclination to deal with race questions" can be noted.[34] Incidentally, several works dealing with race questions would become very much in vogue in France after the war, as Bernice Baumgarten of Brandt & Brandt rightly remarked in 1945 to Hoffman—"Apparently, judging from the inquiries we have had, any book having to do with the negroes in the United States is popular."[35]

The Overseas Editions were published by an *ad hoc* concern, Overseas Editions Inc., under the same management as the Armed Services Editions, a series of books in English intended for the US soldiers stationed throughout Europe; Overseas Editions Inc. was to acquire rights to translate and produce the books, but final approval of the translations rested with the OWI. Interestingly, French and German translations in the Overseas Editions series far outnumbered Italian titles.[36] Because of the Occupation and the collaboration of the Vichy regime, France was apparently regarded as a highly sensitive country for cultural rehabilitation or disintoxication. With preparations delayed, Harold Guinzburg in London reported that notwithstanding their enthusiasm for the books, the French worried about the underlying imperialist tendencies of British and American publishers, and were expressing concern about the protection of their own publishing houses.[37] For American trade publishers, however, such a venture was at least a twofold success: they had done their bit for the war effort and American cultural propaganda, all the while preparing for post-war international markets; in the process they also demonstrated the extent to which they had embraced the American culture of planning.[38]

This wartime public-private collaboration was briefly continued after the hostilities had ceased, through the USIBA, a non-profit export corporation that was meant to act as "an instrumentality [serving] as a common meeting ground for industry and government."[39] Although short-lived, incorporated in January 1945 and defunct by early 1947, it provides an interesting outlook on the problems faced by publishers, and their willingness to expand their book markets overseas to counter what they viewed as the predominance of the cultural action of the British Council and the National Book Council. Very much the product of the Book Publishers' Bureau, USIBA was actually modelled on the British Council. The Book Publishers' Bureau's position paper emphasized how they

> would like to see the U.S. book as freely available in other countries as those of any other foreign supplier. The industry believes that by thus giving other peoples an opportunity, at least, to become familiar with the purposes, ideals and consequences of our culture it is doing a public service as well as furthering its own particular interests.[40]

For Frank Ninkovich, this "cartel" was indeed quite extraordinary for the simple reason that it went against the well-known individualism of publishers,[41] which, with the difficult balance between business and government interests and the lack of currency in many foreign countries, would ultimately bring about its demise. Under the guise of fostering cultural relations through books, the USIBA was intended to serve as intermediary between US and foreign publishers, by supplying them with information, and possibly facilitating the exchange of foreign rights. The inevitable propagandistic tone notwithstanding, the USIBA was to function very much as a book agency, or in the words of Ninkovich, "the sales agent abroad for U.S. publishers, [. . .] supported by dues and commissions from its sales."[42] Its very existence therefore demonstrated the need for such agents, as US publishers most often did not know the foreign markets, could not always tell the sound publishers from the unsound, and consequently were not in a position to negotiate the best, if not the most lucrative, matches. This concern was indeed expressed some ten years later during a Princeton Conference on "Books Abroad" sponsored by the culturally oriented United States Information Agency (USIA), underlining how this ignorance constituted an obstacle to the development of books as better "ambassadors of good will":

> The mutual ignorance, in the main, of American publishers about the capabilities of foreign publishers and the potentialities of foreign markets for American works in translation, and of foreign publishers about how to find good American books and contract for them, is a major impediment to increased commerce in this area.[43]

Certainly American publishers would stand to gain from an improved familiarity with French publishers, in order to assess their capabilities and thence the potentialities of the French market. In this context, co-agents appeared as the perfect intermediaries, who might act as diplomats of sorts, in the service of Americans.

Matchmaking and Information Gathering

The war, and the years following the conflict, demonstrated that books were "a unique medium for transmitting ideas and for encouraging reflective and long-lasting mutual understanding . . . keys to cultural development, catalysts to trade, and unparalleled (but 'neglected') ambassadors of American culture."[44] As they helped to transfer books and ideas from one country to the other, agents were certainly adjuncts to diplomacy, whose missions closely resembled those of diplomats. For Jeremy Black, diplomacy may indeed be considered as "a privileged aspect of general systems of information-gathering, of representation, and of negotiation," to which editors, publishers, and agents certainly contributed.[45]

One of the diplomatic services rendered by French co-agents was, in fact, information gathering. Depending on the quality of this information, they would in turn establish their credentials with US publishers and book agencies, and found the trusting relationships required. This was all the more important in the last two years of the war as the moral and political turmoil in French publishing made it a particularly shifting and elusive field. The structures remained largely those of the pre-war years, but small new imprints had appeared, and those houses which had been aryanized during the war were restored to their former owners, while some of the bigger publishers did not always manage to maintain their dominant position, shaken by the investigations into possible collaboration with the German during the war.

As early as 1944, the *Conseil National de la Résistance* (National Resistance Council) demanded that publishers as well as writers be tried, and the *Commission d'épuration de l'édition* (Committee for the purging of publishing) was created, modelled on the *Commission nationale des écrivains* (National Committee on Writers). The various changes brought to this *Commission d'épuration de l'édition*, which was never given an official status, are symptomatic of the uncomfortable position of those sitting on these "juries": the very transformation of the former into a *Commission consultative d'épuration* (advisory commission) in February 1945 reveals how difficult it was to decide who, in the final instance, would be the judges. In addition to these special committees, publishers whose acts of collaboration were evident were brought directly to trial and charged with intelligence with the enemy. The various trials and accusations lasted nearly a decade; the duration of such legal procedures in itself was difficult to bear, as suspicion seeped outside literary and editorial circles, permeating public opinion.

Yet, in spite of *Résistants'* call for a hard line, few publishers were actually convicted, convictions being more often than not light in the eyes of those who had deliberately shunned collaboration and risked seeing their business closed down.[46] Those who had contributed to the aryanization of Jewish publishers—Jean de la Hire, who had published pro-German works and participated in the selling of Ferenczi to a German owner, or Louis Thomas, who had connived to take over Calmann-Lévy . . .—were sentenced, though some were rehabilitated with the second Amnesty Act of 1953[47]; Denoël was summarily assassinated, three years before the end of his trial and his ultimate acquittal in 1948. Yet others, not the lowliest in the pantheon of Parisian publishers, although strongly suspected of getting too cozy with the enemy, either saw their cases dismissed, or were handed a light sentence.[48]

French historians, literary scholars, book historians, and sociologists have never ceased to wonder about these thorny issues, but here is not the place to take up the ongoing debates.[49] Yet a word to clarify the context: to this day, Gallimard, whose case was dismissed in October 1946, has crystallized many of the suspicions, to some extent becoming the "publisher one loves to hate." Its enormous prestige, its beautiful catalogue, and its predominance account for both the fascination exerted by the publishing house and the continuous suspicions. This case also presents a perfect example of the complex wartime entanglement of the economic and intellectual.[50] Several reasons have been invoked to explain some surprising acquittals, among which is habitually mentioned the defense of Gaston Gallimard by some of his impeccably moral authors and employees of the young generation born out of the *Résistance*. Indeed the epitome of the French *intellectuels*, such as Jean-Paul Sartre—who sat on the *Commission d'épuration*—or André Malraux, or of the former generation, like Jean Paulhan, rose to defend the publisher.[51] Most publishers were able to prove that they had been pressured into banning books and publishing dubious works, either in favor of the Vichy regime or by notoriously fascist authors, which served to ultimately exonerate them. This now classic narrative is countered by several elements: the 140 publishers who had signed the *convention de censure* (censorship convention) with the Germans and approved the Otto list of banned books in September 1940, had done so *even before* Pétain's announcement of an official collaboration with the Third Reich in October of that year.[52] Moreover, as we have seen in the case of Jacques Schiffrin's departure from Gallimard—the reasons for which were never officially disclosed—Jean-Yves Mollier has convincingly argued on the basis of evidence found in the archives of the *Syndicat des Editeurs* restricted to scholars *in totum* or partially since the post-war era, that many editors and publishers had in fact willingly collaborated, either out of ideological or political sympathies, or on economic grounds.[53]

In light of this all-too brief overview of the political, economic, and legal complexity of French publishing in the immediate post-war era, one is led to wonder to what extent publishers and agents on the other side of the Atlantic could indeed fully grasp the goings-on in this foreign market.

In his 1944–1945 correspondence with his American and British partners, Michel Hoffman regularly attempted to clarify the situation, reporting on French publishers and fellow agents. His presentations are not devoid of personal grievances. Agents themselves shared in the climate of bitterness and suspicion, as this draft letter to Bernice Baumgarten of Brandt & Brandt on the subject of James G. Cozzens' foreign rights reveals,

> I happen to know that Mrs Bradley, a lady agent of this town, has also approached Mrs. Hill about the Cozzens copyrights. I also know she has been busily writing to you, Mrs Scialtiel, another colleague of mine is also intending to write you about some authors or other . . . . *Now I do not want to say anything against both of those ladies and I find it quite natural that they tried to do as much business as they could during the occupation and shortly after it, my agency being closed as I was away first in the army and then in the Resistance movement.* However now I am back again and have resumed business as exclusive representative of A.M. Heath & Co. Ltd. and therefore as your exclusive representative for France, I do not think anybody ought to be butting in any more I am sure you feel about it in the same way as I do. (my emphasis)[54]

Aside from the vigorous and legitimate defense of his prerogatives as exclusive French representative of the Heath agency in London and Brandt & Brandt in New York, I cannot help but note the cynicism of the preterition, added to the underlying suggestion that Jenny Bradley and Marguerite Scialtiel[55] had taken advantage of his absence, as though his predominant position had possibly been threatening their own activity. Hoffman's seemingly casual mention of his own whereabouts during the war, in contrast with the other two agents, signaling that he had been on the side of Germany's enemies, was probably intended as a means of establishing his political uprightness and, therefore, his trustworthy position.

Given Hoffman's origins, however, this emotional response to what he considered unfair business practices takes on a particular and personal resonance. Interestingly, Hoffman's pointing to his war record also served as a reminder, and perhaps a defense, of his particular position as a man in a largely feminine agenting business. In fact his correspondence strikingly underlines the overwhelming presence of women agents on both sides of the Atlantic, as also attested by the list of members of the American Society of Authors' Representatives. As James L. West has noted, in the US male-dominated publishing industry, women found in agenting a field where they would face less discrimination, and in fact, one of the "earliest and best ways" for them to enter publishing.[56] The representation of actresses on the European stages was also largely feminine, as Maggie Gale has shown, drawing a list of women play agents that included Paris-based agents Marguerite Scialtiel and Ninon Tallon. As British play agent Kitty Black once surmised, perhaps women were "temperamentally suited to dealing with private problems as well as literary dilemmas, with methodical minds to register details of contract and remember anniversaries and celebrations."[57] Certainly the growing importance of clerical training in the interwar years, and the construction of the exclusively feminine position of secretary in France, also help to explain the number of women agents.[58] At a time when the domestic ideology continued to hold sway, the tasks of agents, which could be performed from one's own apartment, were also acceptable for women.

Hoffman's letter was in fact addressed to one of the better-known American women agents, Bernice Baumgarten. Originally hired, interestingly, as a secretary by the New York Brandt & Brandt agency, by the 1940s Baumgarten had rapidly become one of their best agents and was indeed reputed as one of the best agents in New York.[59] The high regard and affection in which she was held by publishing luminary Bennett Cerf, as attested by their correspondence between 1927 and the 1950s, seem to second this opinion. In 1953, Cerf sent Baumgarten an affectionate Christmas note, declaring, "A Merry Christmas to you and, to be quite serious for a change, I honestly think that one of the nicest things that happened to me in the publishing world this year was getting to know you better."[60]

Brandt & Brandt had been founded by Carl Brandt in 1913 as an adjunct to the Mary Kirkpatrick Dramatic Agency. By 1928 it was known as Brandt & Brandt, and would soon move to the top of its class, along with Curtis Brown, Ltd.[61] Baumgarten, who had married writer James Gould Cozzens in 1927, developed close relations and friendships with several authors, including Samuel Hopkins Adams, and represented Dos Passos, John Gunther, Wallace Stegner, and John P. Marquand, whose bestselling works were actively sought out by French publishers after the war. Besides Baumgarten's clients, the firm also represented modernist poets and novelists James Oppenheim, Jessie Fauset, and E.E. Cummings, poet Stephen Vincent Benet, as well as many writers of bestselling fiction, such as Frederick Faust (Max Brand) or Stewart Edward White, authors of westerns, or Bessie Breuer. From 1948 to 1952, they handled the rights of Raymond Chandler. In fact, after the war, Brandt & Brandt would provide the French with contacts for many authors of popular crime and detective fiction then in vogue. It was through their London representative, A.M. Heath, that Hoffman ultimately obtained their representation in France after the war.

In January 1946, Hoffman, writing to a business acquaintance who had escaped to the United States, once again underlined his position,

As far as I am concerned, I may say that I am part of that most fortunate category of persons who were spared the horrors of captivity and of Hitler's camps. It did not take me very long to rebuild and even develop my pre-war business concern . . . .[62]

Hoffman was a survivor himself, having escaped the Bolshevik repression and the Nazi regime, although not on a par with those who had survived the concentration camps.

In November 1944, Curtis Brown London struck a cooperation agreement with Hoffman, whereby he became their exclusive representative in France. As in the case of most such cooperations, no formal contract was provided, just a simple letter outlining the terms. Hoffman thus replaced in this capacity Marguerite Scialtiel who had worked for the agency's Paris Bureau in the 1930s. For Mary Ann Gillies, the London Curtis Brown agency was certainly on a par with J.B. Pinker as a challenger to Watt, and a contestant in the second phase of literary agenting. With roots going back to 1899, a quarter of a century after A.P. Watt had established his own office, it was created by the American Albert Curtis Brown, who, after learning the newspaper trade as a "cub reporter" and at various jobs for the *Buffalo Express* in the early 1880s, had been sent to London to work as correspondent for the *New York Press*. As he recalls in his autobiography, *Contacts*, *The New York Press* had agreed to let him sell several features—special topical articles, or illustrated features—to Sunday papers; thus was begun the Curtis Brown Syndicate, or International Publishing Bureau, which he ultimately sold during the First World War to continue the business of his agency. Although he stressed in his 1935 memoirs that "it was stray chance that led [him] into a new corridor of publishing,"[63] it was precisely his prior experience in the newspaper trade, and his contacts with both American and British magazine editors, that surreptitiously led him to this rather new profession. Continuing to head the International Publishing Bureau, by 1905 he was conducting business under his own name, Curtis Brown Ltd. Early on, his keen acumen enticed him to develop different departments and take on different associates. This would ultimately guarantee the perennity of his agency, contrary to J.B. Pinker, whose success rested solely on his own talent for discovering new talents, ultimately leading his business to disappear for want of satisfactory successors.[64] Curtis Brown strongly believed that the emergence of the agent would lead to an improved distribution of power between author and publisher, to the advantage of all parties involved. Curtis Brown not only represented some of the most popular and important authors and politicians of the first half of the 20th century, his advice on English publishing conditions was also sought out by American publishers such as Frank N. Doubleday.

Brown's self-conception as diplomat is evidenced in his recounting of his own—unsuccessful—endeavors to bring about reciprocal copyright relations between the United States and Russia around 1915, both by printing features in the leading literary papers such as *The Spectator*, and engaging in correspondence and negotiations with the Russian Ambassador in London, the US Secretary of State, and American Ambassador to the United Kingdom, Walter Hines Page, formerly a publisher with Doubleday.[65] Significantly, Curtis Brown's narrative of such diplomatic endeavors is associated, in his memoirs, with his apparent belief that the international exchange of literature "between the various peoples so obviously in need of better understanding of each other," might induce "touchy neighbours [. . .] to read each other's most notable books, and get each other's viewpoints" so that it "would be possible to reduce the misunderstandings that lead to war."[66] This warranted his effort to establish an international clearing-house "for the exchange of book-publishing rights between the various countries that form part of what we call the publishing world,"[67] and the opening of branches in Berlin, Milan—closed in 1931—and Copenhagen, as well as Paris, and of course, New York.

The New York branch, which would prove so valuable to Hoffman, was opened in the summer of 1914, just before the outbreak of the war. Alan Collins, a former editor with Doubleday, was called in to head the New York office in 1935. Collins, already a prominent member of the Society of Authors' Representatives, became president of the US agency when it was sold to him in 1941. Other influent personnel in the British publishing world made their debut with Curtis Brown in London, before flying from the nest, sometimes leaving with some acrimony: Nancy Pearn, formerly in charge of the continental and transatlantic rights, David Pollinger and David Higham would leave to form an agency of their own, and former agent Michael Joseph established his publishing house the same year that Collins was brought to work in New York.[68] Curtis Brown was for a time associated with Hughes Massie, the latter leaving in 1913 to found his own agency. Another agent, John Farquharson, had worked as manager of the English Books Department at Curtis Brown.

Since the 1940s, agents' code of ethics has made it very clear that like lawyers and doctors, they are not to advertise. But in 1927, here is what an aspiring author could read in the *Who's Who in Literature*? under the name "Curtis Brown":

> Representatives in the principal European capitals. This company, which represents a large number of the leading authors, has its own New York offices devoted exclusively to the work of its clients, and with a large and experienced staff. The company makes a specialty of securing a market throughout the world for English and American books, films and plays, and for European works of international importance.

It would in fact be hard to find fault with this self-promotional description: by the outbreak of the Second World War, the agency had placed material and taken in as clients H.G. Wells—an "intermittent good friend"—Winston Churchill, David Lloyd George, George Bernard Shaw, A.A. Milne, D.H. Lawrence, Ford Madox Ford, W.H. Auden, Christopher Isherwood, but also Theodore Dreiser, T. S. Stribling, Frank Norris, William Faulkner, and John Steinbeck. For George Greenfield, a former agent with John Farquharson, in the 1940s Curtis Brown was "the biggest London literary agency."[69] Brown himself claimed in 1935,

> Most of the leading American publishers send to us their book-rights to be placed abroad; many of the English publishers deal through our clearing-house with American publishers, and we are now occasionally disposing of French and Italian rights for German publishers, and vice-versa, besides an increasing stream of book-rights to and from London and the Continent.[70]

Several continental branches were opened between 1914 and 1935, including a Paris office, where Marguerite Scialtiel made her debut as agent.[71] Contacts with French agents, such as the William A. Bradley agency, are evidenced in the archives. As can be gathered from later correspondence between M. Hoffman and the US branch of Curtis Brown, the different branches established in different countries operated independently, although there were several instances of mix-ups between the London Office and the New York Office, since the latter did not establish a foreign rights department until after 1944, and both London and New York were brought to negotiate the rights to US authors.

Hence the foreign rights of many American authors were in fact handled by the London office.[72] London had signed agreements for the representation of all translation rights not retained by the authors publishing with Harper & Brothers, Farrar & Rinehart, Doubleday, Doran, and Thomas Y. Crowell, in addition to which it periodically handled foreign rights for other US giants such as Bobbs, Merrill; Dodd, Mead; Houghton, Mifflin; Coward McCann; and Random House.[73] Needless to say, for Hoffman the agreement must have appeared a potentially lucrative one, as long as the French co-agent could find adequate French publishers for the works, that is, provide good matchmaking services. For him, matchmaking depended on an agent's capacity to determine who would offer the most appropriate "home" for a book; thus it certainly entailed discrimination between publishers on literary, business, *as well as* political grounds. To all accounts, in this period Hoffman's views echo the discourse of the *Comité Consultatif de l'épuration* in distinguishing the "sound" from the "unsound" publishers, based on the issue of collaboration with the enemy.

In early 1945, writing to the manager of Curtis, Brown London's Foreign Rights Department, he politely offered his opinion on the agency's recent sending of books directly to French publishers,

> A publisher may ask for a book or even extend an offer for it and yet offer—from *our* point of view—an unsatisfactory home for the work in question. This is especially true to-day when all publishers are running after British and American books (even those whose attitude under the occupation was not irreproachable!) and firms and/ or authors who have a representative on the spot should I think in their own interest leave it to his judgment to find the local publisher who a) has the kind of literary output into which the book in question fits in best, b) can afford to pay the best price and c) offers the necessary political requirements.[74]

Hinting at the great potential in the translation rights market of the period, Hoffman was obviously attempting to convince his British partners of the advantages of having Continental representatives for both British and American agencies. As far as the French book business in 1944–1945 was concerned, one could not dissociate the literary from the political, and in spite of what did filter in the English-language professional or trade press, only local agents were fit to sift through those French publishers, hungry for British and American books.[75] Even the best price offer, theoretically, would not be acceptable if the political standing of the publisher was deemed unsatisfactory.

Further evidence of Hoffman's political distinctions can be found in an annotated list of important French publishers sent in 1945 to Alan Collins, President of Curtis Brown, New York. Concerned with matchmaking for American as well as British works, Hoffman details those houses that already published foreign authors and foreign literature series—which, borrowing from the French, he calls "collections"—or were about to create one: Plon's Les Feux Croisés, "often regarded as the best 'collection' of foreign authors"; Albert Pigasse's Editions du Masque "*Le Masque*," "the best French detective collection, containing all the best Anglo-American thriller writers"; or again Robert Laffont, who were "preparing a good collection of foreign authors," presumably a reference to the "*Pavillons*" series.[76] Although Hoffman ultimately signed fewer contracts with Laffont than with other publishers, this imprint might reasonably have been at the top of his list. Founded in 1941 in Marseille, located in the free zone, after moving to Paris Laffont had built its reputation on its refusal to collaborate with the enemy. Furthermore, it was one of the few houses which guaranteed translators a royalty on sales, a good way of securing excellent translations for the many titles suggested in part by American professor Albert Guérard who scouted for the French imprint. On the political front, although

Hoffman took great care not to incriminate publishers directly, the style and length of commentaries on this list of publishers suggest his own preferences: Fayard is presented as an "Important firm, connected with reactionary and royalist circles before the war but not particularly compromised through collaboration with the Germans"; Denoël—who had published both Céline's anti-semitic works and Communist Elsa Triolet's books during the war in spite of anti-Jewish censorship—was subtly labelled "not a very hot proposition," with "Denoël in jail awaiting trial." As for Grasset, Hoffman merely mentioned its current management by a temporary administrator, as its founder was then resting in a "mental home," not alluding to the fact that he was awaiting trial for collaboration with the enemy.

His strikingly brief presentation of Gallimard—granted, the publisher presumably needed no long introduction to US agents—as opposed to his lengthy description of Albin Michel, outlining the recent sales he had concluded with the latter, set the tone for much of the later business correspondence. In short, Hoffman does not appear to have been particularly eager to do business with Gallimard, for various reasons that might have changed over the years. In 1944–1945, it may have been the cloud of suspicion hovering over the publishing house: as early as August 1944, when Paris was being liberated, the French press had stigmatized it as being "pro-German," and considered it one of the publishers that should definitely be purged.[77] The handling of French translation rights for Richard Wright's *Native Son* illustrates Hoffman's reluctance and preferences.

In January 1945, informed that Harper & Brothers were negotiating for a publication of Wright's *Native Son* in Argentina, Sonia Chapter asked Hoffman to get them a good offer in France.[78] *Native Son* had been published in 1940 as a Book-of-the-Month Club selection, consequently becoming a bestseller, which, aside from its literary quality, certainly made for its attraction around the world.[79] By mid-February Hoffman cabled back with an offer from Albin Michel, with whom he had worked before the war, and who, he claimed, completely trusted his judgment. Although the offer was not extraordinary—a $1,000 advance against a 10% flat royalty—Sonia Chapter seemed about to accept it, but, upon learning that Marcel Duhamel, one of the best French translators at the time, had already translated part of the work, she eventually proceeded to await a better offer from the translator. When read between the lines, Hoffman's reply to Chapter is redolent of the climate of suspicion of the times:

> Duhamel also wrote Gallimard that you granted him the rights of this book. As you remember you wrote me (on Jan. 24) that Harper's got an offer from Hermes of Buenos Aires and could I get a quick and better one. I thereupon wired Albin Michel's proposition less

than 24 hours after receipt of your letter. Now, if it is a matter of translation, Albin Michel would be very glad to let Duhamel do it for them. In any case I am in rather a foolish position toward Albin Michel who is my best and oldest customer. I told Gaston Gallimard of A.M's [Albin Michel's] offer and I do not mind staging a competition between them to improve the terms but I would much rather have Michel do it than Gallimard at the end because he is independent of the Messageries Hachette sales chain and gives his books more attention and better publicity than Gallimard who turn out a lot and then forget about them (it being Hachette's business to look after them.) As a result Gallimard very seldom achieves high sales, "GONE WITH THE WIND" being a glorious exception as it practically sold itself.[80]

This rather irritated reply suggests the difficult position of agents in relation to publishers, as Hoffman's primary goal here, aside from getting the best offer for Wright, was clearly to please Albin Michel and maintain the trusting relations he had always cultivated with the French publisher. He probably knew Gallimard to be a logical choice for *Native Son*, with Duhamel close to the house—hence his suggestion that Duhamel translate the book for Albin Michel—yet he clearly undermines Gallimard's capacity to actively promote and sell the work. In passing, his criticism of the main sales and distribution chain, Messageries Hachette, echoes the general diffidence toward its monopolistic tendencies, which had earned the structure the nickname "Green Trust."[81] As Mollier wrote, the idea that Hachette perhaps did not distribute all the books entrusted to it by the publishers under contract—who were prohibited from verifying the stocks—was a fantasy that fuelled many of the criticisms endured by the distributor.[82] Moreover, Messageries Hachette had been suspected as early as the fall of 1944 of collaborating with the enemy, and although they had not been convicted, suspicion continued to hang in the air.[83] Did Hoffman manage to cast doubt on Gallimard's capacity to stand by their books and authors? Did he play this card only to counter the power of the distributor? Or was he concealing ulterior, political reasons? Ultimately, Curtis Brown—Sonia Chapter denied having ever promised the rights to Duhamel—decided to follow Hoffman, not wanting to alienate Albin Michel. *Native Son* was finally published under their imprint, in Duhamel's translation, and negotiated with improved terms and a gradual royalty scale.[84] This fight also reveals that Hoffman, like other local agents, both defended the proprietor of rights and French publishers. This staging of competition between Gallimard and other publishers would not be the last for Hoffman.

Hoffman apprised his transatlantic business correspondents of larger issues concerning publications in French, as he was well aware of another form of competition that had resulted from the war. The war situation in fact highlighted the necessary distinction between language rights and territory. The paralyzing of French publishing had indeed led publishers and printers in French-speaking countries—mainly Belgium, Switzerland, Canada—as well as French publishers in exile in other countries, including the United States, to step into the breach, and publish what could not be issued in France. The prior selling of world French rights to such publishers often irritated Hoffman and his fellow agents, who found it difficult to ascertain the availability of some foreign authors' French rights after the war. Throughout 1945, Hoffman was repeatedly faced with the embarrassing situation of offering a French publisher a book whose rights had already been sold in Canada or in another French-speaking country.

As the war ended, such publishers began to wonder about future prospects; some, like the Canadian firm Editions Variétés, believed they could fill the gap with cheap books, beyond a transitional period of reconstruction. From this editor's point of view, this was not necessarily detrimental to French culture:

> We are sorry that Paris is likely to be slow in recovering her publishing preeminence, but it is probably a wholesome situation for the world in general that Montréal, New York, Rio de Janeiro, Buenos Aires, Lausanne and other centers have had this experience with high-grade French publishing. Their success is added evidence of the vitality of French culture; and if they continue to publish French books, the world, and France herself, cannot fail to profit in the end.[85]

This point of view was certainly not shared by the French, especially concerning those neighboring countries whose geographical proximity to Paris allowed foreign publishers and printers—in Belgium or Switzerland—to distribute their books to French readers easily. For many in Paris, Swiss publishers had taken what was seen as unfair advantage of the wartime situation. This brought up the contractual issue of language rights versus territory/world rights, a thorny issue offering a breach for piracy, with which US and British publishers also contended in the post-war era in their competition for the free world market. By the fall of 1945, Hoffman informed Sonia Chapter of Curtis Brown London that, following the advice of the *Syndicat des Editeurs* (publishers' union), the French government had taken a series of measures amounting to a strict restriction of importation—if not the barring—of books in French printed in Belgium or Switzerland. He contributed his opinion that, in these conditions, granting world rights for the French language to Swiss or Belgian publishers was not in the best interest of US authors, who would not see these books distributed to the wider French-reading public.[86] This problem was further complicated by the fact that several

Swiss imprints, for example, also had subsidiary branches in France, where they could legally distribute books, thus continuing to compete with French houses. While he appeared to defend French publishers, Hoffman was not about to pass on potential deals for French rights outside the country's frontiers; he proved his astuteness by distinguishing between reliable and unreliable publishers outside the French territorial boundaries, again on political grounds. Writing to Sonia Chapter of Curtis Brown in London on the subject of the Franco-Swiss publisher Jeheber who had inquired into future business ventures, he evidently balanced ideological standards with business interests:

> You know my attitude to the question of publishing French books in Switzerland and I told him about some of the grievances we have against the Swiss publishers. On the other hand, I acknowledged that every possible discrimination is necessary between firms that have only come into being during and owing to the occupation of France by her enemies and have largely profited by it and such Swiss publishers that have always had an honest and established business, as in the first place Jeheber himself whose firm exists [sic] for centuries and with whom I myself have transacted business as far back as 1934.[87]

In this case, it is difficult to ascertain firmly whether Hoffman chose to downplay his moral scruples to secure business prospects, or whether indeed he believed Jeheber to be a reliable and honest publisher. It is very likely that his business correspondents abroad, with no opportunity to verify the standing of the smaller Continental houses, would take his advice.

Political and ideological concerns seem to loom over the early postwar business transactions, requiring Hoffman to explain the context to his overseas partners, as a cautious yet not completely unbiased intermediary. By all accounts, material difficulties also raised delicate matters necessitating both pedagogical skills and—literally—classic diplomacy.

Agenting: A Diplomat's Game

In the last two years of the war, national and international communications remained complicated, and merely obtaining reading copies for publishers proved quite arduous. The circulation of books was facilitated by the classic diplomatic channels, and French co-agents relied on the offices of the OWI/US Information Service (USIS) or the British Embassy in Paris to access books.[88] These channels proved especially necessary in the case of US bestsellers, as the possibility of French publishers acquiring the rights depended on the rapidity of their decision and, consequently, on their getting the book as early as possible—at any rate, before competitors. Relations with these American diplomatic services were useful in more ways than one, as they might sometimes provide introductions to new business partners—Hoffman was given Baumgarten's contacts by Peter Jennison from the USIS—or contribute to hastening a publication process.[89] Contacts between Jenny Bradley and John Lackey Brown, Assistant Chief of foreign publications at the OWI and foreign correspondent for the Sunday edition of the *New York Times* were certainly fruitful for the Bradley agency. On another level, the USIS sometimes provided paper to publishers, as with Albin Michel in April 1945, to speed up the publication of Kinnan Rawlings' *The Yearling*, which had been delayed since before the war.[90]

As we may surmise from his correspondence with both Brandt & Brandt and Curtis Brown Hoffman was anxious to establish his credentials with his transatlantic partners, by illustrating his business sense and his thorough knowledge of the local book trade. Not infrequently, he was also asked to verify and clarify contracts signed with French publishers before or during the war and, in some cases, to recover advances or royalties that had been mislaid. Even as he attempted to broker new contracts, his trustworthiness seemed to depend on his ability to set the record(s) straight in a transitional period leading to the consolidation of relations in the post-war era.

Hoffman's business in the last two years of the war testifies to the state of confusion regarding contracts for French-language rights signed before the conflict, due to the interruption of business. Hoffman was contacted by French translators, asking him if he might inquire into the whereabouts of work completed but never published; at the same time, he was asked by US agents to investigate the publication of books contracted for in the years leading to the war, as special ad interim copyright had been granted on both sides of the Atlantic. While some failures to publish were relatively understandable, others were more surprising, as in the case of James Gould Cozzens' *S.S. San Pedro*: Gallimard had acquired French rights in 1934, yet in November 1946 Hoffman was still expecting a copy, only thinly concealing his irritation with the house whom he considered, "a terrible crew really."[91] The book was ultimately published in 1950, which raises the question of why Cozzens and his agent, Bernice Baumgarten—who, as of 1927, was also his wife—accepted such conditions. Were they willing to wait, comforted by Gallimard's outstanding reputation? Or, more prosaically, did Cozzens not expect much from the French translation of his work, in terms of revenues and/or international reputation?

In November 1945 Bernice Baumgarten of Brandt & Brandt asked Hoffman to look into the matters of Bessie Breuer's first novel, *Memory of Love* (1935) and *The Daughter* (1938), as well as several works by Dos Passos, whom they had represented for a time. Besides shedding light on the confusion caused in publishing by the war, the stories of what became of these works each highlight a specific facet of how publishing was being conducted in different French houses. After some investigating, Hoffman wrote back in January 1946: Dos Passos' works had been acquired by several French publishers over the course of time, from avowed Communist imprint Editions Sociales Internationales, to Gallimard, through Maurice-Edgar Coindreau. Hoffman reported that the Editions de la Nouvelle Revue Critique—to which in 1939 he had sold the French rights to Dos Passos' *Adventures of a Young Man*, the first of the *District of Columbia* trilogy—being unable to bring out the book because of the war, had ceded their rights to Gallimard, who had in the meantime acquired the other volumes in the trilogy.[92] Brandt & Brandt—who were exacting and extremely rigorous on contractual matters, as Hoffman would often remind his French partners and correspondents—as well as authors and the Writers' Guild, did not appreciate or even accept such transfers of contract. On a strictly legal level, a new contract should have been drawn up as a new publisher came into the picture. Dos Passos having left Brandt & Brandt in 1940,[93] it is possible that such a contract was indeed signed without the agency being informed. It is most likely that Editions de la Nouvelle Revue Critique ceded the rights without telling either the author or his agent. In 1961 the Authors' Guild was still warning authors against such practices, specifying that—at least in the United States—if a publisher's bankruptcy was indeed one of the contingencies where a contract could be terminated without the author being notified, in such cases the rights should automatically revert to the author.[94] Probably the conditions caused by the war reduced many other French publishers to such necessities, and American authors, agents, and publishers chose to turn a blind eye while publishing was rebuilding in Paris. As we shall see, the war indeed justified a number of doings that would never have been accepted in peacetime; in this case, Dos Passos surely did not suffer from the change, as his French publications were "upgraded" from a relatively small imprint to the Rolls Royce of French publishing.

Other publishers, however, were intent on upholding ethical business standards in spite of the war. Although perhaps difficult to believe, the following story, as told by Hoffman, of the whereabouts of two of Breuer's works was certainly not unique, and illustrates concretely the impact of the war on the international book trade:

> The translation of THE DAUGHTER was entrusted to Melle Claudine Chonez who started it in Spring 1940 but has lost the manuscript as well as the original during the exodus from Paris in June 1940 when the German planes were machine-gunning the refugees on the roads. The American copy of MEMORY OF LOVE was confiscated by the Germans from Albin Michel's office in 1941. So the first thing to do is to send us both original editions. [Albin] Michel will have them translated immediately and put into print as priority property.[95]

Hoffman, who emphasized that Albin Michel could not be held account-able, as this was a clear case of *force majeure*, was subsequently au-thorized to inform Brandt & Brandt of the new terms offered by the publisher: Robert Esménard, head of Albin Michel, was willing to trans-form the $150, initially agreed upon as a fixed sum for the rights of the two works, into an advance against a 10% flat royalty.[96] Although the French franc had been devalued from its pre-war value, Hoffman presented this as an unmistakable advantage for Breuer, the price of French books having risen since 1940 when the books should have been published in the first place. *The Daughter* and *Memory of Love* were ultimately both translated by Claudine Chonez and published by Albin Michel as *Katy* (1949) and *Souvenir d'amour* (1956).

These are two examples of different attitudes taken during the war, and of efforts made to ease the transition toward renewed business nego-tiations. The two cases above were relatively easy to solve. Others, such as the publication of translations by underground imprints, presented yet another form of challenge for local agents to sort out. The French texts of John Steinbeck's *The Moon Is Down* have been commented upon from a translation studies perspective by Jean-Marc Gouanvic, in an at-tempt to compare the Swiss edition, generally cited as the product of war censorship, with the French text by Yvonne Paraf-Desvignes published by Editions de Minuit, which is viewed as "conforming" to Steinbeck's original.[97] The story of the French edition published by clandestine pub-lisher Editions de Minuit, is more than just a story of its popularity or conformity, for it reflects the complexity of transatlantic copyright law, as well as the subtleties of its application in wartime.

When Jean Bruller of Editions de Minuit decided to publish a trans-lation of the novel, he knew that another translation had previously been published by Swiss publisher Marguerat in 1943. Minuit's trans-lator, Yvonne Paraf-Desvignes, therefore inserted a note indicating that the new text, issued under the title *Nuits noires*, was, contrary to the prior *Nuits sans lune*, unaltered and uncut. Minuit's translation was published illegally and clandestinely, while Marguerat had acquired the French rights in 1942 from Steinbeck's agents, McIntosh & Otis, which indeed made the Swiss publisher the legal owner of those rights.[98] In 1945 Editions de Minuit reissued *Nuits noires* in its first public series, "*Sous l'oppression*," and endeavored to normalize the situation, sending McIntosh & Otis a sum for the royalties due Steinbeck on the clandes-tine edition. Minuit had apparently been notified by Gallimard—who had published the last of Steinbeck's titles before the war—that they had infringed their own option rights on Steinbeck's work.[99] McIntosh & Otis assured Minuit that the only conflict was, in fact, with Marguerat, who was the sole legal owner of the French rights to the text and had in-deed stepped in, claiming that this money was due him. The matter was still pending in 1959, when McIntosh & Otis asked Hoffman, who had become their exclusive representative in 1949, to handle this complex problem, which he did and was ultimately commended for.[100] In 2015, the Hoffman agency continues to handle Steinbeck's French rights.[101]

This case is particularly interesting inasmuch as it highlights some of the concessions publishers and authors, as well as agents, were willing to make in the name of higher moral ideals during the war. Contrary to Hoffman's sales arguments regarding Breuer's *Memory of Love* and *The Daughter,* some infringements and irregularities could be defended on a moral level. Nevertheless, it also suggests that once the war was over, business was to continue as usual, options respected, and royalties paid . . . As Mildred Lyman of McIntosh & Otis wrote to Editions de Minuit in 1946, when the agreement had been entered in 1942, the general consensus was that, due to its content, *The Moon Is Down* should be published urgently, and in as many languages as possible; consequently, the significance and value of the book, being so contingent on the war, would not warrant a publication after the conflict, and neither Steinbeck nor McIntosh & Otis felt, at the time, that they were infringing Gallimard's rights, but rather, doing a public service.[102] The correspondence on the matter, extending between 1946 and 1959, clearly shows that Minuit were never criticized for their clandestine edition, hailed by Lyman as "a magnificent job." In the process, however, Gallimard's option on Steinbeck's next book was either shunned by the US agents, or very possibly had lapsed as a result of their failing to publish Steinbeck's *Grapes of Wrath*, whose rights they had acquired long before 1947—in 1939.

Signs of the changes wrought by the war are visible at other points in the transactions, especially in the contracts that were signed during the conflict. New or temporary clauses appeared, once again evincing the parenthetic nature and the particular constraints of the period. The lack of paper was undeniably a central concern for all involved in the production of books, be it in the United States or in France. As Hoffman wrote to Sonia Chapter of Curtis Brown London when he was gradually resuming his business activities,

> The post-war prospects for translations on the French book market are excellent and we should be going through a tremendous boom right now if it were not for the practically complete lack of paper. As it is, we must confine our activities to preparatory work and wait for the actual full scale publishing to resume at the end of the war.[103]

By 1944 the authorized allotment of paper for books had dropped to 1% of the 1938 allotment.[104] This had several consequences on the US-French book market: Hoffman feared that it might induce French publishers to pass on "big American novels" which required large quantities of paper, and which they would no longer be able to afford to print. As this might prove a deterrent for Americans wishing to pursue business with France, local co-agents had to be as reassuring as possible, while at the same time they were expected to present a faithful account of the situation. Another consequence of this shortage of paper and other material was the extension of publication delays negotiated by French publishers and agents. Even before the war, the standard publication times were understandably longer in France than in the United States, as the process of translation had to be taken into account; on average, while 12 months were generally stipulated in US contracts, French language contracts proposed times from 12 to 18 months. Some French publishers inserted a new clause in their late-wartime contracts, extending delays, not within 18 months of the date of agreement, but from the date of cessation of hostilities with Germany, which certainly afforded them some time to polish the translation. Yet for pre-war as well as for post-war contracts, differences may be identified between publishers and/or agents. Knopf seems to have been reluctant to grant more than 12 months publication delay, either before the war or in 1945. As for the extension of 18 months as of the end of the war, it featured in fact in few French contracts. At any rate, the clause of publication date was not to be regarded as secondary, as it was—and still is—a termination clause, regularly invoked by American agents threatening to annul contracts.

Still, French publishers were not alone in taking "advantage" of the war in their contracts. On the other side of the Atlantic, some publishers also began to insert in their domestic contracts a "war clause" meant to exempt them from responsibility in case of unexpected excessive delays in publication and, in some cases, granting them the right to terminate a contract without further ado. This "notorious" clause, as the Authors' Guild put it, declared that a publisher could not be held responsible for delays "caused by any wars, civil riots, strikes, fires, Governmental restrictions, or other similar or dissimilar circumstances beyond its control." This widely encompassing clause was used abusively by some publishers who continued to insert it in the late 1950s.[105] As far as transatlantic foreign rights are concerned, the war also impacted the wording of contracts. Wartime agreements—sometimes as late as 1947—included specific wartime clauses such as that prohibiting the publication, sale, and distribution of French translations in countries "at war with the United States or occupied by the enemies of the United States," a consequence of the 1917 Trading with the Enemy Act, which had been renewed in 1942. Indeed, among the goals for which this act had been designed, was the protection of interests in property rights.[106] The Trading with the Enemy Act was, however, not the only measure restricting trade; as we shall see in the following chapters, restrictions on foreign exchange and the lack of foreign currency in France, entailing non-convertibility of the franc, were crucial obstacles to international trade in the post-war era. Some agents seem to have found a way to pursue business in spite of these barriers, extending the time of payment of advances in such a manner as to allow for the transfer of funds to the United States "immediately upon the opening of foreign exchange." Still, this type of clause was not a common addendum, as failure to remit payment of advances in due time *theoretically* resulted in the termination of contracts. As we shall see, considering the post-war conditions, some agents and publishers—sometimes under constraint—afforded their French counterparts a relative degree of latitude on these matters.

The aftermath of the war left French publishers and agents in a state of relative disarray. Still, in spite of censorship, readers had continued to read during the conflict, and foreign, especially American, fiction, was in demand. As US publishers ventured into new foreign markets, or attempted to reconnect with former partners, co-agents played an invaluable role as counselors. Indeed, Hoffman and fellow agents were ideally positioned as commercial and cultural intermediaries. Tracking down pre-war contracts, verifying and renewing terms, they also guided US publishers through the intricate web of French publishing, which in those years was not immune from larger, political and ideological complexities.

Notes

1 Mollier, "L'édition française dans la tourmente de la Seconde Guerre mondiale," 127–138.
2 See Poulain, *Livres pillés, lectures surveillées,* 306–314. Poulain underlines the role of the few who did actively resist.
3 The *Propagandastaffel* was the name of the German wartime propaganda services.
4 On publishing and censorship during the Occupation, Pascal Fouché's *L'Edition française sous l'Occupation, 1940–1944* is a must. See also Mollier, "L'édition française dans la tourmente de la Seconde Guerre mondiale."
5 Poulain, *Livres pillés, lectures surveillées,* 339.
6 The *Propaganda Abteilung* was a Propaganda Department within the *Propagandastaffel.*
7 Poulain, *Livres pillés, lectures surveillées,* 334.
8 Hubert Forestier, "L'Edition française en 1941. Cent éditeurs vous parlent . . .," in *Liber. Cahiers du Livre,* 2° fascicule, Octobre 1941, repr., Fouché, *L'Edition française sous l'Occupation,* vol. 1, 227ff.
9 Poulain, *Livres pillés, lectures surveillées.*
10 Ibid., 207.
11 As shown by Sapiro, Vercors (Jean Bruller), founder of the clandestine imprint Editions de Minuit, Albert Camus and Jean-Paul Sartre are certainly the most emblematic of this generation. On the clash of generations in publishing and the literary world, and the notion of "moral capital," see Sapiro, *La guerre des écrivains, 1940–1953* (Paris: Fayard, 1999).
12 Luey, "The Organization of the Book Publishing Industry," 29.
13 Gillies, *The Professional Literary Agent in Britain,* 34.
14 See Beal, "Theodore Stanton." Beal outlines three categories of services rendered by the literary agent, to authors on the one hand, and to publishers on the other: literary, clerical/financial, and diplomatic (15–17). While I

agree with her categorization, based on agents' representation of authors, I here consider the adjective "diplomatic" in a slightly different light, taking my cue from a general definition of diplomacy provided by Jeremy Black, as "a privileged aspect of general systems of information-gathering, of representation, and of negotiation" (*History of Diplomacy*, London: Reaktion Books, 2010, 12). Co-agents' missions are, metaphorically and literally, particularly similar to those of other diplomatic agents.

15 Hench, *Books as Weapons*, 65.

16 See Tebbel, *A History of Book Publishing in the United States, Vol IV: The Great Change, 1940–1980*, 6.

17 Ibid., 58.

18 Luey, "The Organization of the Book Publishing Industry," 43.

19 Tebbel, *A History of Book Publishing*, 60.

20 Ibid., 98.

21 The Book Publishers' Bureau had been organized in 1938 to replace the National Association of Book Publishers (1920–1937), which in turn had replaced the defunct American Publishers Association (1900–1914).

22 Minutes of the Meeting of the Board of Directors (Harvard Club), November 10, 1943—Random House Records, 1925–1999—Butler Library, Columbia University—Correspondence MS# 1048, box 135.

23 Hench, *Books as Weapons*, 185.

24 See Curtis Brown, *Contacts*, 210.

25 His son, André Schiffrin, relates this episode in the now classic *L'édition sans éditeurs* (Paris: la fabrique éditions, 1999), translated into *The Business of Books: How the International Conglomerates Took Over Publishing and Changed the Way We Read* (New York: Verso, 2001). His bitterness, so completely understandable, is thinly veiled in this passing remark: as late as 1999, "Gallimard continues to deny what had happened during the war, claiming to the press that my father had left France in 1939, in spite of all the evidence to the contrary" (18).

26 I am indebted to John B. Hench's *Books as Weapons* for the following developments.

27 Hench, *Books as Weapons*, 45.

28 Ibid., 58.

29 Ibid., 59.

30 Ibid., 91.

31 Ibid., 84.

32 Blanche Knopf, undated observations, quoted in Hench, *Books as Weapons*, 166.

33 On the French cultural practices during the war, see in particular Jean-Pierre Rioux, *La vie culturelle sous Vichy*. Rioux has underlined the extraordinary vitality of these practices, suggesting that already the French were moving toward mass culture. See Rioux, "Ambivalences en rouge et bleu: les pratiques culturelles des Français pendant les années noires," in Rioux, *La vie culturelle*, 41–60.

34 Hench, *Books as Weapons*, 103.

35 Bernice Baumgarten to Michel Hoffman, December 3, 1945. BRH. HOF. AG.16.01.

36 In the list of Overseas Editions provided as appendix in Hench, one finds twenty-two French, twenty-three German, and five Italian titles (*Books as Weapons*, 270–274).

37 Hench, *Books as Weapons*, 89.

38 Ibid., 65.

39 Ibid., 183.
40 Quoted in Hench, *Books as Weapons*, 182.
41 See Frank A. Ninkovich's seminal work on US Cultural Diplomacy, *The Diplomacy of Ideas: U.S. Foreign Policy and Cultural Relations, 1938–1950* (Cambridge: Cambridge University Press, 1981), 92ff.
42 Ninkovich, *The Diplomacy of Ideas*, 92.
43 Peter Jennison, "How American Books Reach Readers Abroad," in "American Books Abroad," *Library Trends*, 5, no.1 (July 1956): 8.
44 Curtis G. Benjamin, *U.S. Books Abroad: Neglected Ambassadors* (Washington, D.C.: Library of Congress, 1984), v.
45 Black, *History of Diplomacy*, 12.
46 Jean Bruller, aka Vercors, was among those in favor of a radical purging.
47 Following a first Amnesty Act of January 1961 that released individuals sentenced to less than 15 years for collaborating with the enemy during World War II, another Amnesty Act was passed in August 1953. This second act granted amnesty to a very large group of people.
48 For specific trials and details of this complex period, see Fouché, *L'Edition française sous l'Occupation,* and *L'Edition française depuis 1945*, Poulain, *Livres pillés, lectures surveillées*, Sapiro, *La guerre des écrivains,* and Anne Simonin, *Les Editions de Minuit, 1942–1955.*
49 See Fouché, *L'Edition française sous l'Occupation* and *L'Edition française depuis 1945*; Mollier, "L'Edition française dans la tourmente de la Seconde Guerre mondiale," Sapiro, *La guerre des écrivains,* and Elisabeth Parinet, *Une histoire de l'édition à l'époque contemporaine* (Paris: Seuil, 2004).
50 Another myth surrounds the house's archives, which were long renowned for being off-limits to scholars and biographers, thereby fueling the aura of secrecy around the publishing house. For his seminal biography of Gaston Gallimard, which is also a house history, writer Pierre Assouline did not have access to the publisher's archives.
51 See also Pierre Assouline, *Gaston Gallimard, Un demi-siècle d'édition française* (Paris: Balland, 1984), 378ff.
52 See Assouline, *Gaston Gallimard*, 366.
53 Mollier, "L'Edition française dans la tourmente de la Seconde Guerre mondiale."
54 Michel Hoffman to Bernice Baumgarten, draft, February 18; 25, 1945, BRH.HOF. AG 16.01.
55 After working for the Paris office of Curtis, Brown, Marguerite Scialtiel was head of the Bureau Littéraire International.
56 James L. West, *American Authors and the Literary Marketplace Since 1900* (Philadelphia: University of Pennsylvania Press, 1998), 88.
57 Kitty Black, quoted in Maggie Gale, *West End Women: Women and the London Stage, 1918–1962* (London: Routledge, 1996), 63.
58 Caren Irr clearly links the tasks of a literary agent with those of secretarial labor. Caren Irr, *Pink Pirates. Contemporary American Writers and Copyright* (Iowa City: University of Iowa Press, 2010), 44–45. On the training of French women in the interwar years, see Michelle Perrot, "Qu'est-ce qu'un métier de femme?" *Les femmes ou les silences de l'histoire* (Paris: Flammarion, 1998), 201–207, Sylvie Schweitzer, *Les Femmes on toujours travaillé. Une histoire du travail des femmes aux XIXe et XXe siècles* (Paris: Odile Jacob, 2002).
59 On Bernice Baumgarten, see Philip L. Fradkin, *Wallace Stegner and the American West* (2008; repr., Berkeley and Los Angeles: University of California Press, 2009).

60 Bennett Cerf to Bernice Baumgarten, December 18, 1953, Random House Records, MS 1048 Box 135-Folder Brandt & Brandt.
61 See *The Writers' and Artists' Yearbook*: in 1922 the agency was still listed as Brandt & Kirkpatrick; by 1928 it had been renamed Brandt & Brandt.
62 Michel Hoffman to George Strem, January 7, 1946, BRH.HOF.AG.16.02. Strem, a literary agent with Literary Services in New York, had written Hoffman at length about his son contracting malaria. Hoffman apparently did not feel in a very commiserating mood when he wrote his reply.
63 Curtis Brown, *Contacts*, 1.
64 On this subject, see Gillies's conclusion, *The Professional Literary Agent in Britain, 1880–1920*, 165–172.
65 Curtis Brown, *Contacts*, 219–221. "I doubt if my dream of being godfather to Russian copyright will ever come true" (221).
66 Ibid., 223–224.
67 Ibid., *Contacts*, 223.
68 See Curtis Brown website, http://www.curtisbrown.co.uk/about-us-sf.aspx.
69 George Greenfield, *A Smattering of Monsters. A Kind of Memoir* (Columbia, S.C.: Camden House, 1995), 83.
70 Curtis Brown, *Contacts*, 225.
71 Jack Kahane recalls "taking over" the Curtis Brown offices on the Place Vendôme in Paris when he established his publishing house in 1938 (*Memoirs of a Booklegger*, 204).
72 See Sonia Chapter (Curtis Brown London) to Michel Hoffman, November 14, 1944, BRH.HOF.AG.09.01. Hoffman was appointed exclusive representative of Curtis Brown, yet remained free to negotiate French rights for other English or American agents; Curtis Brown was to be Hoffman's exclusive representative in the United States and England for English-language rights of French authors.
73 See Sonia Chapter to Michel Hoffman, February 13, 1945. BRH.HOF.AG 09.01.
74 Michel Hoffman to Sonia Chapter, January 7, 1945. BRH.HOF.AG. 09.01.
75 The magazine *Books Abroad* reported regularly on the situation of French publishing (19:4, Autumn 1945).
76 Michel Hoffman to Alan Collins, October 24, 1945. BRH.HOF.AG.15.03.
77 See Fouché, *L'Edition française sous l'Occupation*, volume II, 163ff.
78 Wright had signed with the Paul Reynolds agency, yet his foreign rights for *Native Son* were handled directly by Harper.
79 See Laurence Cossu-Beaumont, "Popular Books and the Marketing of African American Best-Sellers," *Race, Ethnicity and Publishing in America*, ed. Cécile Cottenet (Basingstoke: Palgrave Macmillan, 2014), 193–209.
80 Michel Hoffman to Sonia Chapter, March 7, 1945. BRH.HOF.AG. 09.01.
81 Hachette's nickname, the "Green Trust," originated in the color of its minivans used to distribute the newspapers and books.
82 Mollier, *Édition, presse et pouvoir en France au XXe siècle*, 144.
83 See Fouché, *L'Edition française sous l'Occupation*, vol. 2, 183–184; 199. Hachette had put up a defense, printing a booklet recalling how the Germans had requested to commandeer their buildings, and how they had refused to give in to Head of Vichy government Pierre Laval's pressure to let the Germans obtain a sizable part of Hachette's capital.
84 Michel Hoffman to Sonia Chapter, April 18, 1945. BRH.HOF.AG.09.01.
85 Anon., "The Editor Parenthesizes," *Books Abroad*, 19, no. 1 (1945): 98.

86 Michel Hoffman to Sonia Chapter, October 25, 1945. BRH.HOF. AG.09.01.

87 Michel Hoffman to Sonia Chapter, October 12, 1945. BRH HOF. AG.09.01.

88 See Michel Hoffman to Sonia Chapter, September 20, 1945, BRH.HOF. AG.09.01. See also Michel Hoffman to Bernice Baumgarten at Brandt & Brandt, April 24, 1945, BRH.HOF.AG.16.01: he had asked to obtain a copy of bestselling author Marjorie Kinnan Rawlings' *Golden Apples* through the USIS.

89 Jenny Bradley's ongoing correspondence between the 1950s and the early 1980s is evidence of the friendly relations she entertained with John Lackey Brown.

90 Michel Hoffman to Bernice Baumgarten, August 9, 1945. BRH.HOF. AG.16.01.

91 Michel Hoffman to Bernice Baumgarten, November 28, 1946. BRH.HOF. AG.16.01.

92 Michel Hoffman to Bernice Baumgarten, January 4, 1946, BRH.HOF. AG.16.01. The last volume of the trilogy, *The Grand Design*, not yet issued in the United States, was published in 1949.

93 See Virginia Spencer Carr, *Dos Passos: A Life* (1984; repr., Northwestern University Press, 2004), 405–406. Carr notes that Dos Passos actually continued to ask for Baumgarten's advice throughout the year following their severance, which underlines the quality of the agent's work.

94 The Authors' Guild "Your Book Contract," 10.

95 Michel Hoffman to Bernice Baumgarten, January 4, 1946, BRH.HOF. AG.16.01.

96 Robert Esménard (director of Albin Michel) to Michel Hoffman, January 4, 1946, BRH.HOF.ED.FR.34.02. Esménard also offered to improve slightly the 1940 advance on Ethel Vance's *Escape,* another of the books they had contracted for before the war and had not been able to publish within the contractual delay.

97 See Jean-Marc Gouanvic, "John Steinbeck et la censure: le cas de *The Moon Is Down* traduit en français pendant la Seconde Guerre mondiale," *TTR: Traduction, terminologie, rédaction*, 15, no. 2, (2002): 191–202.

98 Mildred Lyman for McIntosh & Otis to Editions de Minuit, May 2, 1946, BRH HOF.AG.13.06. Marguerat had been sold the rights through Denyse Clairouin's Paris agency. Interestingly Clairouin, also a noted translator, had joined the Résistance during the war.

99 See Mildred Lyman for McIntosh & Otis to Editions de Minuit, May 2, 1946, copy to Michel Hoffman, BRH.HOF.AG.13.06. Gallimard had published French translations of *In Dubious Battle* (1940), *Of Mice and Men* (*Des Souris et des hommes*, 1939) and had acquired the French rights for *The Grapes of Wrath* in 1939, publishing it in 1947. A new translation of *The Moon Is Down*, under the title *Lune noire*, was published by JC Lattès in 1994.

100 See Caroline Sauer for McIntosh & Otis to Michel Hoffman, April 20, 1959, BRH.HOF.AG.13.06.

101 In early 1964, McIntosh & Otis informed Hoffman that they would from then on negotiate continental rights through A.M. Heath in London, thus adding an intermediary; they made an exception, however, for Steinbeck, whose rights would be handled directly between Hoffman and the New York agency.

102 Mildred Lyman to Editions de Minuit, May 2, 1946. Copy to Michel Hoffman. BRH.HOF.AG.13.06.
103 Michel Hoffman to Sonia Chapter, December 4, 1944, BRH.HOF. AG.09.01.
104 See Fouché, *L'Edition française sous l'Occupation*, volume II. Appendices, "Déposition du Ministère de la Production industrielle, 19 décembre 1945," repr. 343.
105 "A few publishers, notably Macmillan, were still slipping the contract-terminating war clause into some gullible authors' contracts more than a decade after the end of World War II, and several years after the end of the Korean War," (Authors' Guild, "Your Book Contract," 7).
106 Samuel Anatole Lourie, "The Trading with the Enemy Act," *Michigan Law Review* 42, no. 2, (October 1943): 205–234. Online, accessed July 16, 2014. Section 3 of the Trading with the Enemy Act of 1917 made it unlawful "For any person in the United States" "to trade, or attempt to trade, either directly or indirectly, with, . . ." "an enemy or ally of enemy".

3 New Markets for the Taking: 1946–1955

The war had provided American publishers with new opportunities and incentives to develop foreign markets, for which they scrambled in the immediate wake of the conflict, setting the stage for the following decade. Even as the moral turmoils of French publishing slowly receded, the post-war era was a moment of innovations on both sides of the Atlantic, with the emergence of new houses, and the creation of new outlets such as series, aided by the development of paperback publishing. Internationalization of US publishing increased, with American publishers opening foreign branches and book agencies multiplying around the globe. Conjointly, American cultural diplomats were beginning to envisage what wonderful ambassadors books might actually be in the process of peacekeeping.

In this context, the long move toward the signing of the Universal Copyright Convention in 1952 was a logical step for America, although it might be conceived as a belated effort to finally comply with international copyright law. Once again, the political rationale combined with commercial factors: if the United States was to win the new Cold War "battle of the books," American copyright owners needed to obtain better protection in foreign countries. As Herman Finkelstein remarked in his analysis of the UCC,

> The importance of an international copyright convention of universal application cannot be minimized. We are living in an age when every encouragement must be given to the free interchange of ideas. Today commerce in books and periodicals is just as important as commerce in physical goods.[1]

In 1954, Joseph Dubin couched his own analysis in the typical Cold War discourse of the times, when he wrote "The impact and importance of this Convention to the peoples of the free world may, in some measure, have been the cause for the absence from the Convention of the Soviet Union and her satellite lackeys."[2] Yet to hail the final realization of the "universal republic of letters" was certainly excessive, for the United States, although not a member, had benefitted from the advances of

Berne through its "back door," and obtained protection of its copyrights in many Western countries through bilateral treaties, as it had with France. American analysts—jurists—were prompt to underline how the Universal Copyright Convention had been the work of the United States, and indeed to this day the text is seen as a general concession to the latter. If the Convention adopted the principle of national treatment, as Berne had, it went counter to Berne in that, although it relaxed several copyright formalities, it did not completely dispense authors with such, requiring that there be affixed in the appropriate places the copyright notice. The United States would thus be granted better protection abroad without having to resort to the back door arrangement, without having to adopt the principle of moral rights.

Even with the ratification of the UCC by US Congress in 1955, the book trade between the United States and France continued to be regulated through the 1891 bilateral treaty. Yet the UCC is a sign of the growing importance of the United States as an exporter and importer of books after the war. The same impulse that led to this treaty was instrumental in shaping the networks of transatlantic agenting.

Post-War Publishing in the United States and in France

American and French publishing in the post-war period share several features, although one often finds that essential innovations and indeed, revolutions, developed later in Paris. Furthermore, French publishing faced obstacles unknown to American publishers, as the years between 1945 and 1955 continued to be plagued with suspicion and publishers were still being brought to trial for their wartime activities on charges of intelligence with the enemy. Some, like Robert Laffont or Gallimard, were rapidly acquitted; others, like Bernard Grasset, or Jean de la Hire and André Bertrand, who had presided the Editions du Livre moderne during the war, were convicted. Some of the new houses that had appeared during the war ultimately failed to fulfill the hopes and promises they had raised: Edmond Charlot, first publisher of Albert Camus, who had transferred his publishing house from Algiers to Paris after the Liberation, was a meteor, reaping several estimable literary prizes before falling into financial difficulties in 1950. Even Editions de Minuit initially suffered from bad management and disorganization in the early post-war era.[3] Nevertheless, business picked up rapidly, the production of books resumed and increased slowly, from 9,522 titles in 1946 to 16,020 in 1948; by 1947 the title output was double that of 1945.[4] Several "reading campaigns" organized by the *Syndicat National des Editeurs* (National Publishers' Union) between 1949 and 1952, further helped publishers to recover from the war. By 1950 the printing trade had caught up with its pre-war level.[5] The number of translations into French rose sharply, rising from 81 titles in 1944 to 1,088 by 1948.[6]

Consolidations and the rise of mass marketing were certainly characteristic of publishing in both countries, although they did not develop at
the same rate and on the same scale, due in part, but not only, to a difference in territory size. Beth Luey has shown that in the post-war years
US publishing took a decisively market-oriented turn, as expansion and
competition—for the paperback market and for authors, leading to a
considerable rise in advances—further moved publishing into corporate
capitalism, thereby making publishers' "sense of uniqueness" as cultural
industries increasingly difficult to sustain.[7] The acquisition in 1944 of
Grosset & Dunlap by a consortium of publishers, comprised of Random
House, Harper's; Little, Brown and Scribner, and the subsequent combination of Grosset & Dunlap with the Curtis Publishing Co., resulting
the next year in the creation of the paperback house Bantam Books,
foreshadowed the 1950s as a decade of mergers and acquisitions.[8] On
the French side of the Atlantic, publishers also began, more timidly, to
acquire competitors' catalogues or even houses: Gallimard taking over
Denoël in 1952, and Hachette acquiring the catalogues of Tallandier and
Grasset two years later are examples of such a phenomenon. Nevertheless, the cutthroat competition for authors that US editors were submitting to, agreeing to pay huge advances in order to remain in the market,
had not yet reached French shores, possibly due to the scarcity, if not
outright absence, of book agents orchestrating the bidding in the domestic market. In addition to this, until 1957 the absence of firm contract
legislation made it quite easy for French publishers to maintain their
self-promotion as "gentlemen of letters," friendly craftsmen doing their
best in the interest of their authors. Across the Atlantic contracts were
becoming ever more complex and standardized, through the impetus of
professional organizations such as the Writers' Guild or the Society of
Authors' Representatives.[9] Jean Zay's bill on the *droit d'auteur*, defeated
in 1936, had attempted to standardize publishing contracts, namely insisting that publishers were under the obligation to render clear accounts
to authors on the sales of their books, and to signify the price or royalty
for which the work was contracted. So that although the French *droit
d'auteur* is sometimes held to guarantee the highest protection for authors, until 1957 French publishers were in fact under no obligation to
issue a clear publishing contract, thereby diminishing this protection.

Another post-war revolution was the rise of the mass market book.
Both book clubs and paperback books had been pre-war inventions, but
they truly revolutionized publishing in the United States after 1945. In
France, contrary to the United States, the early success of clubs was not
based on their commercial appeal, but rather on the material quality
of the books offered. While the first book clubs appeared in the mid-
1920s in the United States, a phenomenon prominently illustrated by
the Book-of-the-Month Club that thrived during the war and continued
to flourish and diversify in the late 1940s, the first clubs were launched

in France in the mid-1940s, with the Club français du livre created in 1946, issuing high-quality books, followed by the Club du livre du mois (literally, the Book of the Month club) in 1949.[10] Seeing the success of such independent ventures, publishers would later join the movement. In 1952 Gallimard, Laffont and Hachette together set up the Club du meilleur livre, taking great care to conceal their ownership of the club so as not to alienate booksellers. Booksellers themselves, who soon saw the negative impact of such clubs on sales, launched the Club des libraires de France in 1953.[11] In effect, while independent and publisher-affiliated clubs in the United States developed in large part as a consequence of ongoing distribution problems, the early clubs in France were rather experiments in excellent publishing, which chose to offer their members high-quality reprints, beautifully bound under covers designed with care; editions were small, the print run for the Club français du livre averaging 3,000, and paperbacks were not in order. Again, French book clubs were not then synonymous with commercial success, but they contributed to stimulating book design after the war, as trade publishers gradually understood the use of designers and began to hire them.[12]

The modern paperback, dating back to 1841 with the Tauchnitz paperbound "Collection of British Authors," and its follow-up the Albatross Modern Continental series created in 1932 which set the average size of British and American paperbacks, was possibly the prime factor in the revolution of modern publishing.[13] American paperbacks were directly influenced by Allen Lane's Penguin Books in England (1935), which opened a US branch in 1939 under the direction of Ian Ballantine, and by Robert De Graff's Pocket Books, published by Simon & Schuster. As we shall see, the pocket book also spurred the creation of new series. For the American market, book historians must distinguish between mass market paperback houses, specialized only in the publishing of paperbacks to be distributed through channels other than traditional bookstores, and trade paperbacks; in France however, modern paperbacks developed after the war as specific trade house series, although the fact was sometimes concealed. The huge print runs of mass market paperbacks, their wide distribution—from 95 million copies sold for a little over $14 million in 1947, to 270 million copies selling for $40 million in 1952[14]—and the subsequent shift to serious fiction, in turn spurring the rise of advances to authors, changed the way trade publishing was conducted. As Beth Luey notes, when trade houses began developing their own paperback series, they would sometimes consult paperback publishers before offering contracts to authors. Indeed, the issuing of paperbound editions fast became an important subsidiary right in publishing contracts. In France, the *"Livre de Poche,"* established in 1953 by a concealed Hachette branch, the Librairie générale française, is generally considered as the first modern paperback series, although, as Elisabeth Parinet suggests, the Belgian Marabout series in 1949 had been a first—and failed—attempt to import the Penguin model to France.[15] Parinet also underscores the fact that what was hailed as a new publishing phenomenon was, indeed, not novel, as cheap popular libraries of literary classics had already existed in the 19th century.[16] As Isabelle Olivero further underlines, cheap series of contemporary novels had been launched as early as the 1880s, with great success: Fayard's *"Modern Bibliothèque"* (1904) and *"Le Livre populaire"* inaugurated the "era of one hundred thousand," in reference to the number of copies sold.[17] The gradual development of paperbound "pocketbook" series by French trade publishers throughout the 1950s is important because these were often series that readily welcomed foreign, and indeed American fiction in vast title numbers. For Parinet, the *"Livre de Poche"* benefitted from two phenomena: the wartime banishment of American fiction and authors in France, which induced a great enthusiasm for American authors, and the notion of modernity associated with American fiction, which in turn actually bestowed a tinge of modernity on the imprint, notwithstanding the existence of several predecessors, as noted.[18]

The multiplication and expansion of French series actually constituted a boon for American authors, who found therein the most comfortable— and, for their French publishers, lucrative—lodging. In 1945 were created three series of note, Charlot's *"Les Cinq continents,"* Robert Laffont's *"Pavillons,"* and Gallimard's detective series *"Série Noire."* It is worth mentioning that the first two were founded by "new" publishers that had emerged during the conflict. Gallimard's *"Le Point du Jour"* series, created in 1949, would in 1954 feature an acclaimed anthology of American literature.[19] Again, series, of both detective and foreign literature, were not new, as the example of Stock suggests. Following on the wings of Ferenczi's successful *"Le Roman policier"* launched in 1916, in the mid-1920s and 1930s important detective series had been created, *"Le Masque"* by Albert Pigasse, *"Le Domino noir"* featuring titles by Rufus King, and the British Edgar Wallace, Gallimard's *"Le Scarabée d'or,"* and most famously, *"L'Empreinte,"* which featured exclusively British and American authors—John Dickson Carr, Philip MacDonald, Dorothy Sayers, Ellery Queen, Mignon Eberhart, F.W. Crofts, Anthony Berkeley, Rufus King, Austin Freeman, Henry Wade, Nicholas Blake, Jonathan Latimer, Patrick Quentin, Eric Ambler . . .[20] For Alain-Marie Bassy, series were emblematic of the 1900–1950 period in French publishing, ushering in its modernization and truly organizing the field of production.[21] Certainly the competition between detective fiction series, namely Gallimard's *"Série Noire"* and Sven Nielsen's *"Un Mystère,"* organized the field of production for US detective and hardboiled fiction in France; their success and rivalry, as will be shown later, provided unique opportunities abroad for American authors.

Books Abroad and the Beginnings of Cultural Diplomacy

The post-1945 era saw an increase in the internationalization of publishing in the United States, as British houses opened branches in America, and US publishers either established continental and Canadian branches or organized new international sales departments and divisions, as McGraw-Hill did in 1946, soon followed in the 1950s by Doubleday, Macmillan, Viking, and Wiley.[22] The correspondence files of publishers and agents also attest to the development of international publishing contracts, as business partnerships or simple negotiations were progressively being carried out around the world, often through agents: from Germany, Denmark (through the Foreign Publishers' Service or the Bookman Literary Agency), to Finland, Norway, Hungary (with the Syndicate of Czech Authors), to Italy, Spain, Israel, all the way to Argentina through agent Lawrence Smith. The rise in the number of translators in the United States, from over 200 in 1948 to over 400 five years later, is further evidence of US publishing's growing interest in foreign literatures.[23] Between 1950 and 1955, translations from the French accounted on average for over 25% of all translations, and for over 34% in the case of works of literature and fiction.[24]

The number of English-speaking countries in the world, along with the rise of English as the new lingua franca in the post-war world, allowed Americans to export books in English to a variety of places, including some of the developing countries. Translation of American books for specific countries was thus only complementary to this side of the business. Taking into consideration the relative unreliability of book sales and export statistics, any figure ventured below needs to be examined cautiously, and in any case, will only offer a global picture.[25] According to John Tebbel and Beth Luey, pre-war foreign sales of books represented for US publishers approximately 5% of total sales, in volumes.[26] In 1956, Dan Lacy, formerly of the Book Publishers' Bureau, claimed in a Foreign Affairs essay that the volume of US books exported had at least trebled, or even been multiplied by four relatively to pre-war figures, while the average export value of said books was estimated around $40 million.[27] Malcolm Johnson on the other hand, basing his calculations on statistics provided by the Department of Commerce, estimated the number of volumes shipped abroad in 1953 at 25 million volumes.[28] If this figure is to be trusted, we may consider that for 1954, the number of copies sold abroad, relative to the total number of copies sold by American publishers, represented a proportion of 3% to 5%.[29] As for works in translation, there are no available statistics on the number of foreign rights sold by US publishers and/or book agencies, but the recurrent featuring of Americans on the list of most translated authors established by the French Cercle de la Librairie,[30] tells of the worldwide, sometimes enduring, popularity of both classic and contemporary, literary and popular authors: Edgar Allan Poe, Harriet Beecher Stowe, Mark Twain, James Fenimore Cooper, Louisa May Alcott, Herman Melville, Theodore Dreiser, Jack London, Ernest Hemingway, John Steinbeck, Louis Bromfield, Pearl Buck, William Faulkner, but also Erle Stanley Gardner, Thomas Merton, Zane Grey, Mickey Spillane, and John Dickson Carr. As it is, between 1948 and 1955, translations from American English fiction or literature constituted an average of 25% of the total number of translations published in France, while translations from English-language works, without distinction of country of origin, were already dominating the market, and continue to do so.

This relatively new emphasis on international publishing was further sustained by the US government's growing and propagandistic interest in distributing American books abroad as weapons of what was later named cultural diplomacy. If books had been, in the words of W.W. Norton, "weapons in the war of ideas," there was no doubt that they were to become valuable "ambassadors of good will and information,"[31] as the Cold War gradually gripped Europe. As a matter of fact, France, along with Italy, was a particularly sensitive country in which to test the value of propaganda through books, for it was viewed by Americans as one of the Western European countries most susceptible to Soviet Communist influence.[32] Although the power of the French Communist Party at the time should not be downplayed, the threat of rampant communism was certainly overemphasized by the US government to secure the support of public opinion and of Congress in favor of its overseas information programs: the presence of Communists in the French government up to 1947, growing demonstrations of anti-Americanism, as well as the supposed superiority of the Soviet book export program, were all reason enough to increase US counter-offensives, first through the International Information Agency (IIA) within the State Department, then by means of the independent United States Information Agency (USIA). In a 1954 essay on "The Foreign Distribution of American Publications," Malcolm Johnson, who had served on the board of the Council on Books in Wartime, wrote,

> The Russians know, as again we are learning, that the book is a means of spreading their viewpoint with a permanence nothing else possesses .... The lasting value of books, their durability and permanence, is a point too often overlooked in our attempts to place a picture of America, our way of life, our arts and letters, our education, and our technology before the people of other nations.[33]

As editor for Doubleday, Doran, and having participated in the wartime campaign for books abroad, Johnson surely had an unmistakable interest in selling and distributing US books around the world with the support of the government. As the Cold War fever heightened in the mid-1950s, the Department of State looked further into the use of books to promote the truth about America; in 1955, a conference on the subject of books abroad was held at Princeton, sponsored by the Advisory Commission on Books Abroad in the Department of State, appointed in 1952 by Dean Acheson. Peter S. Jennison, who had worked for the US Information Service (USIS) in Paris,[34] contributed a—biased—report on the French situation that was certainly in keeping with the mood of the period.

> The Paris bureau of the *Chicago Daily News* recently estimated that there are at least six book shops in Paris which are devoted almost exclusively to the sale of Communist literature, and which offer the works of Marx, Engels, Lenin, and Stalin in either Russian or French. Two volumes of Marx and Engels which cost 24 rubles ($6) in Moscow cost 360 francs ($1) in Paris. *Das Kapital*, which cost 20 rubles ($5) in MOSCOW, cost 360 francs ($1) in Paris. (The comparative dollar prices should not be construed as indicating a heavy Soviet export subsidy.) "Works of the basic American political philosophers," the bureau reports, "are difficult to buy in France because of the high cost of American books and the current shortage of American foreign exchange available for the purchase of books." Prices "are excessive" from the French point of view. A book costing $5 in New York is priced at 2,250 francs, the equivalent of $6.40. There are reputed to be thirty-eight French publishing firms more or less controlled by the French Communist Party, the bureau states.[35]

This quotation raises a number of comments and interrogations, not least the fact that Jennison was here quoting a single source, albeit a reputable and serious newspaper, to support the idea that Communist literature was dominating the sales of foreign books in Paris; moreover, these "wild" statistics are based on a survey of a mere six bookstores. As for the thirty-eight publishing firms controlled by the Communist Party, Jennison had earlier cited a figure of 700 "active" publishers in the country.[36] For all the highly detailed, hence supposedly authentic figures provided in this *Daily News* report, the names of those publishers would certainly have been useful to determine the actual danger.

Although overemphasized here, the popularity of "Communist literature" in the world was supported by *Index Translationum* statistics: among the most translated authors in the world between 1950 and 1955 featured quite prominently Stalin, Lenin, and Marx, and for 1955, translations of the works of Lenin (291), Stalin (200) far outnumbered those of Nobel Prize laureates Pearl Buck (32) and Hemingway (35), of the bestselling E.S. Gardner (50), or even the socialist Jack London (55).[37] Yet, the great disparity between the number of translations for Russian and American works does suggest that Cold War propaganda had found its way into a new battle of the books.[38]

More interesting here is the *Chicago Daily News* Bureau's state-ment on the excessively high cost of US books, due to the problem of dollar shortage, which would plague transatlantic book—and other commercial—exchanges for much of the 1950s, as we shall see in the last chapter. Suffice it to say at this point that France's soft currency throughout the second half of the 1940s and until 1958, and the ensu-ing lack of convertibility automatically raised the prices of commercial importations, leading, indeed, to "excessive prices" for foreign products, including books. The Informational Media Guaranty (IMG) program, which allowed media producers to sell their materials to foreign coun-tries with dollar shortages, and accept local currency in payment, pro-vided a partial solution to this problem in France, between 1951 and 1958. These payments were then given guaranteed convertibility into dollars by the US Treasury.

In order, therefore, to palliate the popular and massive misunder-standing, misquoting, misrepresenting, and misinterpreting of Ameri-cans and American culture in France, "the flow of American books—of all kinds—to France" had to be "substantially increased,"[39] taking into consideration the existing institutions and agencies already working in that direction. In the late 1940s and early 1950s, under the impetus of the State Department, several institutions were founded to help promote a better vision of American culture through books, which, indirectly, might enhance the book export possibilities. Aside from the financial issue, which to some extent could be remedied through IMG, American publishers and members of the Advisory Commission on Books Abroad understood that, in order to sell and distribute books more effectively, these had to be better known by the French. In effect, the US govern-ment could count on a variety of institutions or programs, such as the USIS libraries and binational centers, to be found in such cities as Paris, Marseille, Lille, or Lyon, or the independent American Library in Paris, founded in 1920 by the American Library Association, with the purpose of bringing the "light of books" "after the darkness of war."[40] During Dean Acheson's 1950 "Total Diplomacy Campaign," trade and text-book publishers donated a number of books to higher institution and local libraries, initiating wonderful collections of American books in the Universities of Aix-en-Provence and Lyon among other institutions. As Dan Lacy of the Book Publishers' Bureau noted in 1956, these venues were the "natural centers for the reception and dissemination of ideas from abroad."[41] So that even before the establishment in 1953 of the USIA (United States Information Agency) as an independent information agency, intended to improve the effectiveness of American Cultural pro-paganda/diplomacy, such channels and institutions served to offer French intellectuals, editors, and publishers with bibliographic information, if only by providing them access to the trade magazine *Publishers' Weekly*, whose subscription rate proved onerous for many at the time in France.[42]

As we have seen for the late wartime period and its immediate after-math, exportation of books abroad was a goal shared by both the private and the public sector, and it is likely that governmental cultural propaganda efforts did help US trade publishers to make their "products" better known and ultimately sell them in France. Yet, the dependency between private and public sectors was not without its difficulties. One of the obstacles to the successful exportation of books, as highlighted in Chapter 2, was the lack of familiarity of most American publishers with the French market; knowledge of the avenues of the market could be provided, specifically, by scouts and local agents. We might recall that one of the missions of the short-lived USIBA had been to facilitate the negotiations of book rights very much in the way of agents. Concerning publishers and agents, one might wonder to what extent they were expected to abide by the State Department's foreign policy and Truman's "campaign of truth." Did they, would they, in a gesture akin to self-censorship, decide not to sell the rights to books openly critical of America, or even suggestive of criticism? After all, were those books not providing a "full and fair picture" of the nation? How would they reconcile their business interests, with those of the nation? And if American publishers and agents were willing to promote an image of America that was most likely to act as corrective to Soviet Communist propaganda, how would they ensure the participation of the French? If French publishing and the literary scene were so susceptible to Communist influence, how could Americans ascertain the "faithful" translations of those works? These were tasks that would fall to the local agents; as we shall see, several of the works of popular fiction and of literature, published in France at the time, and that transited through Michel Hoffman's and Jenny Bradley's agencies, were decidedly not the prime choice of cultural propagandists.

Shaping Transatlantic Agenting

The Hoffman, and to some extent, Jenny S. Bradley correspondence for the period between 1946 and 1955 sketches out a picture of the transatlantic book trade at a time when US publishers were discovering the possibilities for continental market expansion, beyond their historical relations with the United Kingdom. Here are revealed not only the partnerships and networks that structured this trade, but also what was expected from local agents or co-agents, by publishers on both sides of the Atlantic, as well as by other agencies.

As we have seen, arrangements had been made in 1944 between Hoffman and several agencies, as with Curtis Brown in London. His contacts with this highly reputed London agency had enabled him to sell French rights of a number of US authors who were being handled either directly or by way of US agents represented by Curtis Brown in Europe. Through Harper's, for example, he negotiated the rights of Dorothy Cameron

Disney, Merle Curti, or Richard Wright. The terms of their agreement, accepted by Hoffman, outlined the mutual and exclusive character of their arrangement, with Hoffman agreeing to make all sales of French literary property to either British or American publishers exclusively through Curtis Brown London, while they in turn agreed to make all sales to French publishers of literary property controlled by them exclusively through Hoffman. Both agencies remained free, however, to negotiate sales on behalf of other owners or agents.[43] What should be understood here is that American or British agents might handle foreign rights for *some* or *all* of an author's works, which sometimes created awkward situations for the local co-agent. The longevity and reputation of the London agency had brought them the exclusive representation of several great US publishers, who sometimes retained authors' foreign rights, so that when Hoffman joined forces with them, he was afforded with incredible, albeit indirect, contacts with Harper's, Farrar & Rinehart, Doubleday, Doran & Co, and Thomas Y. Crowell. In addition to these prestigious catalogues, Curtis Brown also negotiated quite a number of works published by Bobbs-Merrill; Dodd, Mead; Houghton, Mifflin, W.W. Norton, William Morrow, Coward McCann, and Random House. The mere joint representation of British bestselling detective fiction author Peter Cheyney, who enjoyed terrific success in France, was in itself a boon for Hoffman; the prospects of representing some of the best works of fiction and literature issued by these big publishers must have been literally awesome. Although no exclusive representation was obtained from Harper's when they terminated their contract with London, other publishers—Doubleday in 1946, William Morrow in 1947— did propose to negotiate directly through Hoffman.

In 1945 Hoffman became the representative for Curtis Brown in New York, which was headed by Alan Collins. The situation at first proved slightly puzzling to Hoffman, who found that some US authors were handled exclusively by the London office, while some British authors were represented by the New York bureau . . . . For British and American agents working for Curtis Brown for the distinct branches on each side of the Atlantic, this arrangement was not necessarily profitable, as it proved confusing on many counts. Although British-born, American agent Naomi Burton seems to have found her British counterpart quite incompetent in some matters.[44] In effect, at least until 1946, Curtis Brown London handled foreign rights for US authors also represented by the New York office, for authors with other US agents who worked with Curtis Brown London as their representatives, as for foreign authors who had granted their foreign rights to their US publishers, who in turn used the services of the London agency for the sale of continental rights. Under Collins's impulse, in 1946 the New York branch finally set up a Foreign Rights department, comprising Naomi Burton [Stone] and Gertrude S. Weiner, with Nellie Sukerman at the Accounting

Department. Curtis Brown, New York brought in a substantial part of Hoffman's American authors of detective fiction, including Patrick Quentin aka Hugh Wheeler and R.W. Webb, Jonathan Stagge, Ellery Queen, Jonathan Latimer, and Mickey Spillane, as well as popular best-selling authors Fannie Hurst and Betty Smith; furthermore, the agency was big enough to successfully bid for some publishers' exclusive representations for foreign rights, including those of E.P. Dutton, A.S. Barnes, and MacRae-Smith. Hoffman's arrangement with Curtis Brown, and the apparent satisfaction he brought to his US partners, led Alan Collins to refer him to other American agents, such as Leah Salisbury.

Hoffman's pre-war contacts with the British agents at A.M. Heath in turn landed him a fruitful collaboration with US agency Brandt & Brandt. In February 1945, writing through the courtesy of the US War Information Bureau where Peter Jennison was working, he explained to Bernice Baumgarten that after unsuccessfully attempting to obtain a visa for the United States, he was now resuming his affairs and wished to deal directly with them—therefore to stop splitting commissions with A.M. Heath. Evidence in the contracts shows that Brandt & Brandt, who had worked with Jenny Bradley prior to the conflict, continued to operate through their British representative in addition to a local agent in France. Still Hoffman's collaboration with reputably one of the best agents overseas, and the breadth of the Brandt & Brandt representation, were to provide many contracts for the French agent. Indeed, the US agency represented some of the leading bestselling authors of the mid 1940s and 1950s, from authors of middlebrow fiction—Marjorie Kinnan Rawlings, J.P. Marquand, J.G. Cozzens, Wallace Stegner, or Budd Schulberg—to more popular genres—Thomas Costain's historical fiction-romances or Max Brandt's literary westerns—to the mystery and detective fiction writers that would bring the tremendous success of such series as the "*Série Noire*" or "*Un Mystère*": Mignon G. Eberhart, Leonard Q. Ross, and king of *noir* fiction Raymond Chandler. Brandt & Brandt would prove to be among the most meticulous and rigorous partners Hoffman had to contend with.

Although Curtis Brown and Brandt & Brandt were possibly the most profitable of Hoffman's transatlantic connections, the latter did not end here: as early as 1946 Hoffman could flaunt his agency's exclusive representation in France of Maxim Lieber and of McIntosh & Otis, who happened to be the agents of one of the authors most translated across the globe, John Steinbeck. Today, Lieber is perhaps best remembered for his ties with Whittaker Chambers and his spying for Soviet Communists, which makes his association with Hoffman, an exile from the 1920s Bolshevik regime, slightly surprising. Yet it is highly probable that Hoffman was not apprised of this before Lieber was subpoenaed before a HUAC commission in 1950.[45] Be that as it may, in the 1940s Lieber did represent some of the best American literature, including the works of Erskine Caldwell, Saul Bellow, John Cheever, Langston Hughes, and Carson McCullers.[46]

Still, Brandt & Brandt and Curtis Brown provided only part of Hoffman's business contacts. By all accounts, the agent's line of business could not have been conducted without a solid network of trusting relations with French publishers, who in turn relied on him to supply them with various kinds of information. As we have seen, as part of agenting, matchmaking involved finding the best publisher for one particular book or one particular author, sometimes shunning the most lucrative deals in order to secure a publisher who would ensure effective promotion of the book and, if possible, a lasting publication "trail" for the authors' next books. This brought Hoffman and his fellow French agents to develop ties and correspond with numerous publishers, who did not all operate out of Paris. Judging from the correspondence, Hoffman entertained privileged, even friendly and personal, relations with Albin Michel's Robert Esménard, Sven Nielsen of Presses de la Cité, Armand Pierhal at Robert Laffont, Frédéric Ditisheim, founder of the Franco-Swiss Editions Ditis in 1945, and Pierre Javet at Julliard.[47] Interestingly, apart from Albin Michel—founded in 1900—all the others here named belonged to the new, postwar generation of publishers whose search for legitimacy was somehow facilitated by the suspicion thrown on the older generations. On the other hand, the relations between Hoffman and the famed house of Gallimard were often strained, which cannot be accounted for solely by their suspected wrongdoings during the German occupation. A large part of the correspondence with Marcel Duhamel, editor of the "*Série Noire*," and Dionys Mascolo, then in charge of foreign literature acquisitions, reflects Hoffman's frustration. His irritation would be caused by the delay in Mascolo's replies, or the sometimes inconceivably low royalties offered, or with Gallimard's repeated practice of changing items—royalty rates, addition of an option clause—in contracts, sometimes even after the contract had been signed by one of the parties.[48] These difficult relations, and Gallimard's status as the King of publishers, led Hoffman, whenever he could, to favor other publishers, in particular Albin Michel or, in the case of detective fiction, Nielsen's Presses de la Cité. Quite possibly the rub lay solely in the relations between Hoffman and Dionys Mascolo; indeed Hoffman 's correspondence with Duhamel quickly warmed as the two men seemingly became quite friendly, even personal—the two men shared an enthusiasm for tennis[49]—and Hoffman readily acknowledged the high quality of Duhamel's translations.

Hoffman's networks reached beyond publishers to encompass translators. Besides the acclaimed Duhamel and Coindreau who translated almost exclusively for one publisher, a host of translators—the *Index Translationum* for 1948 listed over 600 translators working in France—were constantly in search of jobs, and agents acted as welcome intermediaries for those who had few connections in the publishing world. As suggested by some of the agents' archives, after the war many women found in this occupation a source of income to supplement the loss of their husbands'. Hoffman's role ranged from finding out the whereabouts of a translation transmitted before the war, to placing texts translated spontaneously, prior to any contract, to commissioning translations, a service for which he deducted a standard 10% to 15% from the publisher's fee.

As co-agent, Hoffman was expected to provide each of the parties involved in the negotiations with different services, all in the best interest of the owner of the rights. However, the interests of rights owners did not always coincide with those of the buyer. In such cases, the agent served as buffer, making use of his diplomatic skills. The French importation of US literature and fiction operated, like any other market, on the law of supply and demand, with US publishers and agents offering available translation rights to the works they controlled, while publishers on the other side of the Atlantic might add to these "spontaneous" offers demands of their own. Indeed, French publishers often relied on local agents to supply them with bibliographical information on books they might have read about in trade journals or been presented by USIS lists and exhibits. In turn, Hoffman and other French agents scoured *The New York Times* and *Publishers' Weekly,* also making good use of their connections with US agencies and publishers to supplement this information, pointing out the bestowal of a literary prize, a selection overseas by the Book-of-the-Month Club or another book club, or an imminent movie adaptation, all likely to enhance the popularity of a work and even turn it into a lucrative bestseller on both sides of the Atlantic. Any such guarantee of potential success offered by the agent could make a difference and result in a contract; indeed, in spite of the enthusiasm for US fiction at the time, the acquisition of foreign rights at a moment of great monetary imbalance, with the rate of the franc constantly fluctuating, remained risky for French publishers. This might explain why the various French inquiries focused regularly on the same group of US authors, as publishers preferred to speculate on "safe havens."

French publishers would then ask local agents to inquire about ownership and availability of rights. Contrary to the French market, where fundamentally all the rights were vested in the publisher, ownership of subsidiary or secondary rights in the United States is much more fragmented, sometimes making such inquiries tricky for French agents: one agency might control all or partial rights to an author's works, sometimes separating foreign novel rights from foreign serial rights; or, in cases where authors had changed representatives, one agent might control rights to earlier titles and not those to the more recent works. While some French publishers seemed to keep abreast of US ownership situations, others were grateful for the help of agents. Perhaps because she herself was Franco-American, Gladys Delmas at Presses de la Cité was particularly knowledgeable in matters of ownership. An exchange between Hoffman and D. Mascolo regarding the availability of foreign rights to the hardboiled detective novel *A Taste for Violence* by the very prolific Brett Halliday (aka David Dresser), illustrates the complexity and the need for agents. In 1949, in search of the owners of said rights, Gallimard had first been advised by Hoffman to contact Jenny Bradley, then told by A.M. Heath to get in touch with . . . Hoffman. This merry-go-round prompted Mascolo to demand clarification, complaining somewhat ironically to Hoffman how "very difficult it is for us, poor little French publishers, to find out who controls which book, who in Paris represents this or that foreign agency."[50] Complying with this demand, Hoffman replied,

> I myself hate it when I do not represent all the books of an author, but unfortunately this happens (as in the case of Brett Halliday) where part of his work is published by a house which controls the translation rights and another part by a publisher who leaves these rights entirely in the hands of the author or his representative. There is unfortunately nothing I can do about it. (my translation)[51]

Once ownership and availability of rights had been established, local agents might advise publishers on which offers might best help them to acquire foreign rights, especially when several houses might be vying for the same author. Hoffman would highlight not only the importance of a literary prize earned across the Atlantic, which would influence the amount of the advance and possibly the royalty scale, or would present the expectations of specific US publishers or authors. For, if US publishers did not know the French market very well, in the same way the smallest among French publishers presumably knew little about their US counterparts, much less about the way agents actually negotiated.

Demands and expectations from Hoffman's American counterparts, especially Curtis Brown and Brandt & Brandt, were considerably greater than those of French publishers, and resolutely profit oriented. In 1946 the tone was given by Gertrude Weiner, in charge of the Foreign Rights department at Curtis Brown, New York, "One of our ideas is to get you more business and ourselves more business."[52] By April 1947, their Foreign Rights Department was being expanded, and the New York office was about to launch a full-blown operation to obtain the representation of US publishers. In this perspective, local agents were vital assets, and collaborations certainly meant a full commitment on their part. Gertrude Weiner explained their objective to Hoffman: through their combined effort, French publishers would in time become accustomed to contacting agents rather than American publishers in their search for French rights. She insisted that maintaining a durable business relation would depend on him, highlighting the need for loyalty, and requesting that Hoffman endure competition and be prepared to push for deals:

> It will be of the utmost importance, therefore, that you make an all-out effort to push our books. Of course, we have full confidence in you, and together I know we can achieve the goal we have set for our Foreign Rights Department—that is, of making it the most active and successful one of its kind anywhere.[53]

Weiner's note evinces the American agency's efficacy and no-nonsense approach to business. Hoffman had already begun helping Curtis Brown to secure publishers' representation, agreeing to meet the President of E.P. Dutton & Company, Elliott B. Macrae, who had come to Europe on a business trip earlier that year, and had apprised him of the French publishing situation.[54] In the same manner, Hoffman had introduced Doubleday's Donald Elder to several publishers in the summer of 1946.[55] Hoffman undoubtedly felt the thinly veiled pressure in this letter, and although he assured Weiner of his "whole-hearted co-operation [sic]," he also underlined the crisis in publishing and bookselling on the French side of the Atlantic. He argued that the huge number of rights acquired in 1945 and 1946, more or less glutting the market, and the various bankruptcies were indeed endangering the Franco-American foreign rights market. Perhaps not wanting to dampen Weiner's enthusiasm, aware of the business opportunities that lay ahead, he ended his reply thus,

> In spite of all this we are looking forward with optimism because the interest for foreign and especially American literature is still considerable and even if the number of sales is to go down we believe that the value of royalties perceived shall go up after the elimination of many worthless publishers.[56]

Although his assessment of the situation cannot entirely be refuted, Hoffman's reply does appear as an attempt to anticipate failure by deflecting the blame onto the market conditions.

Meanwhile, in order to obtain results, Curtis Brown aimed at further rationalizing their work. Even before the foreign rights department was given the final go-ahead, in the fall of 1946 a new system had been launched, whereby Hoffman was sent advance information on books to be published by the agency's clients, in the form of short summaries. These were intended to save French publishers time in their decision making, all the while sparing Curtis Brown the cost of sending review copies of titles "which would have no chance whatever of a sale."[57]

This was certainly an interesting way of promoting books, although many of the summaries Hoffman received were marked as "too American books." The rationale behind this system was to spare local agents from reading the books, thereby saving them time and energy.

Local French agents, upon entering into exclusive representation contracts for US agencies, were to expect another form of pressure from agents, publishers, or authors. Although a number of authors seem to have had little interest in the sums they might reap from the sale of their foreign rights, content with the popularity afforded them by the translations, others however were intent on obtaining as much as possible. Hoffman often found himself pushed by his American partners to raise royalties or advances. What they may have failed to understand is that France's economic and monetary situation certainly did not encourage publishers to be, had they in fact even wanted to, as liberal as their transatlantic counterparts on the matter of advances. The American inflation in advances was attested to by the sums offered by the paperback publishers, starting around $500 to $2,000, rising to $35,000—in 1951, for Mailer's *The Naked and Dead*—and over $100,000 for James Jones's *From Here to Eternity* in 1953.[58] Between 1945 and 1955 average advances ranged from $500 to $1,000 for novel rights in the United States, sometimes reaching $2,500 for great luminaries or publishers' protégés; French publishers rarely extended American authors advances beyond $500.

For Hoffman, the demands of an author such as the bestselling Thomas Costain, represented by Brandt & Brandt, were especially taxing. A Canadian journalist, Costain had taken to writing historical fiction with great success: at least three of his novels, The *Black Rose* (1945), *The Moneyman* (1947), and *The Silver Chalice* (1952) featured on the *New York Times* bestseller lists. These coups must have gone to his head: in 1947 he stated his claims for the French rights of *The Moneyman*, a Book-of-the-Month Club selection, refusing any advance under $5,000. Hoffman's initial reaction to these terms conveyed by Baumgarten was to explain that

> .... no French publisher is likely to consider such an advance as it would represent roughly the accumulated royalties of 20,000 copies (at 10% and a published price of 300 francs) and you understand of course the impossibility of such a thing.[59]

However, neither Hoffman or Costain relented, and in 1949 the agent was able to obtain from Hachette an advance of $2,000 with a royalty scale of 8% to 3,000, 10% to 6,000, 12% to 9,000, and 15% thereafter, which the author ultimately accepted.[60] In this instance, Hoffman had gone almost beyond the call of duty, negotiating for the book for close to two years, and obtaining what no French author was offered at the time, a 15% royalty below 10,000 copies sold. In his view, this was certainly not sound policy, and he intimated to Baumgarten that it was perhaps best to search for the "best possible publisher instead of the highest possible advance."[61]

This case is illustrative both of Costain's—and indeed, his American agent's—awareness of the marketability of his books, and of their relative ignorance of the terms conceded outside the United States. Clearly, as early as the post-war years, US agents were intent on playing the new foreign markets, readily orchestrating competition among rival authors. Needless to say, the bigger an author's advance, the larger is the commission. The field of detective fiction was certainly one that could be profitably plowed in the mid to late 1940s, as French publishers vied with each other to bring out unknown and famous authors in their series. In November and December of 1948, Gertrude Weiner of Curtis Brown acted on behalf of Ellery Queen to get Hoffman to raise French offers for several of their novels. Ellery Queen, a pseudonym chosen by Frederic Dannay and Manfred Bennington Lee, was by then a celebrated name in the field of detective fiction, both for their own works and for the publication of others in their magazine, the *Ellery Queen Mystery Magazine*, which was also published in a French version. Their position in the field presumably made them privy to information on the terms that were at the time being offered to other mystery and detective fiction writers around the world, and Weiner used this information to suggest that Queen was actually being bested by Raymond Chandler, James M. Cain, Helen McCloy, or Bruno Fisher. Much in the manner of an errand boy, Hoffman was asked to negotiate with Albin Michel to obtain at least as large an advance, and royalties as good as those offered Bruno Fisher. In less than two months, between late November 1948 and mid-January 1949, Hoffman twice negotiated to bring the advance on a par with, then above Fisher's, and reported back three royalty scale offers, so that the Dannay-Lee duo could rest assured that their name "in the mystery field is better than any of the above."[62] Although it might have been quite uncomfortable for Hoffman to repeatedly bargain for better terms, the detective/mystery genre was so lucrative for everyone involved in the transactions, that he apparently complied without much of a fuss. Furthermore, in the case of Ellery Queen, Hoffman's most cordial, if not friendly, business relations with Albin Michel must have made the negotiations easier.

Competition

By the early 1950s, American publishers and authors who hoped to publish their works in Europe had understood the necessity of enlisting the services of US agents; most often these agents worked through a continental British representative, who before the war had most prominently been chosen among the list of A.M. Heath, Curtis Brown (London), A.D. Peters, and John Farquharson. Sensing that there was business to be made with foreign rights, some US publishers after the war started to retain translation rights, sometimes cutting off American intermediaries, to handle business directly through continental agents, which presented a dual advantage: maintaining close contact, at minimal expense for the agency. Several US publishers retained foreign rights on the following basis: 75% of the sums were granted to the author, and 25% to the publisher. This was decidedly not in favor of the author, as compared with the 10% or even 20% commission to be split between the US and the continental agents. In some instances, publishers retained an excessive 50% of the proceeds from foreign rights. In effect, the US Book Publishers' Bureau seems to have heeded the Publishers' Association of Great Britain's 1943 advice to hold on to "continental translation rights" during the war, as these might "prove to be of considerable value after the war," and slightly modified their traditional practice of leaving ownership of these rights to authors.[63] Being mainly in business with agencies, Hoffman saw this shift as a threat of sorts, since, if the trend continued, he might well lose part of his American business.[64]

Some American publishers' decision to bypass US or British agencies and deal directly with individual continental agents, prompted a form of competition among local agents, as evidenced by the misunderstanding between Hoffman and Cass Canfield, former president and board chairman of Harper & Brothers. Assuredly the exclusive representation of a foreign publisher secured a flow of books whose rights could be negotiated on the French market. Hoffman, who during a trip to London in June 1946 had mistakenly understood that he was to act as sole exclusive agent for Harper's who were to terminate arrangements with Curtis Brown in London, received a harsh wake-up call when Canfield chose to work with Jenny Bradley. Having sold a number of titles for Harper, through Curtis Brown—not least Richard Wright's *Native Son* and *Uncle Tom's Children*, Glenway Wescott's *Apartment in Athens* and *Pilgrim Hawk*—Hoffman presumably thought, almost naturally, that he would continue to do so. In an apologetic letter acknowledging his own possibly confusing discourse, Canfield explained that prior personal ties with the Bradleys had influenced his decision to work primarily with Hoffman's competitor regarding the French market.[65] Obviously hurt by this decision, Hoffman was thus reminded of the edge that the Bradley agency had, due to its long history and most probably also, to the multiplicity of contacts made by William A. Bradley, both as a Paris socialite and a Columbia alumnus.

Authors themselves could sometimes, unwittingly or not, make things difficult for local agents, when attempting to arrange terms on their own. Paris agents were also very much aware of outside competition, which made it all the more important that they should "perform" well for their collaborators. Indeed, competition came from three different actors in the field: American publishers, French publishers' scouts, and other local agents. I have already suggested the form of rivalry with the latter which is revealed in the numerous references, not all very kind, made to Jenny Bradley throughout Hoffman's business correspondence. In addition to his disappointment at seeing the Bradley agency obtain the exclusive representation of Harper & Brothers, Hoffman was to endure repeated small vexations. Before 1945 Jenny Bradley had conducted business with Brandt & Brandt, and Hoffman complained that agreements continued to be signed with her agency even after he had become their French representative[66]; furthermore, some book copies seem to have been sent to him by mistake, whereas they had been intended for Bradley.[67] Although Hoffman did pass these copies along, this was cause for bitterness, and he seems to have conveyed his irritation to Gertrude Weiner of Curtis Brown, New York, who in turn grew weary of having to reply to Bradley that Hoffman was now negotiating for them. Writing on the matter of Bradley's enquiry about the French rights to Guy Endore's *Methinks the Lady*, Weiner explained to Hoffman that she had informed Jenny Bradley that she was to turn any French inquiry on the subject over to him, adding

> As you know, I have done this before in connection with other matters. Does she ever comply? I am wondering if it is worthwhile to write her such letters. Please let me know, as I would hate to continue to do so, if my letters just end up in the waste paper basket.[68]

Hoffman does seem to have got along better with publishers than with most of his colleagues. His correspondence with several Paris agencies testifies to his competitive drive. To an inquiry by Agence Littéraire et Artistique on the availability of the French rights to Fiorello La Guardia's memoirs, he curtly replied that the placement of these rights was "in his hands," underlining how his 15 years in the business certainly placed him in as good a position as they to negotiate foreign rights. There followed a brief and paternalistic reminder of the agent's ethics, suggesting that Agence Littéraire et Artistique had ignored an important rule of thumb, to the effect that agents have to transmit any publisher's inquiry to the actual representative of the work or author.[69] Hoffman's opinion on his fellow French agents, as expressed to his US partners, is also evidence of his eagerness to become a key intermediary in the transatlantic business. He once claimed to George Strem, an acquaintance who had emigrated to the United States and opened a representatives' agency, that he was the first book agent in Paris, who could place any title provided it be a genuinely first-class work.[70] He regularly derided the contracts passed before his time by Betty Winkler, wife of Paul Winkler, founder of the Opera Mundi news syndicate and agency, or by fellow agent Marguerite Scialtiel. The latter, who had worked for Curtis Brown's bureau in Paris before and during the war, and as an early director of Albatross Press, had been quite active in the negotiating of Anglo-American crime and detective fiction, before the war, introducing Ellery Queen in "*L'Empre-inte*" series, and Erle Stanley Gardner in Gallimard's Detective series. Hoffman's slowly gaining ground in this particular field after the war partly explains why he felt the need to put her down. As he wrote to Curtis Brown's Gertrude Weiner in 1949,

> I am sorry to say that the majority of the contracts which Miss Scial-tiel passed for detective stories with NRC [Nouvelle Revue Critique] before the war were deplorable: a small outright sum with no limita-tion . . . . The Ellery Queen titles they (NRC) acquired on a normal basis have reverted and I have resold them to Albin Michel as you know. The others however are I am afraid irretrievably lost owing to the rotten pre-war contracts.[71]

In some instances Hoffman's bad-mouthing certainly did hurt his rela-tions with overseas representatives. Upon learning that Ruth McKenney, bestselling author and a favorite of Naomi Burton's, was dissatisfied with his services and had decided to change French representatives, he apparently lashed out against her newly chosen French representative, Authors Publishers International Agency (APIA).[72] This regrettable change might have been caused not only by Hoffman's failure, or re-luctance, to obtain contracts for McKenney, but also by his seemingly "cool and brush-offish" manner with the author, which suggests that he might not have been as comforting as would have been expected from an agent.[73] Could McKenney's decision have been prompted by the—albeit conservative and stereotypical—understanding that women agents were better suited to protect authors' egos, endowed as they were with nat-ural caring predispositions, as play agent Kitty Black wondered? To all accounts, this did not help Hoffman to ingratiate himself with either Weiner or the much appreciated and reputed agent Naomi Burton.

His determination to remain the exclusive intermediary for his US partners sometimes led him to overreach himself, as when, in an effort to counter Press Alliance, the US branch operations of Paul Winkler's leading European syndicate Opera Mundi, he offered to syndicate press material, for which, as he admitted, his agency was insufficiently staffed.[74] Although the reason alleged for his reaction—the confusion of authors whose rights would then be handled by several agents—made good business sense, we may surmise that Winkler's leading position in the European press syndication, and his opening of a US branch in 1938, were in fact potentially threatening to any French agent.

From Hoffman's perspective at least, relations between French agents were far from cordial, as he intimated to Alan Collins in 1947, "You know of course that it is not an easy thing to get agents to sit at one and the same table and even to co-operate . . . . "[75] Although she herself claimed to co-operate regularly with fellow agents, Jenny Bradley had felt Hoffman's reluctance to collaborate, as the slightly offended tone of the following extract attests,

> As I told you when I had the pleasure of meeting you in person, the fact that you almost never answer my letters is disheartening, leaving me to think that it may not be very useful to write you . . . . Besides, could you please tell me quite frankly if you are interested in collaborating on works whose rights you control . . . . Personally, I have always encouraged such collaborations, but if you prefer to do things some other way, I quite understand and keep and will refrain from disturbing you.[76]

Assessing these tensions, one cannot completely set aside the gender equation. The fact that his main rival, Jenny Bradley, was one of several women agents with whom he was competing, presumably made it slightly more difficult to "sit at one and the same table." As suggested earlier, women in France made up a majority among this small group of professionals, just as they did among New York agents in the mid to late 1950s, if the records of the Society of Authors' Representatives are to be believed.[77] While legal studies remained largely out of bounds for French girls, the "clerical revolution" of the 1920s and the new specialized training for young women resulting from various educational reforms, had provided women with secretarial skills that some among the more "literary" could put to good use in the agenting profession: many of the better-educated young ladies had been offered general higher education courses in stenography, typing, but also commercial law, accounting, and foreign languages—usually English, but also German and Italian. To some extent, the competences and virtues of the "*femme de papiers*" (women clerks) were transferrable to the agenting profession.[78]

In spite of these inevitably competitive relations, it was Hoffman who suggested and indeed set up, in 1948, the professional organization of literary agents, modelled after the American Society of Authors' Representatives whose statutes he had requested from Alan Collins. For this purpose, as he explained to Gertrude Weiner, he was willing to co-operate and even split commissions with those of his rivals—all, incidentally, women agents—who sat on the board of the newly founded professional society.[79]

Yet another source of great irritation to Hoffman was the attempt by certain American publishers to circumvent intermediaries by making direct offers to their French counterparts, sometimes after a first contact had been established through a local agent. US publishers were not alone in their endeavors to bypass at least one intermediary; in 1945, Gallimard got in touch directly with McIntosh & Otis on the matter of French rights to several of Steinbeck's books, potentially cutting off the agency's European representative, Curtis Brown London. This prompted the latter's French representative, Michel Hoffman, to warn Sonia Chapter in London, "Please see to it that these agreements are concluded through us and not over our heads if possible."[80] In other instances, copies were "innocently" given out by publishers or editors to individuals acting in a non-official capacity, with the result that a foreign publisher might eventually make an offer, although the copies had been sent for examination purposes only. When the book in question turned out to be a potentially huge success in the French hardboiled detective field—as for instance, Mickey Spillane's first novel introducing Mike Hammer, *I, the Jury* (1947)—the concomitant negotiations by two agencies, Office Artistique International and Agence Hoffman, might cause trouble.[81]

Scouts, either official or not, also added to local agents' difficulties in negotiating foreign rights. In some rare instances French publishers' scouts in the United States merely indicated interesting titles, leaving the publisher to then negotiate with Hoffman.[82] As we have suggested, they might be employed in an official capacity by a publisher, or act as scouts in addition to other services. Maurice-Edgar Coindreau and Marcel Duhamel are two very good examples of not-quite-official scouts, who both suggested and proposed for translation American works they found particularly exciting—albeit in different genres—and translated several of these works for Gallimard, thus leaving their personal "touch" on American literature in the decades following the war. Although Hoffman hailed Duhamel as one of the best translators of the time, he found his acting as unofficial agent on several occasions irritating, as in the case of Richard Wright's *Native Son*. Duhamel had made an offer to Harper's, proprietors of the foreign rights, prior to Hoffman, then apparently continued to negotiate in spite of his being notified by Curtis Brown in London that they controlled the rights; consequently, their representative in France, Hoffman, was to handle the book. When Duhamel claimed that the agency had granted him an option on these rights Sonia Chapter of the London agency denied to Hoffman that she had promised anything of the sort.[83]

By all accounts Hoffman hated to be double-crossed, and insisted that he at least be kept informed when French publishers decided to employ representatives in the United States. The latter might negotiate directly with US agencies on behalf of the French publisher, sometimes offering books that had already been proposed by Hoffman himself.[84] In these instances, Hoffman found himself confronted with individuals whose wide-ranging attributions within a publishing house might from time to time lead them to make offers, although they lacked the business acumen and legal background to carry the offers all the way to the contract stage. More worrisome for him was the setting up by French publishers of full-blown representative operations on the other side of the Atlantic. In 1946 Literary Masterworks, Inc. was founded in New York and advertised as Gallimard's "exclusive agent in U.S.A. [sic]."[85] Headed by Marcel Aubry, these offices were, in the words of Dionys Mascolo, intended to control the payment of American rights to French works and keep watch over the literary market.[86] In August of 1948, Alan Collins of Curtis Brown, New York alerted Hoffman to the subject of an offer made by Duhamel to the Mystery Writers of America, to pay authors of detective fiction "a blanket offer of $300.00 advance against 8% for the first 10.000, and 10% thereafter; guaranteeing a first printing of 30.000 and a 2nd printing of 30.000 within 3 months of the first printing being exhausted."[87] This offer—which actually prompted Ellery Queen, as we have seen, to ask for increased terms for their own French rights—so closely resembled the standard terms for inclusion in the *"Série Noire"* that Hoffman immediately took up the matter with Duhamel. The latter denied being involved and blamed Aubry's Literary Masterworks entirely. Be that as it may,[88] Hoffman strongly resented this campaign organized by a form of "shadow" publisher, feeling it was orchestrated to "push us, French agents, out of the circuit." He further supported his allegations by referring to one of the paragraphs of the above-cited offer, which enticed US publishers to send their books directly to Literary Masterworks, and to inform their French representatives that these titles were no longer on offer for the French market. His words of advice to Duhamel indeed sound like a thinly veiled threat,

> This letter reveals that Literary Master Works Inc. is clearly plotting a campaign against French literary agents whom it seeks to supersede.
>
> Thus it appears to me that unless they distance themselves immediately and most formally from this disloyal form of competition—likely, furthermore, to harm their own interests in New York—Gallimard might stand to lose the benefits of the good relations you have established with me as well as with the other important literary agents in Paris. As for me, I clearly see how this scandalous affair shall be pursued; as Secretary General of the Groupement Professionnel des Agents Littéraires Français, I believe I speak in my own and in my fellow agents' names.[89]

Underneath the braggadocio lies Hoffman's fear of losing an important connection with Duhamel and Gallimard, which in spite of the difficulties already alluded to, was proving ever more lucrative as detective and noir fiction continued to sell by the tens of thousands in France. This letter furthermore proves quite bold, as Hoffman purported to speak not only in his name, but also in the name of the newly founded GPALF (*Groupement Professionnel des Agents Littéraires Français*), which in turn lent authority to his complaint—and his disguised threat of, perhaps, an unrealistic boycott of the publisher. Hoffman clearly wanted French agents to be reckoned with. The accusations were strong enough to move Gaston Gallimard's son, Claude, who by then was working for the publishing house, to reassure Hoffman on his father's firm intentions to maintain his long-standing and excellent relations with Paris agents. As subsequent events would illustrate, this soothing reply was quite possibly just a way of humoring Hoffman. In 1952 three powerful publishers—Hachette, Simon & Schuster, and Gallimard—joined forces to create the French publishing group Editions de l'Atlantique, choosing Simon & Schuster trade book editor Peter Schwed to act as their scout. Schwed was to provide advance information and examination copies of interesting US titles to the group. In answer to a concerned letter sent by Hoffman, Schwed denied that his functions would bring him to compete with French agents. Angered by this hypocrisy, Hoffman once again produced evidence of the editor's contradictions, if not lies, quoting from Schwed's own circular letter to US agents and publishers,

> "You'll have no agency commission to pay to a foreign agent, but I will be responsible for seeing to it that you receive your regular accountings and settlements. You'll probably find it easier to pick up a phone and ask me to have something done than to try to wrestle it out via correspondence abroad. (NOTE to US agents: Obviously, I am in no way competing with you, and when you handle foreign rights for an author, both of you will make out somewhat better by virtue of not having to pay a foreign agent's commission.)"[90]

Just as American and British agents had long been considered parasites by publishers, French agents continued to be seen as thorns in the side of French publishers, and to some extent, of US agents and publishers as well. Competition seems to have stemmed from all sides, and Hoffman fought hard to maintain his position in the Anglo-US-French publishing networks. He considerably strengthened ties with Curtis Brown and Brandt & Brandt, demonstrating an early understanding of the importance of American popular fiction for the French. All the while, he worked through privileged partnerships with French publishers, and attempted to remain on good standing with fellow French agents. There is no denying that local agents proved useful to American rights owners in wrestling out regular accounts, settlements of payment, and in verifying the accuracy of translations. Without them, American authors, agents, and publishers could hardly have made their way through the complexities of French publishing contracts and publishers' idiosyncrasies.

Notes

1 Herman Finkelstein, "The Universal Copyright," *The American Journal of Comparative Law* 2, no. 2 (Spring, 1953): 199.
2 Joseph Dubin, "The Universal Copyright Convention," 89. Dubin's analysis reflects the common fears of the times; the principle of national treatment being considered as a fusion of the US principle, and the idea of the

nationality of the work, as embodied in Berne, "While it is true that works of Iron Curtain authors first published in one of the contracting states would thus be protected in this country, this may be a considered, calculated risk that we would have to take." (102).

3 Mollier, *Édition, presse et pouvoir en France au XXe siècle*, 155.
4 Mollier, "Paris capitale éditoriale des mondes étrangers," 376; and *Édition, presse et pouvoir en France au XXe siècle*, 228.
5 Mollier, "Paris capitale éditoriale des mondes étrangers," 380.
6 Ibid., 376–377.
7 Luey, "The Organization of the Book Publishing Industry," 29.
8 Tebbel, *A History of Book Publishing in the United States, Vol IV*, 349.
9 See Mollier, *Édition, presse et pouvoir en France au XXe siècle*.
10 Founded by Claude Tchou, *Le Club du livre du mois* was a French subsidiary for the Belgian publisher L'Ambassade du Livre.
11 See Parinet, *Une histoire de l'édition à l'époque contemporaine*, 392 and following.
12 Note that book distribution in France remained largely centralized through Hachette in the 1950s (Parinet, *Une histoire de l'édition à l'époque contemporaine*, 393.)
13 Although paperbound books were found as early as the 15th century, the origins of the modern paperback, establishing a tradition of combining reprints of classic and contemporary texts, are generally attributed to Tauchnitz in Germany. Tauchnitz was able to sustain long-lasting business associations with prominent British authors, including Dickens, by paying for reprint rights even before bilateral agreements were fully established in England. See John Feather, *A History of British Publishing*, 2nd edition (London: Routledge, 2006), Mark Rectanus, *Literary Series in the Federal Republic of Germany from 1960 to 1980* (Wiesbaden: Otto Harrassowitz, 1984).
14 Luey, "The Organization of the Book Publishing Industry," 45.
15 Parinet, *Une histoire de l'édition à l'époque contemporaine*, 405.
16 On the rise of French series in the 19th century, see Isabelle Olivero, *L'invention de la collection* (Paris: IMEC Editions; Editions de la Maison des Sciences de l'Homme, 1999).
17 Isabelle Olivero, "The Paperback Revolution in France, 1850–1950," in *The Culture of the Publisher's Series*, Vol. 1, *Authors, Publishers and the Shaping of Taste*, ed. John Spiers (Basingstoke: Palgrave Macmillan, 2011), 80.
18 Parinet, *Une histoire de l'édition à l'époque contemporaine*, 406.
19 In 1954 John Brown's *Panorama de la littérature contemporaine aux Etats-Unis* was awarded the Grand Prix de la Critique Littéraire.
20 Maurice-Bernard Endrebe, "Le roman policier," in *Histoire de l'édition française, Tome IV*, ed. Henri-Jean Martin, Roger Chartier, 256–265.
21 Martin, Chartier, Vivet, ed., *Histoire de l'edition française, Tome IV*, 572.
22 Luey, "The Organization of the Book Publishing Industry," 31.
23 See *Index Translationum* statistics. The statistics were interrupted between 1940 and 1948. For the same period, between 1948 and 1953, the total number of translations published in the United States also doubled, from 290 to 597 titles.
24 See Archives du Cercle de la Librairie, BCL 2.B16-01.01 to 01.07. The figures for the proportion of works of literature and fiction translated from the French are based on my own calculations in the *Index Translationum*.
25 On the problem of statistics, see Laura J. Miller and David Paul Nord, "Reading the Data on Books, Newspapers and Magazines, A Statistical

Appendix," in *A History of the Book in America, vol 5: The Enduring Book, Print Culture in Postwar America*, 503–518.

26 Tebbel, *A History of Book Publishing in the United States, Vol IV*, 122. Quoted again by Luey, "The Organization of the Book Publishing Industry," 30.

27 Dan Lacy, "The Role of American Books Abroad," *Foreign Affairs* 34, no. 3 (1956): 409.

28 Malcolm Johnson, "The Foreign Distribution of American Publications," *Library Quarterly* 24, no. 1 (1954): 115. Johnson signals that this figure does not include books sent over as gifts or in other fashions.

29 This is a very rough estimate, calculated as the ratio of volumes sent abroad to the number of copies sold by US publishers for 1947 and 1954, as provided by Miller and Nord, "Reading the Data on Books, Newspapers and Magazines," 509.

30 Here taking into account authors with at least ten 10 translations, who featured on at least three3 of the nine lists established by the Cercle for 1948, 1950, 1952, 1953, 1954, 1955. Archives du Cercle de la Librarie.

31 Hench, *Books as Weapons*, 182.

32 In 1955, Peter S. Jennison of the USIS estimated that out of the three million members of the Communist Party in Western Europe, two-thirds were Italian, with "the remainder in France." Dan Lacy, Charles G. Bolté, and Peter S. Jennison, ed. *Library Trends* 5, no. 1 "American Books Abroad" (July 1956): 74.

33 Johnson, "The Foreign Distribution of American Publications," 114.

34 See Chapter 2.

35 Jennison, in Lacy, Bolté, and Jennison, ed., *Library Trends*, 82.

36 Jennison, 82.

37 See "études sur l'*Index Translationum*," Archives du Cercle de la Librairie, IMEC, BCL2.B16-01.07. The category of "most translated authors" is based on authors with at least twenty annual translations.

38 The Soviet Union's statistics for the mid-1950s appear all the more propagandistic when we observe the sudden and fantastic leap in the number of translations for Lenin and Marx reported in the *Index Translationum*, between 1948 and 1950: figures rose from 32 to 159 for the works of Lenin, and from 29 to 71 for Marx, with Stalin coming in with 112 translations. Archives du Cercle de la Librairie, BCL 2.B16-01.01-03.

39 Lacy, Bolté, and Jennison, *Library Trends*, 80.

40 Its motto was "Atrum post bellum, ex libris lux." See American Library in Paris website.

41 Lacy, "The Role of American Books Abroad," 415.

42 For more on the role of US Cultural Diplomacy in France, see Martha Bernstein, "U.S. Cultural Policy in France 1945 to 1958," Doctoral thesis (Université de Montréal, 1998), and Brian Angus McKenzie, "Deep Impact: the Cultural Policy of the United States in France, 1948 to 1952," Doctoral Dissertation, History (State University of New York at Stony Brook, 2000) and *Remaking France: Americanization, Public Diplomacy, and the Marshall Plan* (Oxford: Berghahnbooks, 2005).

43 Sonia K. Chapter, Manager of Foreign Department for Curtis Brown, London, to Michel Hoffman, November 14, 1944; and Michel Hoffman to Sonia K. Chapter, December 4, 1944. BRH.HOF.AG.09.01.

44 Naomi Burton to Michel Hoffman, February 7, 1946. BRH.HOF.AG.15.03. Burton contended that the London Office could "mess anything up with the greatest of ease."

45 For more on Lieber, see Michael Denning, *The Cultural Front: The Laboring of American Culture in the Twentieth Century* (New York: Verso, 1998) and Anthony Joseph Sacco, Sr., *Little Sister Lost* (Bloomington: WestBow Press, 2004, 2013).

46 For a list of agents' clients, with dates, see New Yorker Records at the New York Public Library, "Appendix A. References To Notable Authors In Agents' Files" at http://archives.nypl.org/uploads/collection/pdf_finding_aid/nyorker.pdfhttp://archives.nypl.org/uploads/collection/pdf_finding_aid/nyorker.pdf.

47 Nielsen, a competitive publisher born in Denmark, who had first worked in book distribution, became intent on competing with the best detective series, in particular Gallimard's "*Série Noire.*" This, and a budding friendship, might explain why he lent Hoffman money for a—potentially lucrative—trip to New York in February 1949 (Michel Hoffman to Sven Nielsen, May 3, 1949, BRH.HOF.ED.FR.24.03).

48 See Michel Hoffman to Dionys Mascolo, October 11, 1949. In July 1949 Hoffman complained that Steinbeck and Erskine Caldwell, having previously accepted a reduced royalty scale in order to remain with Gallimard, could not possibly agree to be paid a different royalty on hardbound and paperbound copies (Michel Hoffman to Dionys Mascolo, July 27, 1949). On the matter of late contract modifications, see Michel Hoffman to Marcel Duhamel, January 10, 1949, and October 14, 1949. BRH.HOF. ED.FR.33.03.

49 See manuscript letter, Marcel Duhamel to Michel Hoffman, October 30, 1949. BRH.HOF.ED.FR.33.03.

50 See Dionys Mascolo to Michel Hoffman, October 17, 1949, BRH.HOF. ED.FR33.03.

51 Michel Hoffman to Dionys Mascolo, October 20, 1949. BRH.HOF. ED.FR.33.03.

52 See Gertrude Weiner to Michel Hoffman, October 2, 1946. BRH.HOF. AG.15.03.

53 Gertrude Weiner to Michel Hoffman, April 3, 1947. BRH.HOF. AG.15.02.

54 See Gertrude Weiner to Michel Hoffman, January 17, 1947, BRH.HOF AG.15.03, "We are anxious at some future date to become the representative of Dutton on the continent, and anything you can tell him about how you work and the present state of French publishing will, I am sure, be of interest to him and of value in securing Dutton's representation."

55 See Michel Hoffman to Dionys Mascolo, June 21, 1946. BRH.HOF. ED.FR.33.03.

56 Michel Hoffman to Getrude Weiner, April 16, 1947, BRH,HOF AG.15.03.

57 Gertrude Weiner to Michel Hoffman, October 22, 1946. BRH.HOF. AG.15.03.

58 Luey, "The Organization of the Book Publishing Industry," 44.

59 Michel Hoffman to Bernice Baumgarten, July 17, 1947, BRH.HOF. AG.16.01.

60 See Michel Hoffman to Bernice Baumgarten, June 13, 1949, and June 21, 1949, BRH.HOF.AG.20.01. As it turns out, the royalty scale had been mistakenly proposed to Hoffman by a "subordinate editor," but Hachette's acquisitions editor preferred to maintain the offer out of dignity.

61 Michel Hoffman to Bernice Baumgarten, Jan 5, 1949. BRH.HOF. AG.20.01.

62 See Gertrude Weiner to Michel Hoffman, November 22, 1948. BRH.HOF. AG.14.01.

63 See "Minutes of the Meeting of the Board of Directors, (Harvard Club), Nov 10, 1943," in Random House Records, 1925–1999—Butler Library, Columbia University—Correspondence—MS # 1048—BOX 135.

64 See Michel Hoffman to Gertrude Weiner October 7, 1946. BRH.HOF. AG.15.03: "In general I must say that it seems to me rather a menace that American publishers begin more and more to handle the translation rights of their clients and the old arrangement under which we acted for the authors seemed much more preferable. The one thing we must absolutely insist on having is the *exclusive* right to deal with the property. Publishers however do not always appear to be bound by agency arrangements." See also Michel Hoffman to Bernice Baumgarten, October 2, 1946, BRH.HOF.AG.16.01. Commenting upon the reverting of Wallace Stegner's rights to his publisher, Houghton, Mifflin, he concluded, "More and more American publishers seem to want to handle the translation rights of their authors.".

65 See Cass Canfield to Michel Hoffman, June 7, 1946, and June 20, 1946, BRH.HOF.ED.FR.33.03.

66 Michel Hoffman to Bernice Baumgarten, January 29, 1946. BRH.HOF. AG.16.01.

67 Copies of Francis Steegmuller's *Blue Harpsichord* and Max White, *The Man who Carved Women from Wood* intended for Jenny Bradley, had been sent to Hoffman by mistake.

68 "It rather surprises me that agreements are still being passed through Mrs Bradley without my knowledge?" Gertrude Weiner to Michel Hoffman, October 23, 1946. BRH.HOF.AG.15.03.

69 Michel Hoffman to Agence Littéraire et Artistique, May 5, 1948. BRH. HOF.AG.18.02.

70 Michel Hoffman to George Strem, January 31, 1946. BRH.HOF.AG.16.02.

71 Michel Hoffman to Gertrude Weiner, May 24, 1949. BRH.HOF.AG.14.02.

72 See Naomi Burton to Michel Hoffman, July 16, 1948. BRH.HOF.AG.15.02. "Ruth McKenney has the impression that you have not offered the material but she may be wrong about that and in that case, will you let A.P.I.A. (agency) know where the books have been. The A.P.I.A. may be the worst agency in Paris but it is the one the author has chosen and in the face of your conviction that the books cannot be sold, we can't obviously stand in the way of the author's wishes."

73 See Gertrude Weiner to Hoffman, December 24, 1947. BRH.HOF.AG.15.02.

74 Michel Hoffman to Alan Collins, January 30, 1946. BRH.HOF.AG.15.03.

75 Michel Hoffman to Alan Collins, November 24, 1947. BRH.HOF.AG.15.02.

76 My translation. Jenny S. Bradley to Michel Hoffman, February 22, 1945. BRH.C03.B04.D05.

77 A quick survey of the membership of the Society of Authors' Representatives between 1954 and 1960 reveals that women agents—counting agencies headed by women—made up between 40% and 46% of the members of the society. This is not counting the women agents working for the various agencies listed. Society of Authors' Representatives Records, 1939–1991, Chronological Files, MS #1173, Box 2.

78 See Sylvie Schweitzer, *Les Femmes ont toujours travaillé*, 231–238.

79 About Marie-Louise Bataille, translator and French representative of US agent Franz Horch, who was trying to place American labor activist and former Communist Louis Budenz's *This is My Story* in Paris although the French rights were controlled by Curtis Brown, Hoffman wrote in a gentlemanly way, "I agree to share my part of the commission with her. For many reasons I do not want to upset this lady—one of them is that we are both on

the board of the Committee to organize a professional Association of Literary representatives." M. Hoffman to G. Weiner, January 28, 1948. BRH. HOF AG.14.02.

80 Michel Hoffman to Sonia Chapter, March 19, 1945. BRH.HOF.AG.09.01.

81 See Michel Hoffman to Gertrude Weiner, October 7, 1948, and Gertrude Weiner to Michel Hoffman, October 21, 1948. BRH.HOF.AG.14.02. According to Alistair Rolls, the E.P. Dutton hardback first edition of *I, the Jury* sold only around 10,000 copies, while the Signet (New American Library) 1948 paperback reprint sold 6.5 million copies that year. Hoffman was conducting negotiations for French rights even before the reprint edition came out, in December 1948. See Rolls, "An Uncertain Space: (Dis-)Locating the Frenchness of French and Australian Detective Fiction," Alistair Rolls, ed., "Mostly French: French (in) Detective Fiction," *Modern French Identities*, vol. 88 (Oxford: Peter Lang, 2009): 19–51.

82 Albin Michel, whose president was quite close to Hoffman, employed an "agent in America," Robert Chauveau, whose mission was to survey the book output and signal interesting books for possible translation. See Robert Esménard (Albin Michel) to Michel Hoffman, July 11, 1947. BRH.HOF. ED.FR.38.01.

83 Sonia Chapter to M. Hoffman, April 20, 1945, "I am worried about the impression Duhamel has given you that I have promised him the rights in Richard Wright's books. I did nothing of the sort. I was extremely firm with him [. . .] that I had merely left the matter open so that he might try to arrange for terms that would be to the author's advantage." See also Sonia Chapter to Michel Hoffman, September 24, 1945, BRH.HOF.AG.09.01.

84 Michel Hoffman to Armand Pierhal, June 6, 1946, BRH.HOF.ED.FR.34.02.

85 *The Writers' and Artists' Year Book*, 1949, p 219.

86 See Dionys Mascolo to Michel Hoffman, February 17, 1949, BRH.HOF. ED.FR.33.03.

87 Alan Collins to Michel Hoffman, August 24, 1948. BRH.HOF AG.14.02.

88 Hoffman wrote to Alan Collins that he "did not buy it," as Marcel Aubry would never have been authorized to offer such a high advance on behalf of Gallimard (Michel Hoffman to Alan Collins, September 2, 1948, BRH. HOF AG.14.02).

89 Michel Hoffman to Marcel Duhamel, September 1, 1948. BRH, HOF C03B04D05. My translation.

90 Michel Hoffman to Peter Schwed, March 9, 1953. BRH, HOF.C03.B04. D05.

4 Cultural Transfers and Transatlantic Negotiations

Whether well-informed or naïve, misguided or penetrating, the outcome of a passing vogue or a more deeply-rooted reaction, the unprecedented success of American literature abroad is a sociological as well as an aesthetic phenomenon of striking significance.[1]

I have already provided a brief overview of the books and authors negotiated by Hoffman and his fellow agents, and most in demand on the French side of the Atlantic, from middlebrow to literary, from pulp to literary detective fiction. The following pages will examine in closer detail the ways in which transactions for French rights to different categories of American works were carried out by Hoffman. Looking more specifically at the conducting of negotiations, this chapter offers a glance behind the scenes of transatlantic book transfers in the years following World War II, in order to establish the extent to which book agents participated in what has been termed a form of "Americanization" of both French literature and publishing.

Considering the bulk of the demands between 1946 and 1955 from French publishers, and the majority of French rights contracts negotiated by Hoffman, one might choose to classify the contracts along the lines of "brows," as the categories of lowbrow, middlebrow, and highbrow took on a particular significance in the late 1940s, when Russell Lynes and Dwight MacDonald articulated these concepts most forcefully.[2] However operative these concepts might have been at the time, important scholarship has since reconsidered and even denied the pertinence of such cultural stratification, demonstrating the fluidity of categories, and their actual obsolescence.[3] From a cultural historian's viewpoint, Beth Luey has shown that the very idea of middlebrow was passing in the 1960s.[4] Be that as it may, many titles handled by Hoffman certainly qualified as archetypal "middlebrow" Book-of-the-Month Club selections. Yet, as this chapter focuses on commercial transactions, I have chosen not to classify the books according to these categories reflecting literary value, but rather found it made better sense to view them from a publisher's—or an agent's—point of view, that is, considering the target readership. Thus three specific categories of books will be considered: the literary, the midlist novel, and detective/hardboiled fiction. "Midlist novels" are here understood, according to Janice Radway in *A Feeling for Books, The Book-of-the-Month Club, Literary Taste, and Middle Class Desire*, as

> books considered neither avant-garde nor merely commercial in their literary pretensions and neither mass market nor narrowly targeted in their distribution aims. A mid-list book was generally construed as a book of sound quality created for a moderately sized, fairly specific audience of committed readers.[5]

Although the focus is commercial, the question of taste cannot be neglected if one is to understand the "unprecedented success of American literature abroad" as Henri Peyre wrote. The French enthusiasm for American literature and fiction both increased the transatlantic circulation of books, and reflected the scope of such a circulation. Testifying to the quality of and enthusiasm for US literature in spite of the nation's political and ideological misgivings, in January 1951 the literary review *La Gazette des Lettres* listed under the headline "Their favorite translations" the pick of eight critics specialized in foreign literature for 1950.[6] Some of the greatest names in French criticism contributed to this literary magazine. For André Bay, translator and literary editor at Stock; critic and editor Maurice Nadeau, Claude-Edmonde Magny, Max Pol Fouchet, René Lalou, or Gabriel Marcel, translations from American titles predominated, competing with translations of E.M. Forster, Herman Hesse, Dino Buzzati, or Elio Vittorini. Particularly praised were the translations of Henry James's *Ambassadors*, Steinbeck's *The Pearl*, Herman Melville's *Mardi, and a Voyage Thither*, Erskine Caldwell's *Journeyman*, but also works by the newest generation of authors, Malcolm Lowry's *Under the Volcano*, Robert Penn Warren's *All the King's Men*—awarded the Pulitzer Prize in 1947— Norman Mailer's *The Naked and the Dead*, or Mezz Mezzrow and Bernard Wolfe's *Really the Blues*. This list illustrates how selections made by publishers actually bridged the old and the new generations of American writers.

The popularity and impact of American literature in those years have received much attention, and Sartre's 1946 essay "American Novelists in French Eyes," published in the venerable semi-literary—or middlebrow— magazine *Atlantic Monthly* is most often taken as evidence of the French enthusiasm for Faulkner, Caldwell, Steinbeck, Dos Passos, and Hemingway, and proof of these authors' influence on the younger generation of French writers. As the prime gatekeeper of his time, Sartre would forcibly shape both the American vision of French taste, and the French's own view of American literature. He rapidly discarded Dreiser or Henry

James, whose analytical novels he did not find innovative as compared with the French brand of 19th-century novels authored by Zola, Flaubert, or Maupassant; faced with the surprise of Americans who expressed their disapproval of the bleak portrayal, the "filth" and even disloyalty of the novels of Faulkner or Steinbeck, Sartre attempted to respond. He emphasized how these "moralists'" criticism of their country certainly did not provoke in French readers a "disgusted reaction" to America, but on the contrary, admiration for the genuine liberty of such authors who could so analyze their country in all its glory and its gloom. Furthermore, writing from an author's point of view, he chose to emphasize how the narrative innovations of Caldwell, Steinbeck, and Faulkner had in fact come to enrich the works by the new generation of French writers, first and foremost Camus, and Beauvoir herself, who was said to have been inspired by Faulkner's disruption of chronology. In pointing to the new authors writing in the manner of American authors, Sartre was actually already highlighting the conditions for a genuine cultural transfer, through adaptation of a culture and techniques.

This essay, published in a magazine mostly intended for a middlebrow and highbrow readership, calls for several remarks: first, it does not purport to comment on the general reception of US literature and fiction, but focuses on their reception by the writers themselves, which amounts to the reception of "Coindreau literature,"[7] certainly not comprehensively representative by American standards. Second, Sartre does not expand on the fantastic craze for American hardboiled detective and mystery fiction, except for a passing mention of James M. Cain. In fact, the essay opens with the literal exclusion of "popular" bestsellers—*Gone with the Wind* and Sinclair Lewis's *Babbitt*—which, to his eyes, had "had no influence on French literature." Be that as it may, these voluntary exclusions—Sartre was avowedly commenting on the literary influence of US novelists—fail to provide a comprehensive picture of American literature, not to speak of fiction, in France.

In 1947 Henri Peyre, a French linguist who had been teaching as Sterling Professor of French at Yale since 1938, published "American Literature through French Eyes" in the *Virginia Quarterly Review*. Written from the standpoint of one considerably more cognizant of American culture and society than Sartre, this essay clearly takes its cue from the latter, as the very title suggests. Establishing once and for all the—quantitative and qualitative—superiority in France of American over British works, counting for three out of four translated works from the English language, he also reassured public diplomats by asserting that the image of America was then best conveyed in its novels, rather than in other, popular, forms of entertainment. The essay once again posits the primacy of the "American quartet" in France—Hemingway, Faulkner, Dos Passos, Steinbeck—or indeed quintet if one adds Caldwell. Peyre remarked on the preponderance of the South in what we might call "French American" literature, and while he acknowledged the pessimism of US literature, he saw this particular brand of pessimism as

> . . . not the sterile mockery of cynics nor the decadent obsession to soil the beauty of the world. It is the expression of sincere idealism, of lucid faith. It asserts with eloquence that all is not well with the world, but that, by facing realities boldly, we could make life more worthy of being lived.[8]

Peyre offers an interesting development on the supposed thirst for violence of the French, assuaged by their readings of US literature. Not denying the drunkenness, the sex, and debauchery to be found in the works of Henry Miller, Steinbeck's "Wayward Bus," or Caldwell's "Journeyman," he contends that America's image will not suffer from this exposition of the seamy side of life, for only Nazi Germany and perhaps Stalinist Russia would offer the world a literature depicting only "the clean, efficient, moral—and lifeless—face of their country."[9] Yet according to the Yale scholar, what the French are seeking is not gratuitous and entertaining violence, but ". . . something deeper, of which they are in dire need: a message of vitality and a freshness of vision which raise violence and vice to the stature of the epic."[10] Where Peyre further differed from Sartre was in his belief that this epic element, the "raw meat" he found lacking in what he termed an exhausted French tradition of the *roman d'analyse*, could be found, also, in the masters of the hardboiled noir novel, Dashiell Hammett, Raymond Chandler, Horace McCoy, James M. Cain, or the earlier Damon Runyon. By including these highly popular authors and by touching upon the lesser, yet existing, attraction exerted by the "genteel" group of writers like Katherine Anne Porter, Eudora Welty, or Willa Cather, Peyre came, I think, a little closer to the truth of the picture in the late 1940s. Still, where were the other American authors?

The fact that French readers, and not merely French author-cum-readers, were actually not confining their interests to the sacred yet potentially enlarging quartet of great American moderns, was brought home in 1948 by an in-situ observer, Howard C. Rice, director of the Paris United States Information Library. In an essay published in *The French Review*, Rice made a series of observations on French interest in American life and culture, as exemplified by the individuals "of better-than-average education" who regularly patronized the library.[11] His remarks did not purport to express the opinion and tastes of a majority of French readers, yet even so, the standpoint of the US Information Service (USIS) institution does offer a reliable account, highlighting average readers' taste for middlebrow, popular, and bestselling American books:

> In commenting on "American literature abroad" many observers are inclined to concentrate too much on the self-consciously "literary" circles and reviews, and to neglect the tastes of the general

reading public . . . . But even a cursory survey of bookshops catering to a wider public will show the popularity of such authors as Louis Bromfield, Pearl Buck, Marcia Davenport, Taylor Caldwell, Kenneth Roberts—and the inevitable Margaret Mitchell. A complete list of American works published in French translation since the Liberation reveals far more variety than one might suspect—such titles as Gladys Hasting Carroll's "As the Earth Turns" (*Ainsi tourne la terre*)[12], Dreiser's "The Bulwark" (*Le Rempart*), Esther Forbes' "Paradise," J.P. Marquand's "Henry Pulham Esquire" (*L'Honorable Henry Pulham*), and, Marjorie Kinnan Rawlings' "The Yearling" (*Jody et le Faon*).[13]

As Rice went on to demonstrate, French publishers had furthermore become quite aware of the lucrative appeal of the label *"traduit de l'américain"* (translated from American English) . . . In fact, American observers—and some French observers as well—deplored the indiscriminate frenzy of publishers on both sides of the Atlantic, leading, perhaps, to curious selections that certainly did not represent the tastes of American readers themselves. As American literary critic Harry Levin wrote in 1949, if the "currents of transatlantic influence now run eastward rather than westward,"[14] importers displayed a "zeal for immediacy and sensationalism" that made for indiscriminate reading—Gide reading "William Faulkner and Dashiell Hammett with equal attention"—as well as for indiscriminate publishing. However, Levin also very aptly showed that in Europe, and especially in France, translation was being "consummated by imitation, the sincerest acknowledgment of cultural ascendancy."[15]

Peyre had stated that

> The writers of the New World have taught the French a refreshing disregard for composition, a total detachment from such rules as unity of plot, a youthful freedom from artistic restraint. There was a type of writing which aimed neither at pure art nor at eternal values, which cared little for posterity or even for survival. To compatriots of Flaubert and Mallarmé, whose sin is to deify literature, the contrast was salutary.[16]

With the example of Boris Vian, aka Vernon Sullivan's *J'irai cracher sur vos tombes*, Levin picked up what was perhaps the quintessential French homage paid to American literature—and literature of the South, at that: Vian, passing as the translator of Sullivan, a supposed Negro writer whose works were censored in America, had perpetrated a literary hoax evidencing his familiarity with American literature, touching on the quintessentially American phenomena, passing and lynching. His adaptation of US literary history and culture became all the more famous as the book was tried for obscenity; it was in fact just one of several American fake hardboiled novels written by French authors under an American pseudonym in the 1940s, and evidence of genuine, complete, cultural transfers to which, undeniably, agents had contributed from the wings. Léo Malet aka Frank Harding, Raymond Queneau aka Sally Mara, or Serge Arcouët aka Terry Stewart wrote elaborate pastiches of the US genre with an eye to the lucrative rewards of such publications.[17] This was not entirely new: already in the 19th century, French writers Gustave Aimard and Gabriel Ferry—who then had no use for pseudonyms—had become very popular with their Western-like adventure stories à la James Fenimore Cooper.[18] In a context of growing anti-Americanism when US mass culture was seen as debasing, the "American prestige" was thus being revived in fiction after the war.

Translation in Contracts: Some General Principles

As this study contends, if cultural and literary transfers depended, on the one hand, on the French craving for large American novels, and on the other, the talent of transatlantic literary gatekeepers, they were subject to the possibility and quality of translations. In turn, without the protection of US authors' translation rights enshrined in bona fide contracts, controlled by US and local French agents, such important transfers could not have occurred.

Before the ratification of the Universal Copyright Convention by Congress in September 1955, American works in France continued to be protected from piracy—in either British or French editions—under the rules defined in the 1891 bilateral treaty, or through the backdoor to Berne. In 1891 and 1933, commenting on the guarantees offered by the 1891 reciprocal bilateral copyright treaty between France and the United States, *Le Droit d'auteur*—the official publication for the "Bureau de l'Union internationale pour la protection des oeuvres littéraires et artistiques"—reminded its readers that France "guarantees American authors rights not only equal in substance, but identical to those guaranteed to French authors."[19] As for the duration of protection of works, provided the publisher took all necessary measures to protect the text under French copyright legislation, it was considered, under French law, as the author's life plus 50 years, which was actually longer than the US duration of copyright, extending to 56 years as of publication date.

Foreign rights contracts were instruments of this international protection, in turn endowing authors' representatives, both in the United States and in France, with a high degree of responsibility, for indeed, as US agent James Oliver Brown put it in 1967, an agent is among other things, "a protector of rights," or in fact, a "counsel in copyright."[20] When in 1949 Raymond Chandler wrote to Marcel Duhamel that, "[i]n the question of sales in European countries a writer is entirely in the hands of his agent," he was acknowledging merely a fraction of the local agent's services to foreign authors.[21] There was, and still remains, no strict international legislation regarding transactions in foreign rights, so that the drawing of foreign rights contracts rests with the parties concerned; today, as practice or tradition would have it, contracts are usually drawn up by the seller of rights. This means that in the case of French rights, American contracts will prevail, supposing in turn good understanding of the form of such contracts on the part of French parties, and their agreements to be interpreted according to the laws and statutes of the United States—as we shall see, namely those of the state of New York where the majority of publishers and agencies were established.[22]

In the mid-1960s, Paul R. Reynolds of worldwide fame asserted that

> Contracts with foreign publishers are similar to contracts with American publishers, except that they are not full of legal mumbo-jumbo. They are usually drawn up by agents and they are comprehensible.[23]

This statement calls for several remarks: as regards the years between 1944 and 1955, Reynolds' boast was more wishful thinking than actual practice. In fact, his *Saturday Review* article was printed as a way of promoting the New York Society of Authors' Representatives, under the guise of helping writers to separate the wheat from the chaff, in other terms, the good, sound, "legitimate" agents, from the "editorially incompetent" "pseudo-agents." Aside from the traditional deriding of publishers, what Reynolds does underline correctly, however, is that the vast majority of foreign rights were indeed negotiated by agents, thereby suggesting that, by 1965, agents had become regular, even indispensable fixtures in the market for international rights. The contracts negotiated by or with French agents for the period under examination actually reveal a diversity of situations, from a majority of contracts indeed drawn up by US agents, to contracts drawn up by US publishers, when they owned foreign rights to a work, to a few contracts drawn up by French publishers. While the wording differed from one contract to another, the various clauses were in the process of being standardized. In addition to the familiar clauses—similar to those in domestic contracts—sellers of foreign rights had best pay minute attention to the specificities of such clauses entailed by the international situation, the idiosyncrasies of French publishers, as well as to the unique clauses in such contracts.

In both standard foreign rights and domestic contracts there were to be found a royalty clause, outlining the financial terms—advances and royalty scale—under which the work was to be licensed; a grant clause, specifying the limits wherein the publisher could exploit the rights to the work, including territorial limits; several termination clauses, allowing the proprietor of rights to put an end to the agreement, whenever the publisher failed to keep his end of the deal; a copyright clause, ensuring that the author's copyright was protected by the appropriate instance, in the French case, the publisher; the discounts, including the number of gratis copies to be sent to the author; the payment clause, stipulating the method—pattern—of payment and accounting; an option clause, several subsidiary rights clauses, including syndication, or second-serial rights, and an arbitration clause. In addition to these articles, French rights contracts, like other foreign rights contracts, included a clause guaranteeing the accuracy and faithfulness of the translation, as well as protecting the work from any abusive abbreviations or alterations that might be decided without the approval of the author. In some cases, up to the early 1950s, was added the termination "war clause," stipulating that French publishers were not to sell or distribute the translated works in countries at war with the United States, this on account of the Trading with the Enemy Act. The handling of such contracts required an in-depth knowledge of both international copyright legislation and the specificities of French publishing; as we shall see in the last chapter, the payment and syndication clauses were often sources of friction. As for the royalty and the translation clauses, they were respectively overly determinant in the agents' negotiations, thereby revealing the added-value of the local agent's service.

Midlist Novels and Bestsellers

As we have seen, the bestowal of a literary prize, a selection by the Book-of-the-Month Club and/or the appearance of a title on one of the bestseller lists, especially that of the *New York Times*, often resulted in increasing foreign publishers' demand(s) for a particular American novel, and consequently term offers. Well aware of this "bestseller effect," foreign agents scoured both the mainstream and trade press for such information, and were kept abreast of any outstanding paratextual promotion by their American counterparts. In some cases, results fell far below the publishers' initial expectations as noted above, the success of Thomas Costain's historical romances overseas did not transcribe into good sales on the French side of the Atlantic. As Swiss publisher J-H. Jeheber wrote to Hoffman, explaining his decision to decline publication of Costain's *For My Great Folly* and *Ride with Me*, taste was still to be taken into consideration. For Jeheber, the French had "quite different expectations from those of the American public," and the fact that the books had been bestsellers in America certainly did not guarantee success in France.[24] The "bestseller effect," however, did create a form of emulation among French—and foreign—publishers, who often vied for the same authors over a certain period of time. Hoffman, pressed for information on 1939 Pulitzer Prize laureate Marjorie Kinnan Rawlings and other regular Book-of-the-Month Club selected authors such as Fred Wakeman or J.P. Marquand, was thus forced to keep a close eye on the demands of Paris publishers, in order to keep track of who held examination copies, who had made an offer, or whose offer could be topped. All the while, the number of requests for a specific work also allowed him to raise the ante and negotiate better deals.

Marjorie Kinnan Rawlings' attraction among French publishers, and her subsequent success in France, is evidence of the "bestseller" effect, especially when compared with other juvenile titles. Albin Michel had acquired the French rights to Kinnan's *The Yearling* (1938) just before the war, and through Hoffman, who represented Rawlings' agents, Brandt & Brandt, those to *Cross Creek* and *Golden Apples* in 1945. *The Yearling* had been awarded the Pulitzer Prize in 1939, and although initially intended by Rawlings and her Scribner's editor Maxwell Perkins as a story for boys, it had originally been published as an adult novel. Unable to bring out *The Yearling* on time on account of the war conditions, in 1945 Albin Michel offered to improve the terms initially offered Rawlings, and the USIS judged it important enough—at least for the promotion of American Southern culture—to agree to provide paper from US stocks so that it might be rapidly published, and the pre-war contract honored. The popular success of *The Yearling*, as noted by USIS librarian Howard Rice, is evinced by the various French-language paperback reprints in the 1950s—for the *Club des libraires de France* and the Belgian *Club du livre sélectionné* in 1954, for the *Livre de poche* in 1955—affording Hoffman an additional source of revenue from this author's representation, as commissions ranged from 5% to 13%.[25]

From Hoffman's perspective, *The Yearling* proved to be an exception of sorts in his handling of juvenile fiction—although as has been suggested, the novel was not initially aimed at juvenile readers. On several occasions he informed his American partners that juvenile fiction was "a very bad proposition on the French market," and "Westerns," too "puerile" for French readers, would not make interesting series. His reluctance to trade in juvenile fiction was seemingly not shared by all French agents; Jenny Bradley did not shun such deals, when Max Brand's or Henry Larom's Western fiction was in demand on the other side of the Atlantic. Judging from the developments in children's books in America, and to some extent in France, Hoffman's reticence certainly does not appear a sound business move.

If most American trade publishers had been slow to acknowledge the prospects and importance of this area, the creation in 1945 of the Children's Book Council, a promotional and information center, as well as a trade organization, attested to the flowering of this particular sector.[26] Specialized houses were born, trade houses developed or expanded their children's departments, hiring creative—for the most part—women editors, and sales leaped at a fantastic rate. Titles began to sell over 40,000 copies, rising in some cases to 100,000, and in 1947 Simon & Schuster's Little Golden Books sold a record of 39 million.[27] This trend was no doubt heightened by the multiplication of uniform series after

1940—while several 19th-century series proved highly durable. Tebbel notes that by 1955, *Publishers' Weekly*, overwhelmed by the number of children's series, decided to establish a specific list, thereby acknowledging the reality of the phenomenon.

In France, juvenile and children's book series, some very popular, had bloomed in the interwar years, with nearly all the great publishers issuing their own—Ferenczi's "*Le Petit roman d'aventures*" (1936), Tallandier's "*Les chevaliers de l'aventure*" (1933), "*Lectures illustrées de la jeunesse*" or "*Les Romans de la jeunesse*" by Editions Modernes, and of course the perennial "*Bibliothèque rose*" and "*Bibliothèque verte*" published by Hachette. The latter, a pioneer in the publishing of juveniles and of series, held an undisputed dominant position after the war. Why, then, was Hoffman so hesitant to negotiate the rights to juvenile or children's books? The limited staff at the agency—Hoffman worked alone, with the collaboration of a secretary—may have led him to concentrate on other genres and other literatures; another possible, highly pragmatic reason may be that such works did not command as potentially lucrative contracts as adult novels. While the average royalty scale for foreign rights to trade novels began between 8% and 10% to 5,000 copies, juvenile fiction was generally offered 6% to 3,000 copies, sometimes rising to 10% after 10,000 copies. Considering the differences in prices between a juvenile and a trade novel, certainly the energy spent on the one would not exactly yield the same results as the other, and the standard agent's commission of 10% in this instance was perhaps not worth trying for.

Publication of translated literature was, and remains, an economically risky endeavor for publishers, who often acquire French rights at a high price, without any guarantee as to the subsequent sales; hence the general enthusiasm for works that are in demand not only in the country of origin, but elsewhere in the world. The terms offered must take into consideration the cost of translation: some publishers—including Laffont or even smaller ones such as J.B. Janin—as Hoffman liked to point out for his American partners, chose to offer translators a royalty on copies sold, around 2% or 3%, which in the long run always proved advantageous, as translators personally interested in the circulation of the book would logically provide high-quality translations. Still this rather generous practice was far from common, most publishers paying translators a fixed sum. In any case, the choice of a good—costly—translation would necessarily induce lower offers for the proprietor, when total costs were computed. The advance against royalties thus depends on a combination of factors that include the popularity of the author, the sales of the title in the original country, the estimated print run and the price of the book in France, as well as the degree of international fame. In other terms, supply and demand remains a central operating rule in the international book market.[28] One other factor is the negotiating skills of book agents, on both sides of the Atlantic. American authors to this day may be unpleasantly surprised to learn the actual amounts foreign publishers are willing to extend as advances against foreign rights. In many countries, these cannot possibly compare with what they may expect in the United States. Between 1944 and 1955, advances of $1,000, $1,500, $2,000, or even $2,500 were not uncommon among big New York publishers. While some big Paris publishers might offer from $1,000 to $2,000 for important novels whose bestselling potential had already been demonstrated by a book club selection or a prize, the advances extended by small and large publishers alike averaged between $250 and $450, rarely $500, for mid-list and literary novels. Awards and publicity overseas warranted the raising of terms, as Hoffman explained to the small publishing house Editions de Flore, who wished to make an offer for Jo Sinclair's bestselling *Wasteland*, that Harper's would certainly accept nothing less than a $1,000 advance.[29] However large the gap between standard American and French advances, the ratio of 1 to 3, sometimes 1 to 4, was not in the least advantageous to authors, when compared with other countries. Danish and Norwegian publishers appear to have regularly offered advances approximating $200 for mid-list and even literary US authors; advances granted in Argentina, Finland, or Hungary were a far cry from US standards, ranging from $150 per volume, to outright sums.

Similarly, royalty scales could not compare with US standards of the times: according to Alan Collins, head of Curtis, Brown New York, the average royalty scale had "spread" in the early 1950s to 10 % on the first 5,000 copies sold, 12,5% on the next 5,000, and 15% on all sold after 10,000.[30] Exceptional contracts might start at 17,5% on the first 5,000 copies, 20% on the next 5,000, and rise up to 25% above 5,000 copies sold. The vast majority of French publishers did not even consider the possibility of ever reaching 15% at any point. As a matter of fact, the average royalty scale for French contracts offered by small to middle-sized publishers then ranged from 7.5% to 8% on the first 5,000 copies sold, rising to 10% on the next 5,000, then to 12% or 12.5% above 10,000. In a few instances, the more generous publishers, including Albin Michel, might extend a 15% royalty above 15,000 or 20,000 copies sold.[31] In the United States as in France, average stepping points were 5,000.

Just as in American domestic negotiations, the advance and the royalty clause were undeniably the first, essential points taken into consideration in all of Hoffman's negotiations of French rights, and the main subject of his correspondence with US partners. This should not be surprising: as Paul Reynolds explained in the mid-1960s, "[t]he primary function of the literary agent is to obtain for an author as much money as possible," and he will try "to get as high an advance and royalty as the publisher will stand for," for logically, his own commission would rise accordingly.[32] In some cases, however, Hoffman felt he was being pushed to sell books just as he would peddle any other kind of merchandise, including sacks of potatoes, as he wrote in 1947 to Gertrude Weiner of

Curtis Brown on the matter of the French serial rights to Fred Wakeman's *The Hucksters*.[33] Ironically, this novel, published in 1946 by Rinehart & Company, presented a satire of the US advertising world, authored by Fred Wakeman, a former advertising executive and a navy officer. This critique of ad-men, and more generally of the typical American business culture, had rapidly risen to number four on the *New York Times* best-seller lists of that year, selling over 700,000 copies, and was ultimately selected as a title for the BOMC.[34] Immediately following the American success in the fall of 1946, several French publishers expressed interest in the novel. Hoffman, negotiating with Albin Michel and spurred by Wakeman's apparently "tough" lawyers, was able to obtain a very good contract according to French standards—an advance of $750 against royalties, with 10% on the first 10,000 copies sold, 12.5% on the following 5,000, and 15% above.[35] Albin Michel secured the services of "ace translator" Marcel Duhamel—who eventually translated the book with Jean Weil, and arranged to bring out the book at the same time as the film adaptation in the spring of 1948. In the same manner, Hoffman was also able to help Robert Laffont ultimately acquire the French rights to four of J.P. Marquand's literary novels, negotiating separately for two of the author's crime novels with Albert Pigasse's Editions du Masque.[36]

J.P. Marquand, who had started his career writing for mass-market serials, author of the "Mr. Moto" secret agent series, had finally broken onto the literary scene in 1938 when his first literary novel, *The Late George Apley*, was awarded the Pulitzer Prize. His three subsequent novels, *Wickford Point* (1939), *H.M. Pulham, Esquire* (1941), and *So Little Time* (1943), nominated for another Pulitzer, sold extremely well, and the mainstream magazine press soon hailed him as one of the best American novelists. Between 1941 and 1949 Marquand regularly made the best-seller lists, his novels—*H.M. Pulham* in 1941, *So Little Time* in 1943—being featured frequently as Book-of-the-Month Club selections.[37]

This, in addition to the fact that for eight years Marquand had refused that his works be translated, inevitably aroused the interest of French publishers. When in 1946 he finally agreed to negotiate the foreign rights to his works, they came running. Fortunately, Hoffman had by then official and privileged access to the New England "novelist of manners" through his representatives, Brandt & Brandt. After Bernice Baumgarten at Brandt & Brandt suggested Marquand would appreciate coming out in France under the Gallimard imprint, Hoffman replied,

> if you could suggest to me approximative terms for a contract Mr. Marquand would be inclined to accept from a French publisher. I can get practically any good publisher (and of course I do not think it wise to split his books between several firms). Gallimard is very interested but I am afraid that today they are not a commercially interesting firm as they bring books out in very small printings and cannot

reprint on account of their immense priority list. If you have no objections I would try to get a good general contract with one of the most successful younger firms such as Pavois, Laffont or Julliard.[38]

As may be inferred from the above, Hoffman foresaw considerable commercial success for Marquand in France, which might warrant rapid reprintings; this, at any rate, was the argument he used to disqualify Gallimard in favor of other publishers. Truth be told, Gallimard seem to have been quite picky, and their terms were certainly not among the most generous. It appears that "playing hard to get" was ultimately a successful strategy for Marquand, and Hoffman proceeded with extreme caution. In January 1947, he had secured a general contract offer from Robert Laffont, indeed one of the younger and more commercial-oriented houses, for five of his novels, *B.F.'s Daughter, Repent in Haste, The Late George Apley, Wickford Point,* and *Warning Hill.* He did not state the terms, knowing "how difficult Mr. Marquand is and presuming that he may have special wishes asf." and instead lauded the quality of Robert Laffont's foreign literature series, "*Pavillons,*" noting that Marquand "would no doubt feel himself at home in it, side by side with the other New England authors such as Henry James and Henry Adams. Their foreign list also includes works by Graham Greene, Evelyn Waugh, Helen Glasgow, Harold Nicholson, John Hersey."[39] Either Marquand's US sales figures had blinded Hoffman, or this was quite a sycophantic commentary, for Marquand was certainly no Henry James. By mid-February, he had obtained an offer from Editions du Pavois and one from Laffont, the latter slightly better than the former, proposing an advance of $500 per title, against a 10% royalty on the first 10,000 copies, 12.5% above. As was to be expected, Marquand declined and Brandt & Brandt suggested a scale of 10% to 3,000, and 15% above, a relatively exceptional scale for French publishers, and far from what publishers in other countries were ready to extend: in 1948 Marquand had accepted a $200 advance against a royalty scale of 5% on the first 2,000 copies, 7% on the next 3,000, and 10% above for the German-language rights to *So Little Time* acquired by the Swiss publisher Rascher & Cie.[40] Laffont apparently complied, for they brought out the books, including *The Late George Apley* with a foreword by André Maurois. A member of the Académie Française and author of a *Histoire des Etats-Unis* (1943), Maurois was fast becoming an acclaimed and sought-after patron of American works, several of which he prefaced.

The Translation Clause

As the case of Marquand illustrates, rigid as some American authors might have been over the question of translation, they had virtually no control over the choice of translator or prefacer, however competent and knowledgeable. In 1948 Nancy Hale, author of several short stories and of three novels published by Scribner's, asked her agent Harold Ober if she might see the French translation of *The Prodigal Women* (1942), which would feature an introduction by Maurois. Ober's reply highlights both one of the problems of works in translation, and the role of the local agent,

> It is theoretically possible to provide in foreign contracts that the authors shall have the right to approve the translation, but this is very seldom done, partly because of the delays involved and partly because most authors haven't sufficient knowledge of foreign languages to judge the translation anyway. In the present case the French publisher seemed in such a rush to get the book out that I thought it would be all right to go ahead on the usual basis. I have always found our agent in Paris, who reads English very well, extremely careful about the quality of translations. I did ask her to try to get me a copy of the Maurois introduction as soon as possible to show to you.[41]

In this particular case, the French publisher, Le Rouge et le Noir had been in such a hurry to start printing that they had actually commissioned the translation before the contract was signed, which accounts for the fact that they did not wish to be delayed. Ober's response does reflect a general practice, however many contracts did stipulate that the author had the right to see and revise the translation, even turning the approval of the translation into a termination clause. Some authors, who indeed wished to supervise the quality of the translations, sometimes asked a third party to read and verify the text. Yet again, when personal friendships or artistic affinities warranted such collaborations, the author or their collaborator could have the name of the translator specified in the contract, thereby avoiding the trouble of verification.

Indeed, although not all contracts provided the possibility for authors to check the quality of the translations, virtually all did guarantee that the publishers were to provide a faithful and accurate translation, sometimes adding that it should be of "good literary quality."[42] The standard Gallimard contract allowed for submission of the translation to the author, if he/she so requested, leaving the latter a mere 4 weeks to return suggestions or disagreements. In all cases, any alterations were to be accepted in writing by the proprietor. It therefore fell to the local agent, in most cases, to ascertain the quality, accuracy, and faithfulness of the translations, as Ober intimated to Nancy Hale, assuring her of the complete trust he had in their Paris agent, Suzanne Hotimsky. Although the translators' competence was the French publisher's responsibility, the agents shared in this responsibility at different stages and to varying degrees: in the case of first serial rights, whenever the translation had not yet been undertaken by a publisher, Hoffman would sometimes pay for translations so as to provide them to the magazines and newspapers, who either did not read English well enough, or had no money to pay for the translation before actually agreeing to publish it. In other cases, especially when he was on particularly good terms with a publisher, he might participate in selecting a translator, or have translators prepare trial texts for those in search of a new pen. This was facilitated by his contacts with various translators who addressed him in search of work—either looking for titles with available French rights, or sometimes themselves proprietors of the French rights to certain books. Then again, he might transfer translations initially commissioned by a publisher who ultimately failed to publish the text—either for financial reasons, or compelled by the agent's contract to relinquish the rights, the publication delay having lapsed.

For most Curtis Brown and Brandt & Brandt authors, Hoffman was the watchdog and guarantor of translations. He was to make certain that drastic cuts were not made by the translator or publisher indiscriminately and without the author's consent. When the translator of Fannie Hurst's *Lonely Parade* suggested cutting most of the "1900 Americanisms" she found, Hoffman gave her the go-ahead without waiting for Hurst's answer, advising that the cuts should not exceed 10% of the text. In some cases Hoffman could be fierce when it came to defending authors' contractual right to the integrity and faithfulness of the translations. No competent agent would indeed let matters stand, when an author felt he was being wronged. In 1949 Editions des Deux Rives, headed by René Defez,[43] a former Colonel in the French army, published the translation of Gore Vidal's *The City and the Pillar* under the title *Un garcon près de la rivière*. The novel, published in the United States in an expurgated version in 1948, became a literary cause célèbre, as critics refused to review this story of same-sex relations in the post-war period. Still hailed as the first novel to present homosexuality in terms other than deviance—Vidal's characters are avowedly and intentionally all-American boys—it was originally published by a mainstream US publisher, E.P. Dutton. As Curtis Brown had obtained representation of Dutton's catalogue, Hoffman had consequently been in charge of negotiating the French rights. While Gore Vidal apparently deferred to the request by John Lehmann—his British publisher—to alter the violent ending of *Pillar*, where one of the characters kills his former lover, he was not prepared to accept Defez's cuts. Indeed, although he claimed to be satisfied with Gilbert Martineau's French translation, Vidal complained to Hoffman about the cuts, and showed his agent the redacted passages. These evidently belied Defez's defense that he had merely shown Vidal some passages that he *considered* cutting. Moreover, Hoffman also made certain that Defez did not use his intended promotional *bandeau*, which read "From every corner of the United States homosexuals were flocking to New York" (*my translation*). Vidal felt certain this would not help the success of the book.[44] Defez's arguments to refute this accusation were, to say the least, very weak: he protested that Vidal must have stolen a loose scrap of paper on which was written this inconsequential sentence. Protecting his client, Hoffman decided to let this lie slip, writing the former Colonel that he was ready to turn a blind eye to the incident, and agreeing to the chosen French title. It should be noted that, in this instance, Hoffman's assistance was sought directly by the author, who was residing in Paris at the time. This proximity, added to Curtis Brown's pressure to retain the representation of E.P. Dutton, certainly motivated the agent in his defense of Gore Vidal.

If midlist novels were clearly profitable sellers for American and French publishers, they made up only a small proportion of the books handled by the Hoffman agency in the immediate aftermath of the war. As Georges Hoffman notes, hardboiled detective fiction constituted a very lucrative market for the agency in the late 1940s, when his father, Michel Hoffman, resumed his activity.

Hardboiled Detective and Crime Fiction

For French scholar Benoît Tadié, crime fiction was historically the first genuinely transatlantic literary genre. Formally and ideologically moving back and forth between Europe and the United States, the genre developed as authors vied with one another—borrowing plots, characters, ideas—and in this way created traditions that would ultimately unify it into an "international literary field."[45] Viewing the genre from a transatlantic literary perspective, Tadié inevitably refers to Edgar Allan Poe, the legendary "inventor" of crime fiction, showing how several of his works were pirated in the mid-19th century before poet Charles Baudelaire published what would become the canonical French translations of Poe. Tadié notes that some of the early literary historians credited the French Emile Gaboriau with inventing the genre, which first crossed the Atlantic from East to West, to be translated in the Sunday papers. If indeed crime and detective fiction is to be considered as a quintessentially transatlantic genre, there remains much to be said about the material and financial conditions of the cultural transfers that enabled its emergence.

It is by now a well-established fact that the categories of *film noir* and its corollary, the *roman noir*, were defined in France in the post-war years. Although the hardboiled, thriller genre was initially published and developed in the American pulp magazines of the 1920s, notably by Dashiell Hammett and Raymond Chandler, the "upgrading" of these texts to the legitimate *noir* category was undeniably the result of their inclusion in one of the most prestigious popular series in France, Gallimard's "*Série Noire*." The iconic status of the series is such that one cannot examine the importation of American pulp fiction into France in the post-war years without closely considering its role, and more specifically, its workings. Although this section focuses on the importation of the hardboiled genre, it also considers the other closely associated genre of the mystery novel or whodunit, whose popularity did not dramatically wane as a consequence of the rise of *noir*.

As we have suggested, much of Hoffman's business with French publishers involved the negotiation of French rights to American detective, mystery, and hardboiled fiction. Between the beginnings of the *"Limier"* series and 1953, he sold Albin Michel nearly 50% of the English-language titles in the series, and he negotiated approximately 20% of the American titles in Gallimard's *"Série Noire"* series between 1945 and 1956. His roster of authors included some of the most prestigious, coveted, and bestselling genre writers, from Ellery Queen and the Patrick Quentins in the field of mystery, to Raymond Chandler, Erle Stanley Gardner, Jonathan Latimer, Don Tracy, and Mickey Spillane. By all accounts, these were authors who had been represented by either Brandt & Brandt or Curtis Brown for some time, a situation that definitely worked to the advantage of the French agent, in a period when *noir* was in vogue. In the United States, the relation between crime fiction writers and literary agents was fundamental and logical, at least before the advent of the paperback revolution in the mid-1940s, which is not to say that it was an easy relationship, as Chandler's frequent deriding and change of agents attest, and as he himself testified in his 1952 "Ten Percent of Your Life" essay in *The Atlantic Monthly*. As the primary market for this genre fiction was composed of the pulp and slick magazines, writers could certainly benefit from agents' knowledge and working of this market. Indeed, before the 1940s most American agents originally worked mainly, if not solely, on the magazine and press markets, as evidenced by Paul R. Reynolds memoirs. The thirteen or so best mass circulation magazines in the late 1920s and 1930s paid from $350 to $5,000 for a short story, while serials were bought for sums ranging from $7,500 "to an occasional $50,000."[46] Outside the crime genre, authors such as Fitzgerald benefitted from the lucrative opportunities of the slick magazines in the 1930s, selling a number of his short stories to the "slick" *Saturday Evening Post* for sums averaging $4,000.[47] The publishing, as well as money-earning opportunities afforded by such outlets as *Black Mask*, created by George Jean Nathan and H.L. Mencken and home to Dashiell Hammett's early fiction, or later on the better-quality *Ellery Queen's Mystery Magazine*, were very real. The mass circulation of these magazines, made possible by their low prices—from 10 to 25 cents—also contributed to the popularity of these authors.

With the advent of the mass-market paperback revolution in the 1940s, reprint rights went on to represent an increasing proportion of agents' business negotiations, and were a bone of contention. The standard repartition of earnings until the 1960s, 50% for the publisher, 50% for

the paperback reprint house, and the low—1 to 1.5 cents on average—
royalty were a subject of complaint for many authors, but they were
vastly compensated for by the astounding sales figures, since the publishers' low pricing policy was meant to be compensated by the sales.[48]
As Beth Luey notes, the initial print run for Bantam's paperbacks in the
1940s was 150,000, others rose to 500,000, and Erle Stanley Gardner's
would reach figures as high as 1 million.[49] Between 1947 and 1952, the
number of mass-market paperbacks sold was multiplied by nearly three,
rising from 95 million to 270 million copies.[50]

On the French side of the Atlantic, even before the war, detective
fiction writers had also found several publishing outlets, either in magazines or in publishers' series. In the interwar Golden Age of the whodunit, "*Le Masque*," created in 1927 and published by La Librairie des
Champs Elysées founded by Albert Pigasse, was historically the first
series entirely devoted to the publication of mystery novels. Essentially
turned toward England, home to Agatha Christie's novels, it would long
retain its prestige. Pigasse's success led other publishers to emulate his
example, and the 1930s saw the launching of new series specializing
in translations from British or American writers. It was, in fact, the
overwhelming number of British and American authors in those series
that caused their interruption during the war under German occupation: "*L'Empreinte*" founded in 1932 by Nouvelle Revue Critique had
included fiction by John Dickson Carr, Dorothy Sayers, Ellery Queen,
Mignon Eberhart, Henry Wade, Jonathan Latimer, Patrick Quentin,
and Eric Ambler; Le Domino noir published by Editions Alexis Redier,
was another of these series.

Even before "*Série Noire*," Gallimard and his founder had quickly
jumped on the bandwagon, with "*Les Chefs-d'oeuvre du roman d'aventures*." Founded in 1927, this series was initially meant to publish adventure stories, but rapidly came to include mystery novels, such as S.S. Van
Dine's *The Benson Murder Case* or works by Edgar Wallace.[51] Acting
as acquisitions editor for the series, Jean Robert ultimately obtained the
rights to Dashiell Hammett's *Red Harvest, The Dain Curse, The Maltese
Falcon,* and *The Glass Key* after difficult negotiations with Alfred Knopf,
whose terms Gallimard judged excessive. According to Franck Lhomeau,
Gallimard was particularly and minutely attentive to the selection of the
titles and to the quality of the translations, which were paid outright, between 1,200 and 1,500 francs on average. Soon another, more literary,
detective series was added, whose name paid homage to the revered E.A.
Poe, "*Le Scarabée d'Or*," and which counted among its star authors Erle
Stanley Gardner, S.S. Van Dine, and Rex Stout. Even before the ultimate
consecration of hardboiled authors under the "*Série Noire*" imprint,
Gallimard had chosen to emphasize the literary quality of the mystery
genre, setting this series apart from other "popular" series. It is interesting to note that many of these early translations of detective fiction and

hardboiled novels were not published in France as a distinct detective genre, but either in mainstream or literary series to be later repackaged in "*Série Noire*," as in the case of Dashiell Hammett. Their initial inclusion in a more general catalogue of literature, albeit in foreign literature series, certainly made for their ulterior classification not as genre fiction, but simply, as literature. French critic Claude-Edmonde Magny's *L'âge du roman américain* (1948), which drew parallels between Hammett's and Dos Passos', or even Faulkner's, techniques, certainly contributed to their canonization. Chandler himself, in "The Simple Art of Murder," had grouped Hammett with other social writers such as Hemingway or Steinbeck.[52]

In his analysis of Gallimard's early *collections*, Robert Kopp points out the influence of Gaston Gallimard's 1917 and 1919 trips to the United States on his ulterior, and successful, entrepreneurship.[53] Following his second stay in New York in 1919, he decided to turn a new leaf and steer the publishing house in a resolutely commercial direction.[54] This trip might have prompted him to tie, astutely and in very American fashion, "*Les Chefs-d'oeuvre du roman d'aventures*" with the magazine *Detective* (1928), first by offering books from the series to prospective subscribers, then by pre-publishing in serial form the titles from the series.[55] Incidentally, it was Marguerite Scialtiel, an agent working for the Paris offices of Curtis, Brown, who brought a vast number of authors to the magazine, including E.S. Gardner from 1935 onward.

After the war, parallel to continuing series such as "*Le Masque*," several publishers began their own crime and mystery series. The French public, already familiar with the codes of 1930s British and American whodunits, were now being schooled in those of hardboiled crime stories on the silver screen. The now classic and seminal 1955 *Panorama du film noir américain, 1941–1953* authored by Raymond Borde et Étienne Chaumeton distinguished over twenty emblematic movies, among which John Huston's *The Maltese Falcon* (1941), Billy Wilder's *Double Indemnity* (1944), and Otto Preminger's *Laura* (1944), which were screened in France for the first time in 1946. This initiated a period, up to 1950, which is generally acknowledged as the peak in the production of *film noir*. The story of the rapid post-war Americanization of French culture through movies is well-known. Yet, as Robert Kuisel has demonstrated, although French viewers were indeed exposed to this new cinematic style, many remained quite conservative; if given a choice between an American and a French movie, the public would most often prefer to see their favorite French actors.[56] With time, French directors would imitate, then refine the genre, proposing French *film noirs* set in the French context, to an avid public. Duhamel's adaptation, and not merely translation of American popular titles, aligned these closer with French taste.

As Claire Gorrara suggests, these films prepped French viewers/readers for the new style, and the "*Série Noire*" would soon define the standards of American hardboiled detective fiction, joined by *"Un Mystère"* published by Les Presses de la Cité. In the meantime, readers could continue to enjoy the more classic mysteries and whodunits in the style of Patrick Quentin and Ellery Queen, either in series such as Albin Michel's *"Le Limier,"* or in the French version of *Ellery Queen's Mystery Magazine,* entitled *Mystère Magazine*. The French magazine, published by OPTA (Office de Publicité Technique et Artistique), founded by Maurice Renault, published short stories in translation, most of which were taken straight from the American version of the magazine. This, with time, might prove detrimental to French agents' business. On the subject of Patrick Quentin's story *Puzzle for Poppy*, published in *Mystère Magazine,* Hoffman complained to the duet's representatives, Curtis Brown,

> It is natural that I take it for granted that literary material of our authors belonging to the agencies I represent in this country are our cup of tea and nobody else's.
>
> As I pointed out to Mr Collins the French edition of Ellery Queen's Mystery Magazine is doing us a lot of harm. Unfortunately there seems to be not much we can do about it. The least we can expect however is to be notified of sales made to and by EQMM of material by our authors.[57]

Certainly, the fact that Maurice Renault was himself a book agent provided him with a profitable vantage point from which to acquire the rights to a host of bestselling and profitable authors, which was not to the taste of his French fellow agents.[58]

Hoffman, Série Noire, and Its Rivals

Prior to the war, Hoffman had already been providing titles to *"Le Masque"* series. Pigasse specialized in British mystery and crime fiction, whose rights he bought outright. After the war, French crime fiction publishers scrambled over the rights to Peter Cheyney's prolific work, which proved a very good bargain for Hoffman as Continental representative of Curtis Brown in London, who represented Cheyney. While Cheyney was a British writer, he deserves to be mentioned in this study for his Lemmy Caution series centered on an FBI investigator, framed and written in typical American hardboiled style. Cheyney's works sold in prodigious numbers, thereby justifying the enthusiasm of French publishers. Obviously, as of early 1944 at least three publishers were vying for his novels—Gallimard, with Raymond Queneau and Marcel Duhamel hot on the trail; Pigasse's Librairie des Champs Elysées; and Sven Nielsen, for Editions Albert/Presses de la Cité. Duhamel, sent by Gallimard to London to negotiate the rights to Cheyney and other British writers' works even as the war was still raging, was reported to have extorted a promise of exclusivity from Cheyney in London and it seemed that he was about to take home the prize.[59] Ultimately Cheyney's works in France would be published in several distinct *collections*, including "*Série Noire*," "*Un Mystère*," and "*Cosmopolis*" (Presses de la Cité), as well as "*Le Masque*." But in 1944, Cheyney had expressly warned his agents in London that he wished to see his works published in French under a single imprint . . . preferably Gallimard. He thus rejected Nielsen's first offer for *Dark Duet*, considering that royalties of 8% on the first 10,000 copies were quite inadequate. Having started negotiating with Nielsen, and possibly due to his reluctance to handle Gallimard's offers, Hoffman pressed on, getting the publisher to raise the offer to 10% on the first 3,000 copies, 12.5% to 10,000, and 15% above, and specifying that this was an exceptional offer, as French editions bore the cost of translation on the first copies sold.[60] Meanwhile, he was also negotiating on behalf of Pigasse, who had agreed to try out for a few, but not all, of Cheyney's works, offering an advance of 20,000 francs ($400) per title against a flat royalty of 10% on all copies sold, and a guarantee of 20,000 copies payable on publication. Submitting this offer to Sonia Chapter, Hoffman added that Pigasse could certainly publish five or six titles a year, "more than Gallimard could even think of publishing for instance."[61] In spite of Hoffman's warning, and presumably motivated by the offer made by Duhamel in London, Cheyney closed the deal with Gallimard for three titles, ultimately accepting lower terms.[62] But *Dark Duet*, whose translations had already been completed by the fall of 1944, prior to the signing of a contract, was published by Presses de la Cité; in the form of an apology, Hoffman explained to Chapter that this had been advised by Cheyney's former agent, Jenny Bradley.[63] Good-naturedly, and certainly standing to benefit from this competition, Cheyney offered to meet with all three publishers upon a visit to Paris, to "work a little propaganda," and offering to pay for publicity himself.[64] As for Hoffman, he arranged for a good interview of the British author to be published on the front page of the newspaper *Libération*.

This early competition orchestrated by both Hoffman and Bradley prefigures the ensuing rivalry between French publishers; it also suggests the great powers of attraction and persuasion of the Gallimard imprint, even as the famous "*Série Noire*" had not yet been launched by Marcel Duhamel. The series, created by Duhamel and poet Jacques Prévert in 1945, was intended to break with the classic mystery or whodunit, offering readers a particular brand of hardboiled detective fiction that—as the famous 1948 editorial manifesto warned readers—should be handled with caution, for it was filled with "action, thrills, and violence—in all forms, and in particular the most abhorrent."[65] Between 1945 and 1947, the series published two titles a year, which left Duhamel free to pursue other activities, especially translation, and adaptation of American plays. For the first four years, the volumes were translations either of

American titles or British novels *à l'américaine*, and set in America; the first two volumes, indeed, were by Cheyney, negotiated by Hoffman, followed in 1946 by James Hadley Chase's *No Orchids for Miss Blandish*, and ultimately, the first American title, *No Pockets in a Shroud*, by Horace McCoy. At this point the eminently transatlantic nature of the *roman noir* is already attested, as we see British authors writing in the manner of their American counterparts, or for Chase, plagiarizing them, in this instance, Raymond Chandler. In fact, the *"Série Noire"* allowed for a complete cultural transfer of an American genre: The first French authors included in the series, Serge Arcouët aka Terry Stewart, and Jean Meckert aka John Amila, not only wrote under American-style pseudonyms, they set their stories in a—largely fantasized—America. Furthermore, Duhamel would ultimately gather a team of translators, not all literary writers, who did not merely translate, but actually adapted the American texts to suit French taste. This ultimately gave the series a uniformity of tone—in the use of the 1950s *argot* (slang)—as well as a rather entertaining dimension, but from a strictly legal point of view, the "faithful and accurate translation" clause was in many cases far from respected. In 2013 Gallimard reissued Chandler's Marlowe titles in one volume, in new translations by Cyril Laumonnier.[66] Reviewing the new 2013 edition, the French press has amply commented on the strange liberties and bizarre choices of Duhamel's team of translators; yet again, these translations/adaptations may be considered as perfect illustrations of a successful cultural appropriation, and an example of what many publishers were doing at the time. Indeed, the series became an icon of French popular culture, and would ultimately cross over to intellectual readers, as Sartre's later claim attests: the once anti-American intellectual admitted in *Les Mots* that he preferred reading a *"Série Noire"* volume over a Wittgenstein title. Certainly this humorous statement could not have been published in the context of the 1940s Cold War when such large-scale fabrication of fiction was frequently decried by the defenders of French culture.

The year 1948 marked an acceleration for the series. In 1947 the aggregate sales of the first six titles had amounted to over 70,000 copies; the sales of Horace McCoy's *No Pockets in a Shroud*, published in the *"Série Noire,"* are found to be twice those of his *They Shoot Horses, Don't They*, published in Gallimard's general catalog.[67] Considering these figures, Claude Gallimard decided to take the series to a new level, and to market it massively. This implied a new form of distribution, similar to the networks used in the United States for the distribution of mass-market paperbacks, beyond libraries, through newsstands. Consequently Gallimard closed a deal with the "green octopus," Hachette, to distribute the volumes through its network of railroad kiosks and other venues. This scheme required the lowering of prices, yet, in order to reach a viable equation, this meant reducing the number of pages in each volume.[68] Moreover, mass distribution would not be reached, and profits could not mechanically be sustained if print runs remained at 11,000 copies; they were consequently increased to 33,000, and the number of titles published annually was also increased, from 2 between 1945 and 1947, to 13 in 1948, to 26 in 1949 and 1950, to 38 in 1951, 1952, and 1953.[69]

For Duhamel, this meant that he could no longer consider working on the series on the side, organization had to be rationalized, and new titles quickly found. Pressured into publishing ten times as many volumes annually, Duhamel developed closer contacts with American as well as local agents, including Hoffman, and had to pay renewed attention to the American market, especially with the help of Gallimard's scouting agency in New York, Aubry's Literary Masterworks. Competing with Literary Masterworks, between 1948 and 1955 Hoffman never supplied fewer than three annual titles to the series, including titles by Peter Cheyney, Harold Q. Masur, Don Tracy, several Jonathan Latimers, and Chandler's *Little Sister*. Moreover, as his relationship with Duhamel grew progressively more personal in the 1950s, he eventually supplied him with the names of various American contacts, agents publishers, and authors for his business trips to New York.[70] The change programmed in 1948 had other consequences as well: the formatting of the volumes to fit a total of no more than 256 pages inevitably induced massive cuts. Needless to say the cuts were made, in the vast majority of cases, without the author's knowledge.[71] As today's translators are finding out, "*Série Noire*" was not the only series for which cuts were demanded; "*Un Mystère*" published by Presses de la Cité also formatted their French versions, both "materially" and linguistically. It must be said that the rather low rates paid for the translations certainly did not encourage the translators to be more rigorous, and the drastic cuts decided by Duhamel must have come as a relief for them. Now as then, translators of popular fiction did not receive royalties, but were paid a fixed sum, which according to Hoffman, averaged in 1946–1947 15,000 ($130) to 20,000 francs ($170), while literary fiction commanded higher rates. Yet even for literary works, no established rate per page seems to have been set at the time: in 1946 payments began at the rather low rate of 30 or 50 cents a page, sometimes rising to $1.5. By the early 1950s rates had increased, from 60 to 85 cents a page on average. However low the cost of translation might have been considered by the translators themselves, it did remain a factor in determining the advance and royalty rates to be offered to the authors.

Along with these material changes came another, which in turn would represent a hurdle in agents' negotiations. In order both to visibly mark the break with the first series (1945–1947), and to strengthen the quality of the copies which could be damaged by the now massive distribution, Gallimard decided that the new volumes would be bound and sold with a dust jacket. This undeniably emphasized the unity and uniformity of the series, all the while affording Gallimard promotional space on the back jacket and flaps, either to promote their other series—"*Série Blême*," "*Collection Pourpre*"—or, more surprisingly, other staples such as Reynolds ink pens.[72] The downside for authors, however, was that the manufacturing cost actually impacted the royalties, reducing them by 50%. Several authors found this hard to accept, and it most often fell to Hoffman and other agents to explain how this loss might be compensated, both financially and symbolically, by the sales guarantee, and through the prestige of the publishing house. In addition to the sales guarantee, generally fixed at 30,000 copies, was the undeniable prestige of the publisher's imprint, recognized by both authors and agents in the United States, and very soon, that of the series itself, which was generally considered one of the best in the field. This was sometimes enough for Gallimard to retain authors who were regularly offered better deals by other publishers. Others ultimately refused the 50% cut and chose another, albeit less reputed, imprint. The terms extended to authors for inclusion in the "*Série Noire*" were in fact not exactly uniform. To the better-known, in-demand authors, Duhamel offered a $300 advance, a guarantee of 40,000 copies, and a flat rate of 10% (i.e., 5% net royalty); to the less popular or relatively new authors, a guarantee on 30,000 copies, against 8% on the first 10,000 copies sold, and 10% above, which amounted, respectively, to 4% and 5% net royalty for the authors. With prices varying between 150 and 180 francs, roughly equating 45 to 55 cents, this represented guarantees between 180,000 francs and 720,000 francs, that is, for 1949, between $545 and $2,100.

Royalty rates of 4% to 5% were in themselves not very dissimilar from those offered to authors by American mass-market paperback reprint houses in the same period. The main difference was the sales figures: while US houses could expect sales from 100,000 to 1 million copies, sales for "*Série Noire*" rarely reached 100,000, except in the cases of Peter Cheyney or Raymond Chandler. As compared with American contracts for trade editions, authors undeniably stood to lose financially in the process. Cleve Adams, whose *Contraband* appeared in the "*Série Noire*" in 1951, had published with Knopf in 1949 under very different conditions[73]: a $1,000 advance against a royalty scale of 17.5% on the first 4,000 copies, 21% on the next 3,500, and 25% above, the book to be priced between $2 and $3.[74] Even if this was not a common contract, the average scale proposed by US trade houses for the best detective fiction remained much better than the standard "*Série Noire*" contracts.

Be that as it may, Duhamel at least offered royalties to his authors. By mid-1946, Hoffman informed several publishers of the average scale for detective fiction—advances of $200 to $300, against royalties of 8% on the first 5,000, 10% on the next 5,000, and 12% above. While royalties and stepping points varied slightly from one publisher to another, it is worth noting that some publishers continued to purchase French rights outright. In comparison, the *"Série Noire"* contracts remained attractive, but certainly could be improved upon. As the success of the series grew to be almost overwhelming, Sven Nielsen, the owner of Presses de la Cité and a man of excellent business acumen, became intent on launching his own rival series. In 1949, he drew Hoffman into the equation as he began to vie for one of Gallimard's star authors. Ultimately, the negotiations around Raymond Chandler's *Little Sister* demonstrate the centrality of the local agent in the building of such popular and successful series.

Formerly director of the Messageries du livre, a French book exporting concern, in 1944 the Danish-born Sven Nielsen took over the Editions Albert and renamed them Presses de la Cité. Very quickly, he endeavored to build up his publishing house on the translation of English-language books, and in 1949 launched his own mystery and detective fiction series, *"Un Mystère."* Very probably in the hopes of outdoing Duhamel, he secured the rights to Erle Stanley Gardner's prolific and hugely bestselling work, thanks to Hoffman's help, whom he had asked to send from New York as much information about the prolific ex-lawyer as possible. By then, news of Gardner's extraordinary sales had certainly not escaped French publishers: in 1937 the trade journal paper *Toute l'édition* had commented upon his earnings from his pulp stories, estimated at $75,000 a year.[75] Nielsen also obtained, through Hoffman, the rights to a number of Cheyney novels, after the Englishman had freed himself of any obligations to Gallimard whom he considered as having breached their contract for five of his novels, not issued in the contractual delay. As Nielsen told Hoffman, his intention was to launch Gardner in the manner of Cheyney, so that his novels would literally become fixtures for the French readers.[76] Again thanks to Hoffman who, through Brandt & Brandt, was the local representative of E.P. Dutton, Presses de la Cité brought out the very first volume in Mickey Spillane's Mike Hammer cycle. Thus the first five titles published in 1949 included two Stanley Gardners, Spillane's *I, The Jury*, and a Cheyney title. Unlike the *"Série Noire," "Un Mystère"* also included mystery novels, whodunits by the "American Agatha Christie," Mignon G. Eberhart, Patrick Quentin, and Ellery Queen, all supplied, to a large extent, by Hoffman. In 1944, Nielsen struck a lasting friendship with the successful and hugely famous André Simenon, and became his new publisher, after . . . Gallimard. Undeniably, the sales of Simenon's books offered a financial guarantee that would allow Nielsen to lose money on other titles.

The One That Almost Got Away

In 1949, again with the help of Hoffman to whom he had grown quite close, Nielsen attempted to lure another of Gallimard's authors away from Duhamel. Raymond Chandler had requested that payment of advances on the part of Gallimard for two volumes of stories be made in dollars, and in the United States, so that he might cash the money rapidly. When Gallimard did not immediately comply, Hoffman played on the author's dissatisfaction to initiate a competition of his own, in the interest of Nielsen. In September, after informing Bernice Baumgarten of Nielsen's offer, Hoffman wrote to Duhamel to put forth an offer for Chandler's *Little Sister*, without specifying the name of the publisher: a $1,000 advance—as compared with $300—against a royalty scale of 12% on the first 5,000, 15% on the next 25,000, a guaranteed printing of 30,000 copies, and a similar price of 150 francs.[77] Duhamel explained to Hoffman that Gallimard would certainly not match these extravagant terms, which in his view were bound to lead the undisclosed publisher to bankruptcy, unless the book was cut by half, entailing a bad translation. He nevertheless raised his own offer to propose a fixed 12% royalty and a guaranteed print run of 40,000 copies, asking Hoffman to do his utmost to make sure Chandler remained with Gallimard.[78]

Hoffman, caught between his friendship with Nielsen, his relative antipathy for Gallimard, and his acknowledgment of the predominant position of the "*Série Noire*" on the hardboiled fiction market, played the role of middleman to perfection. If, to all appearances he seemed to be acting in the author's interests, he also represented to Chandler's agent the troubles he would personally suffer, depending on the outcome,

> Now, I put this offer up to you (sending a carbon to Mr. Brooks) for what it is worth. I am not urging you to make Chandler accept it because: a) I know he is in direct correspondence with Duhamel and appreciates the imprint of Gallimard on his books, and b) because if he accepts Nielsen's offer the afore-said Duhamel will poison my existence for at least a year (which from my private point of view is not negligeable [sic] at all).
>
> However I think it is my duty as Chandler's agent in France to put this offer before you and if he is a businessman I do not think he will want to turn it down.[79]

Hoffman was very much aware of the need to maintain good relations with Duhamel. Although he did not pressure the author and his representatives to go with the highest bidder, his remarks, in the same letter, on Gallimard's publication of J.G. Cozzens's *S.S. San Pedro*, whose rights they had acquired 16 years before, subtly underlined his mistrust of the firm. As he was in fact writing to Cozzens' agent and wife, he might have intended to trigger Baumgarten's irritation with the publisher. On the American side of the Atlantic, the agent must have known that publication delays had become a specialty with Gallimard; in 1948 the agency had worked in an addendum to a 1945 contract for four of Chandler's

works, summoning the publisher to issue the three remaining novels—
Farewell My Lovely, The Big Sleep, and *The High Window*—on specified dates, at 2 and 3 months intervals between August 1, 1948, and
January 1, 1949. The addendum mentioned that upon non-compliance
on the part of the publisher, Chandler would be

> . . . at liberty to consider the above-mentioned contract null and
> void (and to sell the French translation rights of the unpublished
> works elsewhere) without prejudice to any damages and/or monies
> which may be due him thereunder and royalties which may become
> due him on the sales of those works . . . .[80]

Although admittedly such consecutiveness of publication within the
"*Série Noire*" was perhaps not strategic in terms of stimulating the readers' anticipation, Duhamel had ultimately deferred to Brandt & Brandt.
   Still, although Baumgarten was convinced that Gallimard would not
be able to top the offer, she felt that the reputation and quality of the
imprint might make it worth accepting lower terms. In the meantime,
Duhamel wrote to Chandler to sort matters out, and to ask him for recommendations for *hardboiled* titles. Ironically, his letter emphasizes the
crucial role of the agent in this affair:

> . . . So it takes a letter from your French agent, Mr. Hoffman, and
> quite a nasty jolt to wake me up: I am told that quite substantial
> offers have been made to you . . . . I don't know how you feel about
> this, but I don't think that it is quite fair, since we are publishing all
> your other books, including short stories. We'd hate to lose a great
> name of our "Serie Noire," which has now become, even if I say
> so myself, a national institution, thanks to our choice of first class
> books and the quality of our translations . . . .
>
>   If I am telling you all this, it is because I want you to have a
> clear idea of our background. We lead by a large margin the tough
> detective field and mean to keep on improving. But that cannot be
> done if we have to fear—every moment of our working days—last
> minute competitors who "make a grab" at our authors. I frankly do
> not think anybody can give the public translations or presentations
> half as good as ours. We would have to lower the quality of both to
> offer better terms. However (even though the new rate of the dollar
> is 350 francs, which makes the advance and equivalent to 250,000
> issue) we are sending you $1,000 on "The Little Sister". You will get
> it *immediately*.[81]

Gallimard's generous gesture of raising the advance to $1,000, "*imme-
diately*," that is, to be paid in New York whereas they had up until then
refused to do so, is evidence that they would not let Chandler go. As

Baumgarten would later acknowledge—Chandler would finally remain with Gallimard—Hoffman's work had at least "shaken up" the publisher, who also agreed to extend a 12% flat royalty rate, minus 50% to cover the cost of the binding. Ultimately, Gallimard decided that short stories were not in keeping with the new direction for the series, and the translations of *Red Wind* and *Spanish Blood*—which Duhamel had already ordered—were ultimately ceded to . . . Presses de la Cité, thus affording Chandler better terms on these volumes.[82] To Brandt & Brandt, this affair also showed that in spite of their reluctance and general delaying, even Gallimard could be enticed to pay authors on the spot, and in the United States, provided an agent egged them on. As will be seen in the next chapter, payment—delays, currency, and location—was a regular bone of contention between US parties and French publishers.

Chandler, sensing the anguish in Duhamel's letter, had sent a reply that Hoffman would relish, as it quite exceptionally celebrated agents' positive role, while classically deriding publishers:

> I take the liberty of sending your letter on to my agents in New York, because I have no way of answering its argument, no standards of comparison, no knowledge of the reputation of the other publisher. I am sure you appreciate this. *In the question of sales in European countries a writer is entirely in the hands of his agent.* While I can understand your annoyance at being forced to bid against someone who may have a lower standard in production and translation, etc. than yours, there is of course no possibility of my knowing that such is the fact, if it should happen to be the fact. The same sort of thing goes on here. But in the United States a writer has some possibility of assessing the situation; in France none at all. *Presumably you are a businessman and a skillful one; I must attribute the same virtue to my agent. It is likely that he also is capable of weighing other factors than the initial advance.* Also, with all due respect, I have knowledge of extremely few instances of a publisher voluntarily raising the ante on a writer. It takes competition to loosen him up. The history of publishing in all countries shows that publishers have exploited and defrauded writers shamelessly just as long as they were able to get away with it. If it were not for agents, I have very little doubt that they would still be doing it, that some modern Goldsmith would be selling the entire copyright to some modern Vicar of Wakefield for £5 and glad to get it.
>
> I have always thought it one of the charms of dealing with publishers that if you start talking about money, they retire coldly to their professional eminence, and if you start talking about literature, they immediately yank the dollar sign before your eyes. (my emphasis)[83]

Chandler was thus taking up the publishers' own argument pitting agents as parasites and turning it around to represent publishers as relentless and "shameless" exploiters of authors who pretended to act in the name of the noble calling of literature. In fact, the hardboiled author was certainly not partial to agents, and he changed representatives several times, from Sydney Sanders to Brandt & Brandt, to H.N. Swanson, to Helga Greene, whom he eventually married; but he understood that an author's foreign rights could not be satisfactorily marketed without local agents, who knew the markets well enough to assess potentialities not only in terms of immediate financial returns. As for Hoffman, he had astutely turned a budding competition between Presses de la Cité and Gallimard to his and Chandler's advantage. Incidentally, Nielsen would soon emulate his rival, and deduct the cost of binding from the "*Mystère*" volumes to accrue their sales.

The renewed "American prestige" of fiction in France after the war, the wonderful opportunities provided by the distribution of paperback series, were a boon for local as well as American agents in the late 1940s and 1950s. Aided by the bestseller effect, propped by his transatlantic contacts, Hoffman negotiated an increasing number of contracts and was expected to pay particular attention not only to the royalty clause, but also to the translations themselves. Even as he was to protect the material interests of US authors, he also contributed, indirectly, to the making of a new French fiction culture, providing the leading series of noir fiction with a considerable number of titles. Chandler's tribute to his foreign agent forcefully underlines the part played by Hoffman, Jenny Bradley, and other local agents in mediating not only book rights, but also, quite simply, literature. This was no easy task, as frictions were not only caused by publishers and agents, but also by the international financial and economic policies.

Notes

1 Henri Peyre, "American Literature through French Eyes," *Virginia Quarterly Review* 23, no. 3 (1947): 427.

2 Lynes and MacDonald are authors of two of the founding texts of the low-brow/middlebrow/highbrow debate in the 1950s and 1960s. Russell Lynes, "Highbrow, Lowbrow, Middlebrow," *Harper's* (February 1949): 19–28, and Dwight MacDonald, "A Theory of Mass Culture," *Diogenes* 1 (1953): 1–17 and "Masscult and Midcult: 2," *Partisan Review* (Fall 1960): 203–33.

3 On the emergence of the "middlebrow" cultural category and the ensuing debates, see Michael Kammen, *American Culture, American Tastes; Social Change and the 20th Century* (New York: Basic Books, 1999), Joan Shelley Rubin, *The Making of Middlebrow Culture* (Chapel Hill: University of North Carolina Press, 1992), and Herbert Gans (1970), *Popular Culture and High Culture, an Analysis and Evaluation of Taste*, revised edition (New York: Basic Books, 1999); on the porosity of such categories, see Lawrence Levine, *Highbrow/Lowbrow: The Emergence of Cultural Hierarchy in America* (Cambridge, Mass.: Harvard University Press, 1988). On the passing of the "idea" of middlebrow in the 1960s, see Beth Luey, *Expanding the American Mind: Books and the Popularization of Knowledge* (Amherst: University of Massachusetts Press, 2010), 179 and following.

4 Luey, *Expanding the American Mind,* 179 and following.
5 Janice Radway, *A Feeling for Books. The Book-of-the-Month Club, Literary Taste, and Middle Class Desire* (Chapel Hill: University of North Carolina Press, 1997), 90.
6 "Domaine étranger 1950," *La Gazette des Lettres* (January 15, 1951): 28–29.
7 See Chapter 1.
8 Peyre, "American Literature through French Eyes," 436.
9 Ibid., 431.
10 Ibid., 432.
11 Howard C. Rice, "Seeing Ourselves as the French See Us," *The French Review,* 21, no. 6 (May, 1948): 432.
12 *As the Earth Turns* was a Book-of-the-Month Club selection, reportedly selling 100,000 copies the first month it was issued.
13 Rice, "Seeing Ourselves as the French See Us," 438.
14 Harry Levin, "Some European Views of Contemporary American Literature," *American Quarterly,* 1, no. 3 (Autumn 1949): 273.
15 Levin, "Some European Views of Contemporary American Literature," 265.
16 Peyre, "American Literature through French Eyes," 435.
17 See Claire Bruyère, "Du prestige de l'étranger"; Anne Cadin, "Les premiers romans noirs français: simples exercices de style ou trahisons littéraires complexes?", *TRANS* (online) 11, 2011. http://trans.revues.org/435.
18 See Bruyère, "Du prestige de l'étranger" and Paul Bleton, "La Frontière médiatique du livre," in *Les mutations du livre et de l'édition,* ed. Michon and Mollier, 453–460.
19 Union internationale pour la protection des oeuvres littéraires et artistiques, *Le Droit d'auteur: organe officiel du Bureau de l'Union internationale pour la protection des oeuvres littéraires et artistiques,* Quatrième année, no. 8 (August 15, 1891): 85–96.
20 See Curtis Brown, "Literary Agents," 15; and Hoffman, "Agent littéraire," 40.
21 Raymond Chandler to Marcel Duhamel, October 9, 1949, BRH, HOF AG.20.01.
22 See Emmanuel Pierrat, *Le droit d'auteur et l'édition* (Paris: Cercle de la Librairie, 2005), 350.
23 Reynolds, "Should Every Writer Have an Agent?," 69.
24 J-H. Jeheber to Michel Hoffman, August 1, 1946. BRH, HOF ED.FR.33.03.
25 "Livre de comptes [Account books]—1953–1969," BRH, ED.FR.16.05.
26 For a brief overview of the development of children's books between 1940 and 1980, see Tebbel, *A History of Book Publishing in the United States, Vol IV,* 467–488.
27 Tebbel, *A History of Book Publishing in the United States, Vol IV,* 469.
28 See Jean-Marie Bouvaist, *Pratiques et métiers de l'édition* (Paris: Editions Promodis/UFR Communication Paris XIII, 1986), 89.
29 See Michel Hoffman to Michel Horay, May 30, 1946. BRH, HOF ED.FR.33.03.
30 Alan C. Collins, "On Improving the Lot of Authors, Grub Life on 1952's Grub Street," *The Saturday Review* (February 16, 1952): 14.
31 See for examples the contracts for Christopher Morley's *Thoroughfare,* published by La Nouvelle Edition, offering 10% to 10,000, 12.5% to 15,000 and 15% above; and Albin Michel contracts for R. Wright's *Native Son* in 1945, rising to 15% above 20,000 copies sold, and for Garland Roark's *Fair*

Road to Java in 1950, beginning at 8% on the first 5,000 copies, increasing to 10% on the next 5,000, and 15% above 10,000.

32 Paul R. Reynolds, "The Literary Agent; His Function, Life, and Power," *Saturday Review* (October 8, 1966): 113, and "Should Every Writer Have an Agent?" 69.

33 Michel Hoffman to Gertrude Weiner, October 9, 1947. BRH, HOF AG.15.02. Box 106.

34 On *The Hucksters*' sales, see Susan Smulyan, *Popular Ideologies: Mass Culture at Mid-century* (Philadelphia: University of Pennsylvania Press, 2007): 117.

35 See Michel Hoffman to Gertrude Weiner, October 14, 1946. BRH, AG 15.03.

36 *Thank You Mr. Moto* and *Last Laugh Mr. Moto* were sold to Editions du Masque.

37 In addition, Marquand's *B.F.'s Daughter* and *Point of No Return* became bestsellers in 1946 and 1949, respectively.

38 Michel Hoffman to Bernice Baumgarten, November 8, 1946. BRH, AG.16.01.

39 Michel Hoffman to Bernice Baumgarten, January 16, 1947. BRH, AG.16.01.

40 Brandt & Brandt Contract Files, C0732, Box 26, Folder 10.

41 Harold Ober to Nancy Hale, November 18, 1948, Harold Ober & Associates Papers, C0129. 46: 5.

42 See contract for J.P. Marquand, *So Little Time*, for Rascher & Cie in Zurich, Brandt & Brandt Contract Files, Box 26: Folder 10.

43 René Defez was presumably a wartime acquaintance of Hoffman's; he oversaw the agent's membership of the veteran Résistants' association.

44 See Michel Hoffman to René Defez, June 17 and June 21, 1949; René Defez to Michel Hoffman, June 20, 1949. BRH HOF.ED.FR.42.05.

45 Benoît Tadié, "Essor du récit criminel transatlantique: esquisse d'un champ de recherche," *Transatlantica* 1 (June 19, 2012). http://transatlantica.revues. org/5785. My translation.

46 Reynolds, *The Middle Man*, 17.

47 Reynolds, *The Middle Man*, 17. The adjective "slick" is here used as opposed to the pulp magazines. Slick magazines were better quality and catered to a middlebrow readership, whereas pulp magazines—the term originating in the poor paper quality—were aimed at a lowbrow public.

48 See Leonard Q. Ross's contract with Century Publications for *The Dark Corner*, November 2, 1945. Royalties went from 1 c on the first 150,000 copies sold, rising to 1.5 c on all copies above. Brandt & Brandt Contract Files, Box 30: Folder 23.

49 Luey, "The Organization of the Book Publishing Industry," 43.

50 Luey, "The Organization of the Book Publishing Industry," 45.

51 See Franck Lhomeau, "Les collections de romans populaires de la Librairie Galimard avant la 'Série Noire'" in *Gallimard 1911–2011—Lectures d'un catalogue—Les entretiens de la Fondation des Treilles*, ed. Pascal Fouché (Paris: Gallimard, 2012), 177–205.

52 On this point, see Claire Gorrara, *The Roman noir in Post-War French Culture* (Oxford, New York: Oxford University Press, 2003), 7.

53 Robert Kopp, "Regard sur un catalogue de collections," in *Gallimard 1911–2011—Lectures d'un catalogue,* 163–176.

54 See Assouline, *Gaston Gallimard,* 96.

55 See Lhomeau, "Les collections de romans populaires de la Librairie Galimard avant la 'Série Noire'," 183.

56 See Robert Kuisel, *Seducing the French: The Dilemma of Americanization* (Berkeley: University of California Press, 1993).

57 Michel Hoffman to Gertrude Weiner, January 31, 1949. BRH, HOF. AG.14.02.

58 Maurice Renault and Alice Le Bayon formed one of the Paris agencies until 1958, when they separated.

59 See Assouline, *Gaston Gallimard,* 410.

60 See Michel Hoffman to Sonia Chapter, February 13, and 17, 1945. BRH, AG 09.01.

61 Michel Hoffman to Sonia Chapter, February 24, 1945. BRH, AG 09.01.

62 Gallimard agreed to pay advances of 15,000 francs for *Dames Don't Care,* 20,000 francs for *Poison Ivy* and *This Man is Dangerous,* against royalties of 8% on the first 10,000 copies, 11% above. Sonia Chapter to M. Hoffman, February 27, 1945. BRH, HOF.AG.09.01.

63 Michel Hoffman to Sonia Chapter, March 19, 1945. BRH, AG.09.01.

64 See Sonia Chapter to Michel Hoffman, October 3, 1945, BRH, AG.09.01. A few days later Hoffman dined with Cheyney in Paris and arranged for him to meet Nielsen and Pigasse.

65 Quoted from Marcel Duhamel's 1948 Manifesto-cum-editorial for the series. My translation.

66 In the 2013 volume of Chandler stories, the initial translations by Boris and Michèle Vian were left untouched. The translator, C. Laumonnier, explained on his personal blog that this decision was made on account of the "proper poetics" of these authors' translations, adding that Vian was still very much read and appreciated by the public. https://cyrillaumonier. wordpress.com/2013/11/13/7-enquetes-de-philip-marlowe-les-de-raymond-chandler-quarto-gallimard/ accessed November 30, 2014. In 1946 Vian had authored an "American hardboiled novel" of his own, *J'irai cracher sur vos tombes,* which he presented in a competing series, "*Le Scorpion,*" as a translation from a title by one Vernon Sullivan. Although it is often presented as pastiche, it can also be considered as homage to the genre, and to American literature more generally.

67 The following developments owe much to Franck Lhomeau, "Le véritable lancement de la '*Série Noire*'."

68 Another argument for reducing the number of pages was that thick volumes would not fit on Hachette's *tourniquets* (newsstands).

69 Gouanvic, "Panorama de la traduction-importation de la littérature américaine en France (1820–1960)," 168.

70 See Marcel Duhamel to Michel Hoffman, February 28, 1956. "I am leaving for the United States on April 23rd, and would be quite grateful if you could provide me with all the information useful for my business over there, as I wish to contact as many people as possible (addresses and phone numbers of agents but also of authors you represent whom we have published." BRH, ED FR.33.03.

71 See Jérôme Dupuis, "Polars américains: la traduction était trop courte," *L'Express culture,* October 25, 2012, http://www.lexpress.fr/culture/livre/ polars-americains-la-traduction-etait-trop-courte_1178207.html.

72 See Lhomeau, "Le véritable lancement de la '*Série Noire*'."

73 Cleve Adams's *Contraband* was published for "*Série Noire*" by French born Hollywood film director Jacques Tourneur, director of *Nick Carter, Master Detective* (1939), *Cat People* (1942), *Days of Glory* (1944), or *Out of the Past* (1947).

74 See contract for Cleve Adams, *Contraband*, with Knopf, October 24, 1949. Brandt & Brandt Contract Files, C0732 Box 1.

75 René de la Porte, "L'édition populaire aux Etats-Unis," *Toute l'édition*, no. 362 (March 6, 1937): 8.

76 See Sven Nielsen to Michel Hoffman, March 18, 1949. ED.FR. 24.03.

77 Michel Hoffman to Marcel Duhamel, September 12, 1949. BRH, ED.FR.33.03.

78 Marcel Duhamel to Michel Hoffman, October 5, 1949. BRH, ED FR.33.03.

79 Here Hoffman is referring to C.H. Brooks of A.M. Heath, representatives of Brandt & Brandt in England. Michel Hoffman to Bernice Baumgarten, July 20, 1949. BRH, HOF AG.20.01.

80 July 12, 1948 addendum to August 1, 1945, contract, Brandt & Brandt Contract Files, C0732, Box 4.

81 Marcel Duhamel to Raymond Chandler, September 28, 1949. Copy to Michel Hoffman. BRH, HOF AG.20.01.

82 Hoffman wrote to Bernice Baumgarten on December 29, 1949, exclaiming that they had "been able to more than double the terms," as Presses de la Cité offered advances of $300 for each of the two titles, and a royalty scale of 8% on the first 7,500, 10% above.

83 Raymond Chandler to Marcel Duhamel, October 9, 1949. BRH, HOF AG.20.01. A copy of the letter had been sent by Baumgarten to Hoffman.

5 Bridging the Divide
Frictions and Business Culture

As intermediaries in a domestic marketplace, literary agents are led to mediate between two professional groups, authors on the one hand, editors and publishers on the other. Literary agents operating on a global, or even a merely transatlantic scale, find themselves not only mediating between three professional groups—authors, publishers or editors, and agents—but also between several cultures. Although a common ground must, and will be found, based on both international copyright law and a commonality of practices in publishing, the local agent is most often required to explain and translate local idiosyncrasies for his partners. Working toward an understanding is essential, in order for transactions to be settled as smoothly as possible, and in the best interest of all parties. Viewed from the United States, each foreign country has its own specificities; for US agents, in the 1940s and 1950s Italy and Mexico were countries where success might be achieved if agents agreed not to be in a hurry. French publishing also had its own singularities, which sometimes caused some irritation on the other side of the Atlantic. Hoffman and fellow agents helped to bridge a cultural divide that was also a professional one. Several American publishers regarded French practices with diffidence.

Although the previous chapters inevitably touched upon matters of money, central when one examines the advance and royalty clauses of foreign rights contracts, another important prerogative of literary agents should be examined. In the last resort, agents are bankers who not only make sure the proprietor of rights gets paid, but who also cash proprietors' money, and in the case of international transactions, facilitate money transfers. This role is all the more crucial when proprietors are geographically removed from the place of transaction, as they lack the means to control these different processes. Raymond Chandler, who, as previously suggested, did not look upon agents in a particularly favorable light, thus stressed the importance of the "local fellow" to his agent, Harold N. Swanson, in 1952,

> As to foreign language rights, we have found out here, that is my secretary and myself, by long experience that they are not handled by agents except in the most cursory manner. Frankly, I don't see how

they could be. The only fellow who does anything is the agent on the spot. The English agent and the American agent can't even write a contract; they don't know when royalty statements are due; they don't know if they are paid when they should be paid; they don't even know when the books are published unless they get authors' copies, and they don't always get author's copies. The whole thing is just a bluff.[1]

Although Chandler's excessive dismissal of English and American agents was here presumably due to his own frustrations, his remarks on the remitting of statements and payment, or on gratis copies, strike an echo with the experience of many an author. Keeping track of payments and the actual transferring of money require tedious administrative work. What Chandler was perhaps unaware of, however, were the very complex conditions of monetary transfers in the immediate aftermath of the war, which plagued international imports and exports and required effective action on the part of all brokers, including literary agents. As noted by a contemporary observer,[2] France's commercial—and economic—policy between 1944 and 1957 appeared largely riddled with contradictions: on the one hand, economic reconstruction and growth required massive importations, payable in dollars; on the other, the monetary situation necessitated relative restrictions on importations, and massive exportations, in order to provide the country with foreign currency, and especially reduce the dollar shortage. To stimulate the domestic economy, the government adopted loose monetary policies, leading to recurrent devaluations. This resulted in a complexification of policy, a proliferation of commercial decrees and restrictions, as well as the multiplication of exchange rates, as we shall see. Consequently, multiple devaluations of the French franc and strict control of imports certainly weighed heavily on international transactions. Still other friction points repeatedly jammed the mechanics of international negotiations.

Friction Points

As trivial as this might seem, the very materiality of the correspondence between Hoffman, his American partners, and French publishers, reveals subtle differences in conducting business, which—although not irreconcilable—suggest a gap between the two sides. For instance, each request or note in accompaniment of a book sent by the American agents was short, to the point, and printed on A5-sized stationery; in other terms, one note was to be devoted to a single issue, even if this entailed sending out several such notes on the same day. This allowed agents to organize their files, by author name, title, and date, thereby allowing for quick checks. An agent wishing to know if a contract were still valid, or verifying the date of latest payment, would then rapidly find the information. Conversely, Hoffman's early letters to Curtis Brown and Brandt & Brandt, seemed to pack as many subjects as possible into one or two pages, distinguishing items with the use of capitals and underlining. This made for confusion on the American side of the Atlantic, as Alan Collins of Curtis Brown intimated in the spring of 1946. Hoffman had explained that the layout of his correspondence allowed him to cut down on airmail expenses, which remained quite high in 1946, as compared to the slower boat mail rates. Still, one cannot help thinking that this also revealed disorderly, or at least unsystematized, filing. This was also typical of the makeshift character that still characterized much of French publishing at the time.[3]

For this reason, and in order to keep better track of their authors, American agencies also preferred to use their own contract forms, as did a number of publishers as well. Foreign rights contracts are usually drawn up by agents rather than by the publishers acquiring said rights. We might add that this saves publishers a lot of trouble, and further highlights agents' value in these transactions. This in turn allowed American partners to control the wording of contractual clauses, and bring them as close as possible to domestic contracts. Consequently, the majority of foreign rights contracts were American contracts, and as such, to be interpreted under the laws of the United States; as New York was both the publishing and literary agenting center, agreements were specifically to be interpreted "according to the laws and statutes of the State of New York and the United States of America, regardless of the place of [their] physical execution," as the standard contractual clause went. Surprisingly, this does not seem to have caused too much of an uproar among French publishers. It has now become standard practice for foreign rights contracts to be drawn up by the selling party. In an age when few French publishers sufficiently mastered English, and before most houses had organized their own foreign rights services, this was made possible through the help of agents.

The contracts reveal discrepancies between American and French practices, some petty, others more serious. Perhaps a first, albeit not the most important, point is the number of free copies given to the proprietor. Obviously, a strict comparison between American and French publishers should take into account the disparate economic situation of each country, and more precisely, of each publisher. Still, a global overview certainly reflects these economic differences, but also highlights a shameful French parsimony. Whereas by the mid-1940s, it had become standard procedure among US publishers to give ten free copies to their authors, French contracts stipulated an average range of two to six copies![4] Gallimard, certainly one of the largest French firms and comparable in status to Random House, specified in their contracts for the "*Série Noire*" a number of two gratis copies to the proprietor in 1945, rising to four copies in the 1950 contracts. Exceptions can be found, with some

French publishers sending up to twenty copies of an American author's book, but these figures seem to reflect the average practices of most European countries, from Spain, Germany, Switzerland, or Italy, to England. Of course one might argue that American proprietors, whether authors or publishers, had in fact little use for these copies in a foreign language, which they almost never could read, and certainly would not be able to use for promotional purposes. These gratis copies thus remained tokens of good faith, proof that the book had indeed been published. Local agents received copies for their own files. At any rate, they were perhaps more important to authors than to the original publishers, as a symbolic acknowledgement of their authorship, although the translated texts were no longer theirs, often remaining the property of French publishers.[5] What US agents and publishers most often checked, and continue to verify, was the mention of the author's name and copyright in the first pages.

In cases where authors had retained their foreign rights, to be marketed by themselves or their representatives, the option clause could sometimes be very eloquent of the quality and nature of the publisher-author relationship. In 1961, reflecting upon common practice in the United States, the Authors Guild warned its members, "Under no circumstances should a writer accept options for more than one later work."[6] The multiple option clause typically reflects the classic wish for a long-lasting, fruitful collaboration, on the part of both author and publisher, and one is reminded of the gentleman-publisher's rhetoric with its emphasis on the friendly, mutually beneficial relation—that very relation that agents were constantly threatening to sever, if publishers were to be believed. In the case of contracts being negotiated in a far-away land, most often by several intermediaries, authors had to be extremely vigilant, or entirely trust their local representative to protect their interest. In addition to multiple options, agents had to control the option period, in order to prevent books from being immobilized by publishers who in the last instance might simply choose to pass, while keeping other publishers from making an offer in the meantime. Then again, American authors might sometimes be comforted by knowing that they had struck a profitable and long-term deal with a French publisher, thereby avoiding the future trouble of having to negotiate for each title; as noted above, Peter Cheyney had initially wished for all his books to be published by the same Paris publisher. French contracts often featured an option on the author's next two works, to be exercised within 30 or 60 days. In some cases, they might add an option on a number of former works not previously translated. From time to time, Hoffman had to stave off extravagant requests, such as when a publisher asked for an 18-month option period that would allow them to assess the reception of an author's work recently translated and published, before acquiring his next book, already published in English. As Hoffman explained, depending on the success of the book in the United States, it was utterly inconceivable to take the book out of the publishers' circuit for such a long time, which would have prevented other publishers from making a lucrative offer. Another incident, this time involving Gallimard, further enlightens Hoffman's role as cultural and business intermediary.

In October 1949, possibly irritated by Presses de la Cité's tentative grab for Chandler a few weeks before, Marcel Duhamel asked Hoffman to add a two-month option clause on a contract for *False Bounty* by Frederick C. Davis, aka Stephen Ransome, for the author's next three books, to be published in the "*Série Noire.*" Hoffman replied that such a clause could not legally be added to a contract already agreed upon, and even signed by one of the parties. Was this merely negligence on Duhamel's part? Hoffman then went on to claim that such a general option was certainly not in keeping with the policy of the important foreign agencies he represented. Given what we know about Hoffman's reluctance to negotiate with Gallimard, would his reaction have been different if it had been another publisher asking? The question should not be ruled out; what the exchange between the two men suggests is that, although multiple options might have been commonplace among French publishers, Hoffman was strictly following American policy on the matter; or he might have chosen to hide behind his American partners to refuse and save himself the effort of altering a contract.[7]

We should not, however, consider Hoffman's reply as a mere excuse, for there is ample evidence of other sticking points due to the policy of American agencies. Strangely enough, the general French custom of the 10% allowance for overs does not seem to have occasioned much resistance on the part of authors, publishers, or US agents. Hoffman also proved an adequate pedagogue whenever he had to explain new taxes, such as the reduction of the price of books by 4% decided by the French government in 1952. Yet one decidedly tricky question was that of first serial rights, which were considered quite differently on either side of the Atlantic. American publishers usually received 50% of syndication or second serial rights (i.e., after the publication of the work in volume form), meaning that authors received 25% of these rights, as the share between syndicate-publisher-author was understood as a 50%-25%-25% split. On first serial rights—that is, serialization occurring before the publisher's own publication of the book in volume form—American publishers generally earned nothing, for they logically did not participate in the process. As Alan Collins of Curtis Brown explained to Hoffman, "no American publisher would ever dream of asking for a share in the serial rights prior to publication by him of a book."[8] This, however, was not true for every publisher; some US publishers were known to initially grant the author first and second serial rights, provided they paid back their advance in the case of a first serial arrangement. In fact, throughout the 1940s, Knopf and Random House's standard contracts provided for a publisher's cut of the first serial rights, respectively 25% for Knopf and 10% for Random House.[9] Furthermore, publishers usually stood to benefit from the promotion generated by first serialization. Foreign publishers viewed the matter differently, arguing that, as they were the ones bearing the cost of the translation that would be used by the newspapers and magazines, they should be entitled to part of the proceeds—from a quarter, or a third, to 50%. Hoffman attempted to make his US partners see the benefits of such a system, insisting that this was standard practice throughout Europe,

> As regards the 50% participation of the publishers (which in some cases can even be reduced to 40%) in the serial rights this is a usual thing to which British and Continental authors are accustomed and is really in the authors' interest. You must remember that according to the French common law and the uses of the "Société des Gens de Lettres" every publication of a translated text in a periodical is split—if there is no other agreement—in equal shares between the author and the TRANSLATOR. Now, if you give 50% to the publisher of the book—it is HE WHO PAYS the translator so practically he does not cost you anything but is often instrumental in selling serial rights or getting better terms if he has an interest in the book he is bringing out, publicizing asf.[10]

Even those US publishers who might venture into the acquisition of English-language rights to foreign works did not face the same costs, as they very often had the opportunity of splitting the costs of translation with a British publisher. Hoffman's explanations obviously did not fully convince his US partners. Agents at both Curtis Brown and Brandt & Brandt, who believed that authors should retain their first serial rights in the case of a domestic publication, all complained to Hoffman about this practice, feeling that the proprietor of said rights should at least be granted the right to choose whether or not to grant first serial rights, in addition to a more decent share of the proceeds. Brandt & Brandt especially resented the French publishers' custom of not dissociating first serial rights from volume rights, indeed taking for granted that the ones tacitly and automatically came with the other, and ultimately demanded that distinct offers be made for each title. Once again, this went against French publishers' logic—not only for translations—which is based on the idea that subsidiary rights should all be left in their hands. Indeed, as Hoffman explained, if rights were to be dissociated, many French publishers might actually refuse to acquire the volume rights, for they would not be guaranteed against anyone else—a press syndicate—exploiting the serial rights "under their noses."[11]

Hoffman was therefore called upon repeatedly to sort out cases where publishers in Paris had marketed first serial rights, giving absolutely no thought to the fact that this might be seen as dishonest from an American point of view. In 1947 Robert Laffont serialized Betty MacDonald's *The Egg and I*—which was to appear as the first volume in Laffont's foreign literature series, *Pavillons*—without informing the French agent. From a strictly American legal perspective, Laffont had not acquired the serial rights to MacDonald's famous memoir; Hoffman's irritation upon discovering this breach of contract does seem excessive, or perhaps served his self-aggrandizing. In a scandalized tone, he wrote to Georges Poupet, in charge of press relations for Laffont:

> I was astounded . . . . Needless to say my Agency has always had the best and most friendly relations with the house of Robert Laffont, to whom I have always given the most interesting works among those I represent—something that M. Robert Laffont has acknowledged several times; I will once again try my utmost to be of service to M. Laffont and my friend Armand Pierhal in order to come out of this difficult situation caused by such an ill-advised sale of rights. I have already asked our London office (Mr. Brooks) to intercede with Brandt & Brandt.[12]

A few weeks later Hoffman had sorted things out, obtaining the serial rights for $500. Judging from the above-cited extract, it was of course important for him to remain in good standing with Brandt & Brandt, as well as with Laffont, which was fast becoming an important commercial publisher. At any rate the letter served to emphasize his role as agent— his intimate knowledge of publishers and editors, and his capacity to sort things out in case of a mishap, due to his extended international network. Interestingly, C.H. Brooks is here presented as an employee of the Hoffman agency, whereas he was in fact an agent with A.M. Heath, Brandt & Brandt's independent representative in England. This anecdote also underlines the relentless search for financial profit on the part of Brandt & Brandt. In spite of Hoffman's outrage, serial rights in France were by no means as lucrative as they were in the United States, where many agents had actually built their business on the selling of magazine rights. For one thing the circulation of the press in France could never reach the heights of the American mass-circulation magazines; while the editors of *McCall's* or *Woman's Home Companion* could afford to pay $20,000 or $40,000 for first serial rights in the 1940s and early 1950s, newspapers such as *Libération*, *Le Franc-Tireur*, or *Paris-Matin* could barely extend $1,000 to $2,000—a very good offer—not even matching the rates offered by US small-circulation magazines such as *Harper's* or *Atlantic Monthly*.[13]

In such conditions, Hoffman does not seem to have put a lot of energy into this particular area. Still, he resented having to lose the potential profits, precisely because he believed such rights should not be dissociated from volume rights. Evidently, agents themselves also stood to lose from such dissociation, as Hoffman made clear when the New York offices of Curtis Brown suggested working with a syndication agency, the Overseas News Agency, in order to maximize profits on the sales of first serial rights. In 1947, invoking the detrimental effect of such a dispersal of rights on authors, Hoffman strongly resented what he seemed to perceive as an infringement on his prerogatives, and insisted that first serial and volume rights were undividable, as French publishers also emphasized. Reacting to Alan Collins's claim that such an arrangement would cause no great financial loss, as serial rights represented a minor part of his business, Hoffman replied in anger,

> I am rather upset that you do not seem to see eye to eye with me in this.
> You say: "The financial loss to you would be very small". This is quite beside the point. First of all I do not give a damn about the financial loss in this connection—the confusion in customers' records and loss of prestige which would inevitably result from such a step are much more important to me than the financial loss. Moreover the loss could be very important and not only to me but to the whole Curtis Brown concern and last but not least to our authors. The reason is simple—many publishers shall refuse to buy the *book rights* if they cannot have a share in the serial rights or at least the assurance that somebody else is not going to exploit these under their noses. Many books will thus become unsaleable.[14]

That same year, Laffont proved Hoffman's point, when they refused to sign a publishing contract for Marquand's literary works—*B.F.'s Daughter, Repent in Haste, The Late George Apley, Wickford Point,* and *Warning Hill*—if they did not acquire serial rights in the process. The agent further argued that at any rate the magazine market in France was not a lucrative one, at least not one that would warrant such a "divided offices system." The French agent's show of reluctance might have disconcerted Alan Collins and Gertrude Weiner in New York, yet they accepted Hoffman's representation of French conditions, and ultimately relented. Weiner seems to have been convinced by these arguments, as she put them to Fred Wakeman that same summer, explaining why in foreign markets the dividing of volume and serial rights would in the long run not benefit him.[15]

Still another nagging problem to overcome in transatlantic business relations was the issue of publishers' statements, which American partners either found irregular, not frequent enough, or simply too vague. I should specify that the archives of such large agencies as Curtis, Brown, Ober & Associates, or Brandt & Brandt appear to—rightly—place the blame on French publishers, and not on agents. Then again, the longer the trail of intermediaries, the higher the risk of error on information ultimately provided to the author.

Bi-annual accounting in the United States had been standard practice in mainstream publishing as early as the last quarter of the 19th century, if not before. According to Curtis Brown's Gertrude Weiner, US publishers' general skepticism about the foreign rights market could be accounted for by the fact that foreign publishers were extremely casual about sending regular royalty statements, as opposed to domestic publishers who were used to rendering semi-annual statements on the dot. Furthermore, foreign publishers' statements did not clearly specify which period they covered.[16] Judging from the post-war contracts, many French publishers had taken to submitting semi-annual statements, to June 30 and December 31, proceeding to settle the accounts within a period of 1 to 3 months. Some preferred to render annual statements, usually at the end of the year. In spite of these guarantees, a number of confusing situations arose: sometimes checks were mailed out without the accompanying statement, or royalty statements would consist in vague scriptures on paper without any form of letterhead. Royalty statements issued by French publishers could indeed be confusing: Hoffman repeatedly asked publishers to distinguish between an author's several works, and not to indicate royalties owed for a bulk of books, so that he might clarify his own ledgers. Furthermore, American publishers and agents were continually writing to ask for missing statements, sometimes over periods of 2 years or more. If post-war conditions might have explained this confusion, this continuing practice certainly gave out a negative image of Parisian publishers to their partners on the other side of the Atlantic. French publishers to this day seem to have perpetuated this custom, in spite of warnings on the part of foreign agents that this is cause for termination of contract. In 2001 writer Pierre Assouline confessed that he knew of many big publishing houses in Paris which did not send annual statements to their authors, implying that there might be more oddities not worth mentioning.[17]

In 1946 Gertrude Weiner of Curtis Brown went so far as to make the issue of statements a priority in the early collaboration with Hoffman, as the US agency was about to expand their foreign rights department. Asking Hoffman how effective he might be "as to following up publishers so far as rendering statements are concerned," she insisted that "[a]ssurance of good service in the rendering of statements regularly could, of course, be a strong point in getting the translation rights representation of American publishers."[18] Hoffman seized upon these requests to push his advantage, emphasizing that this was precisely an additional reason why American proprietors should have and trust local agents who were ultimately the only ones who might closely control the rendering of sales statements.[19] Indeed, while in some rare instances authors in the United States might be granted the contractual right to control publisher's accounts, often at their own expense, when removed from the place of publication they were entirely in the hands of their local agent, who was to act in their name and be allowed to inspect the publishers' account books. Agents were thus made to keep and remit statements for all transactions handled for their authors.

Money Makes the Books Go Around

Needless to say, the bickering over the remitting of statements was in fact laments over payment, for in the end, agents are to ascertain that money will make the books go around. As has already been suggested, an agent is, among many other things, a broker and banker, a fiduciary "with respect to all funds received by him for the account of the author,"[20] contractually granted the right to cash monies on behalf of clients. Due to the complexities of the French monetary and economic situation, as we shall see, the central, and indeed, quintessential matter of money in transatlantic negotiations in the post-war era raises at least three interconnected questions: to that of "when" would proprietors be paid, were added the questions of "how" and "where" they *could* be paid.

Complaints on the part of US agencies and publishers as to the delay in, or absence of, payment, abound in the archives. By 1947 the Curtis Brown agency had still not obtained any payment of advances for some ten contracts, including for titles by Ellery Queen, passed with the Editions de la Nouvelle Revue Critique between 1936 and 1940.[21] In the case of unreasonable delays, US authors, publishers, and agents had first to ascertain whether the local co-agent or foreign publisher was responsible. In New York, the Society of Authors Representatives' code of ethics had from early on established reasonably acceptable delays within which agents were to pay their authors/clients—10 days after receiving the money for outright sale of the author's work, and a month for continuing sales.[22] Even before the organization of French agents in 1948, they too had to abide by particular standards, provided publishers themselves did not withhold payment for unreasonable periods of time, which might arouse suspicion of playing the market. However, as already suggested, the consequences of the war and of the inflationary policies between 1944 and 1952 had led several small publishers to either change their programs or to go bankrupt without their US counterparts being informed. Several contracts, as well as translations when they had already been commissioned, simply changed hands in the process without proprietors being notified. American agents paid particular care to these points, asking their local correspondents whenever possible to annul former contracts and draw up new ones.

In effect, the delegation by an author to an agent—be they American or local—to receive and collect the sums owed him was most often specified under the terms of each individual contract for volume rights, rather than made the object of an overarching agent-author contract. Such contracts do exist, but they remain an exception. The agent is thus empowered to act on the proprietor's behalf in all matters arising out of the agreement. Although in some cases of transatlantic negotiations the American agent was to receive payment, in a greater number of contracts the prerogative went to the local agent. In the 1930s Henry Miller asked his agent William A. Bradley in a simple note, to hold all sums due him by his Paris publisher, Obelisk Press. Of course one of the agent's primary missions was to verify statements in order to make certain the correct amounts had been paid by the publishers, check that the royalty scale was indeed respected when sales exceeded the first 5,000 or 10,000 stepping point. While payment for a hundred copies on which royalties had been incorrectly calculated was relatively easy to retrieve from a publisher, in other instances arbitration had to be resorted to. Hoffman, who took over the representation of Henry Miller from the Bradley agency after the war, waged a long and ugly battle with publisher Maurice Girodias, formerly of Editions du Chêne, to obtain back payment for several of Miller's books. Girodias had inherited the rights to Miller from his father, Jack Kahane; the attack for obscenity filed by the *Cartel d'action sociale et morale* in June 1946 against both *Tropic of Cancer* (published in French by Denoël in 1945) and *Tropic of Capricorn* (Editions du Chêne, 1946), had also contributed to boosting the sales of *Tropic of Capricorn*, but Girodias repeatedly failed to transfer the money to Miller. In 1951, he had lost Editions du Chêne to Hachette; in 1954, after years of meticulous perusing of accounts, Hoffman was able to obtain from the Hachette subsidiary, renamed Société Nouvelle des Editions du Chêne, a formal acknowledgement of debt for over 2,9 million francs owed to Miller for the 1949 English-language publication of part one of *The Rosy Crucifixion,* better known as *Sexus.*[23] In the late 1950s Hoffman never tired of reminding Girodias of his financial and personal debt to Miller.

Delay in payment or non-payment, however, was not always due to publishers' wrongdoings or negligence, as other obstacles got in the way of money transfers. In 1948 Harold Ober of the Ober & Associates agency wrote to Nancy Hale, author of the bestselling *Prodigal Women* (1942), which was on the point of being translated into French,

> One very important thing I forgot to mention: at the present time it is not possible to get money transmitted from France to the United States. The money is simply held there to your account. This is true of a great many European countries and simply a result of the general economic situation, so there is nothing we can do about it.[24]

This post-scriptum presented only a very sketchy outline of the difficult situation that plagued transatlantic commercial relations between

1945 and 1955, and indeed until 1958 when the French franc was finally stabilized and France was welcomed back onto the international banking scene. Possibly, this was all Hale needed to know about the dollar gap, whereas the tasks of her local representative in France, with whom she had no direct contact, were growing increasingly arduous. The dollar shortage and the non-convertibility of the franc, in conjunction with import barriers, were then, as they would continue to be in other countries throughout the 1980s, obstacles to a transatlantic book trade. Programs such as the Informational Media Guaranty Program (IMG) are in fact evidence of the importance of overcoming such barriers for the distribution of media products, including books. Post-war economic imperatives, the need to improve the balance of payments, as well as the development of US public diplomacy and its emphasis on US books as weapons against the threat of Communism, resulted in the organization of the IMG under the Economic Cooperation Administration Act of 1948. As Peter Jennison remarked in 1956 in his contribution to the Princeton University symposium on "Books Abroad," the IMG was the "chief instrumentality for overcoming the economic barriers to the importation of American books in countries with severe dollar reserve and credit shortages."[25] The stated intention of the program was to allow foreign countries with dollar shortages to pay for American cultural and media importations in local currency, all the while guaranteeing the exporter the convertibility of foreign currency into dollars. As can be inferred from the discussions on the choice of currency for payment of French rights, this was certainly a way to ease commercial transactions between the United States and France. Exporters would apply to the IMG for the payment of a dollar equivalent, supplied by Congressional funds; in turn, the Treasury Department would deposit local currencies in a specific account, to be used for diplomatic operations and missions abroad.

In 1952 the IMG was transferred from the Mutual Security Agency to the Department of State, then from August 1953 until its demise in 1968, was operated by the autonomous United States Information Agency. These shifts actually exemplify the private-state cooperation typical of the post-war and Cold War eras, as already suggested by the United States International Book Association (USIBA). As Donald E. McNeil explained in 1986,

> IMG was established to eliminate the foreign exchange barrier as an impediment to the free flow of ideas. Although IMG's implicit relationship to economic and technical assistance efforts and its obvious contribution to the stimulation of foreign trade and an improved balance of payments were also considered important, the program's stated purpose, as identified in the 1948 ECA Act and in many congressional documents thereafter, was to serve as an adjunct to the

government's international information activities. Its relocation to
the State Department in 1952 and to USIA in 1953 was logical in
light of this stated purpose.[26]

The implementation of standards for the selection of media products
further underlines the public diplomacy perspective: requests for books,
pamphlets, periodicals, and films were accepted insofar as they definitely
promoted a truthful image of America, and were "consistent with the
national interests of the United States."[27] Any sensationalist, salacious,
or politically dubious character would warrant the rejection of said
product. In such conditions, evidently, textbooks and technical guides
were favored over the crime and detective fiction that made up the bulk
of books in demand among French publishers and readers.

To take in the full measure of the difficulties facing agents and proprietors of book rights, France's monetary and exchange policies require
examination. Like most European countries after the war, France lacked
sufficient dollar reserves to uphold its currency's fixed value to the dollar, as requested by the Bretton Woods Agreement of 1944 which established the gold standard, and the franc remained a non-convertible
currency until 1958.[28] In order to artificially maintain its value to the
dollar, the consecutive French governments advocated, and indeed implemented successive devaluations, which meant that the French franc
was a dangerously soft currency. These devaluations, generally and automatically meant to foster a form of commercial equilibrium, in fact
tended to make foreign investors and businessmen wary of foreign transactions. Thus were brokers, and agents among them, compelled into a
pedagogical mission, made to signal any new devaluation and sometimes
to correct the exchange rates calculated on either side of the Atlantic.
Another aspect of French economic policies consisted in an increasingly
strict control of importations and of all financial transactions between
the French and foreign residents, enacted through a powerful and central agency, the Office des Changes. In short, transfers of monies from
France to a foreign country—as in the case of advances and royalties—
were to be authorized by the Office des Changes, and effected through
appropriate and authorized channels, namely specifically listed banks.[29]

Created in 1939, strengthened in 1945, the Office des Changes represented a centralization of the control of exchanges, as compared with
the relatively loose system that had prevailed between 1931 and 1939.
First administered by the Banque de France, in 1940, it came under the
direction of the Ministry of Finance until 1956.[30] Sadly it must be said
that the fastidious formalities required by the Office des Changes fully
justify the notorious reputation of the French "administration," well
known for its traditional red tape.[31] In 1958 Gérard Marcy noted that
some 500 distinct recommendations had been issued by the Office des
Changes, further complicating an economic policy already riddled with

contradictions.[32] The number of steps to be taken toward clearance was itself a deterrent.

Some French agents or publishers, who were negotiating the acquisition of rights from the United States, had to file with the Office des Changes a request for import licences. The licence would be delivered after the following information had been provided: the names of the importer and the exporter and full addresses, the trade registration number, the nature of the object to be imported, including its weight, the probable date of arrival and port of entry in France, the amount billed, and the nature of the currency used. If importers wished to purchase dollars, the request was to be processed by the Office des Changes clearing house, which issued a visa number to be used for all subsequent correspondence, and by the Ministry of Finance's Import and Export licence division. It was particularly vital that publishers, or agents, depending on who filed the request, not lose this precious visa number, lest they incur additional paperwork. This import licence was one of the documents—along with a certified copy of the contract—necessary to file a request to purchase dollars, as sellers of rights most often demanded payment in dollars; this request was to be filed in no less than five copies. This was not counting the fact that when agents were in charge of the filing process, they paid commission on currency exchange.

After 1945, American agents became increasingly aware of the diffi- culty of transferring money overseas, and French agents strove to main- tain their trust in spite of these difficult conditions for which they could not be held responsible. In the spring of 1946, with the threat of blocked transfers and devaluation looming large, Curtis Brown's Alan Collins anxiously asked Hoffman whether he felt he would be able to make transfers, explaining that many authors were becoming reluctant to ac- cept French offers if that implied having to wait months or years for the money, adding, "heaven knows what will happen to the franc in the meantime."[33] At this stage, Hoffman was still able to assuage his fears: Money transfers were still being processed satisfactorily, although, as he pointed out, they represented a "lot of extra—filling in forms, giving explanations to the Exchange Control authorities, asf. This is the reason why we prefer to send the money off in batches and not for every single contract."[34] By September 1946 the Office des Changes was on strike; a year later transfers were completely blocked, and by the spring of 1948 no dollar authorizations were being delivered and the Office des Changes sent out a circular letter to publishers and agents, informing them that they would stop authorizing contracts with the United States on account of the dollar shortage.[35] They ultimately did by the fall of 1948.[36]

These restrictions on import and the ever tighter control of exchanges exerted a number of constraints and caused complications for authors and agents. First, as Ober explained to Nancy Hale in 1948, in case of non-transferability of monies, the majority of sums due to proprietors of rights, be they authors or publishers, were collected and kept by agents, as non-residents had very few, if any, means of opening a French bank account. In reply to Bernice Baumgarten's inquiry into the matter, Hoffman explained that French agents kept the sums either in their own bank accounts or in authors' accounts taken in their own names.[37] This was nothing new for Baumgarten, as US agents also opened special accounts for their clients, into which they would deposit the sums owed to each client. In fact, the SAR's Code of Ethics made it a requirement that agents not "commingle the Author's moneys with his own," nor "deal with any money received or held on behalf of an Author so that such money will appear to be his own"; indeed, respectable agents were meant to establish a distinct clients' account, to be maintained separate from the agency's general business.[38] What might have struck her, as a seasoned and reputable agent, was the relative lack of distinction between accounts in Hoffman's reply. Since the sums deposited were in francs and could not be transferred outside the country, there remained the question of how to get to it. Authors planning a trip to France might stop by the agency and ask to collect part of the sums to spend in the country; publishers who traded directly in foreign rights might ask their local agent to hand out part of the sums to some of their employees who travelled through Paris; others yet again, not able or not desirous to travel to Europe, might ask the agent to use these sums to buy specifically French gifts for members of their family—such as the much sought-after Paris perfumes! Authors yet again sometimes designated someone travelling to Europe to benefit from the money. France was not alone in this situation: Italian or Israeli publishers also shared the plight of soft currency and restrictions on imports. In the same manner, restrictions weighed on the United States, so that in 1946 commissions owed on sales of American rights to French works negotiated by French agents could not be paid to French bank accounts; fortunately Hoffman had long before opened an account of his own in New York, testifying to the genuinely international nature of his profession. His strategy is also evidence of the interesting role of book agents as surrogate bankers, in an era of complicated financial transactions: Hoffman asked Curtis Brown in New York to deposit part of the sums owed him in his bank account, and hold the other to his agent account, so that they might easily renew his subscriptions to the trade press, and also help to convey this money to his mother who was still living in Russia. This would be achieved through a charitable committee, the *Artists Committee to Aid Soviet Orphans*.

In these circumstances, quite possibly a good number of authors throughout the world never did actually obtain the monies due them for the sale of foreign rights. In certain cases, the amounts were perhaps too small to warrant a time-consuming procedure. Regarding the transfer of small royalty payments, we might correctly assume that most authors and agents simply abandoned any claim to the sums. This increasingly led US agents, publishers, and authors to ask for the sums to be remitted directly in the United States, in order to guarantee prompt payment. Several American authors were adamant about being paid in their own country, notwithstanding the difficulty of money transfers. France was not alone in facing these difficulties: German publishers sometimes worked out of Lichtenstein to get the money out of the country. While the bigger French publishers could indeed work through several channels to defer to these demands, the smaller ones had no such possibility, which in turn made them less attractive to foreign authors and publishers. Yet even the big ones were reluctant to pay in the United States. Only under pressure from authors and their agents, as in the case of Chandler, did Gallimard—in this instance, Marcel Duhamel—ultimately agree to pay advances in New York. Yet in 1949 Dionys Mascolo had forcefully rejected Brandt & Brandt's request that Marcel Aubry, president of Literary Masterworks and Gallimard's representative in New York, pay an advance on their behalf. Aubry's firm, he contended, was not a subsidiary of the publisher, but their correspondent; as such he did not possess enough monies to pay advances. Invoking the higher calling of literature, Mascolo had suggested that the US agents' position was certainly not "*sérieux*," and in a melodramatically offended tone, had ended his explanations to Hoffman in this way, ". . . would American authors, publishers and agents rather not have their books translated, than accept for royalties to be paid with the usual three or four-month delay?"[39] This reply certainly illustrates the typical French publishers' position, hiding behind their literary vocation in order to avoid talking business. As Chandler once wrote to Marcel Duhamel, "I have always thought it one of the charms of dealing with publishers that if you start talking about money, they retire coldly to their professional eminence, and if you start talking about literature, they immediately yank the dollar sign before your eyes."[40]

Sometimes Hoffman was able to transfer funds through London; in other instances the more international French publishers could work through a Swiss subsidiary to get the money out and to the United States. Yet in other affairs publishers parceled out their requests for money transfers, in the hope that the Office des Changes would more readily authorize small sums, rather than the full amount. As Hoffman explained to Alan Collins in 1946, for every money transfer agents "[had] to put in a lot of extra work—filling in forms, giving explanations to the Exchange Control authorities asf. This is the reason why we prefer to send the money off in batches and not for every single contract."[41]

This, however, entailed accounting problems across the Atlantic, for agents were then at a loss to know whether the full amount of advances had indeed been paid.

The Office des Changes procedures took a toll on agents, who grew reluctant to file requests for importation, as the procedure was both costly and time consuming. French agencies, including Hoffman's, were generally not sufficiently staffed to handle these matters efficiently, in addition to the rest of their tasks. Throughout the 1940s and 1950s, Michel Hoffman worked as sole agent in his firm, with the collaboration of competent secretaries. This explains why in several instances, Hoffman readily let French publishers engage in the process, all the more so as they sometimes had better leverage with the clearing house. Dionys Mascolo intimated as much when Brandt & Brandt insisted that Chandler be paid directly in New York,

> If you prefer, instead of paying you the advance, we will file the request with the Office des Changes ourselves and undertake to hasten the process. While you may not have the leverage to hasten the transfer of certain sums, we believe we do, for we have on certain exceptional occasions in the past succeeded in paying monies very quickly.[42]

The delays occasioned by the Office des Changes procedure were a source of discontent for American authors, publishers, and agents, who strove to keep track of payments due by French publishers. These delays were particularly long between 1946 and 1949, from 4, 5, or 6 months to over 1 or 2 years in some cases. Starting in 1949, perhaps as a result of the burgeoning recovery of the French economy, the Office seems to have become more efficient, and delays were kept down to a month at most.[43] When delays became insufferable, French publishers could sometimes appeal to diplomatic channels to hasten the process. In December 1948, when Weiner who had asked whether Albin Michel might not be able to pay an advance due to Ellery Queen in New York, Hoffman replied that

> The advance can of course not be paid in New York immediately but Albin Michel is now working hard to obtain a permit for the first contract (the one with seven titles). It has already been okayed by the Publishers Syndicate and the Foreign Office and is now with the Exchange Control, so there is hope at any rate.[44]

As if red tape were not enough, French agents were also made to bear the impact of four successive devaluations between September 1944 and September 1949.[45] In September 1949, the exchange rate of the franc to the dollar was artificially fixed at 350, and remained at that level until 1957. By the fall of 1949 the French economy had sufficiently recovered, in large part thanks to the Marshall Plan, for the government to stop resorting to devaluations. Between 1944 and 1949, however, with the franc/dollar exchange rate constantly fluctuating, former contracts stipulating advances to be paid in dollars became difficult for French publishers to uphold: an advance of $150 or $250 agreed upon in mid-1947 might be worth several times more in francs 6 months later. In March 1948, Hoffman was able to negotiate with Editions de Flore to honor payment of a $300 advance to Fanny Hurst formerly agreed upon, in spite of the fact that it then represented, in francs, 2.5 times more than it had when the contract had been signed.[46] As Hoffman explained to Sonia Chapter of Curtis Brown in London following the December 1945 devaluation of the franc, it was doubtful whether French publishers would maintain their offers made before the devaluation once they found out how much more they would have to pay, compared with the amount initially envisaged.[47] American publishers were themselves quite aware of this problem; in January 1948 publishers at E.P. Dutton worried that French publishers who had already bought the rights to several titles by Inez Hogan, and even translated them, would ultimately lose interest, following the lack of authorizations delivered by the Office des Changes. They certainly could not afford to wait until the financial condition in France was improved.

More directly, French agents also stood to lose money from the fluctuating franc and dollar exchange rate. Standard procedure had agents collect the advances from French publishers, and remit them to the rights owner. Ideally, such advances should have been transferred as rapidly as possible, so that the agent did not have to hand out a higher equivalent in dollars than had been agreed upon, in case of devaluation. In the postwar age of fluctuations, this also entailed a scrupulously similar understanding and consideration of exchange rates, on the part of agents and on the part of French publishers' accountants. Hoffman was certainly not ready to pay any surplus amount of money due to the errors of an accountant who might have based his calculations on the dollar selling rate instead of the buying rate used for international transfers. As he explained to his nemesis Dionys Mascolo in December 1949 concerning the advances on five Ellery Queen titles, after Gallimard's accountant utterly failed to understand his arguments, Hoffman could see no other solution save to ask the publishers to file the request for a transfer permit themselves,

> Most times payment is based on the average rate to the dollar at Fr. 350. Since the devaluation, it is the first time that a client chooses to apply a rate of Fr. 249, and I really don't see why I should pay the difference of 2 Fr to the dollar out of my own pocket.[48]

These last remarks were insidiously insulting, intimating that Gallimard's accounting department may have purposefully set out to swindle Hoffman. Indeed, they also reflect the curious phenomenon of multiple exchange rates voluntarily established by the French government between January 1948 and September 1949 as a temporary measure to avoid a strong deflationary trend, and ultimately, to restore the "natural" rate

of the franc. At the time, this so-called "graduated devaluation" created, besides the black market rate, a "free market" rate, an official rate,
and an average rate—the latter calculated as a medium point between
the official and the free market rate of the dollar.[49] In addition to this,
until October 1948, France had applied a "privileged" exchange rate
for staple products.[50] In these circumstances, and when every centime
mattered, French agents and publishers—not to mention their American
counterparts—were bound to become confused.

On the other hand, American rights owners and negotiators could
not be expected to accept lesser sums than had initially been contracted
for, and US agents increasingly asked that foreign contracts be drawn
up in dollars as a matter of policy, so as to avoid the consequences of
devaluation. Interestingly, some American publishers continue to ask for
payment in US currency whenever they fear the instability of the dollar,
and some have made it a perennial custom.[51] Whenever he had a chance,
Hoffman refused such arrangements. As he explained to Gertrude
Weiner in October 1948, "It is in every respect advisable I think to make
the advances in francs as the official free rate of the dollar fluctuates all
the time."[52] Again, cases varied depending on the popularity and the
"best-selling" effect of works; in August 1945 Albin Michel did agree
to modify a contract originally drawn up in francs to supply Marjorie
Kinnan Rawlings with dollars instead of soft currency. It should be noted
that Albin Michel was one of the bigger French publishers; other, smaller
houses could not afford to be so generous considering the national lack
of dollars. So as to counter the risks and effects of devaluation, increased
by the delays in obtaining a transfer permit, certain American agencies
devised a cunning—although illegal—"devaluation clause" to insert in
foreign contracts. This became cause for a veritable tug of war between
Hoffman and the Curtis Brown agency in New York, who had conceived
the clause to be so-worded,

> In recognition of the fact that by the time restrictions on withdrawal
> of the franc from France are lifted, the number of francs exchange-
> able for the United States dollar may be increased from the number
> of francs currently calculated as the equivalent of the dollar; the
> parties agree that in such event, after the time that the restriction
> on withdrawal is lifted, the buyer will, upon demand, pay to the
> seller, such number of francs that the seller will have in hand, in
> the aggregate, that number of francs as of the time the restriction is
> lifted as shall be equivalent to the dollar amount at the date hereof,
> in calculating the number of francs payable hereunder.[53]

Weiner, informing Hoffman that Italian agents and publishers had
agreed to this clause, specified that it would of course only be inserted in
case of devaluation, as an increase in value of the franc would ultimately

favor publishers, whereas the measure was in fact devised to protect US authors.

Hoffman balked and warned Curtis Brown that French publishers were not very likely to accept such conditions, which amounted to imposing upon them obligations on matters they could not foresee; for surely they could not predict the end of devaluations, and the problem of the availability of dollars was well beyond their control. He also contested the very legality of such a clause, not to mention the clumsiness of the wording.[54] Gertrude Weiner reluctantly agreed to withdraw the clause and assented, yet her reply suggests that Curtis Brown was by no means abandoning the principle of such an objectionable—from the point of view of their foreign partners—clause. Evidence of similar restrictions can be found in contracts negotiated by other American agents, stipulating that specified dollar advances should be paid regardless of the date of money transfers, or the exchange value of the foreign currency at any given time.

Paradoxically, similar conditions were sometimes requested by French publishers themselves, who sought protection from other deflationary measures. In November 1947, Jenny Bradley wrote Random House to submit a proposal put forward by Flammarion, setting the advance at 120,000 francs, this sum amounting to $1,000 as calculated at the time of the contract, for one of Sinclair Lewis's novels. Lewis's editor reacted quite strongly, explaining to the author that French publishers were typically bound to break contracts.[55] In the face of so much red tape, partners were bound to become irritated, or worse yet, demoralized. Still, the difficulty of international commercial relations was genuinely beyond the control of agents or French publishers.

Like any other transatlantic market, the Franco-American book trade was dependent on the particular commercial and monetary policies of the post-war era. This period also afforded publishers and agents some creativity in the wording of their contracts, to which they would sometimes append surprising clauses. In this context, and in addition to the peculiarities of French publishing, sometimes considered one of the most singular markets, the diplomatic and fiduciary competences of local co-agents were, more than ever, put to the test.

Just as they were compelled to reassure their American partners, and to repeatedly explain differences in practices, they also defended their French partners, namely the publishers. The balance was not always easy to maintain: thus Hoffman would alternately choose to strictly uphold American agencies' standards, and to defend French publishers' interests, as in the case of first serial rights. Furthermore, the intensified internationalization of publishing and the increasing volume of rights negotiated induced new, tedious administrative tasks that fully warranted co-agents' commissions, and justified their existence in the international book market.

Notes

1 Chandler to Harold N. Swanson, December 5, 1952. Online, Bonham auction website. Swanson was also an agent for William Faulkner and John F. Fitzgerald.
2 Professor of Economics Gérard Marcy, 1958.
3 See also Alan C. Collins to Michel Hoffman, March 15, 1946, and Hoffman's reply, March 20, 1946. BRH, AG.15.02.
4 Taking as reference the 1947 Random House contract negotiated with them, the Authors Guild estimated that ten free copies and a 40% discount represented "practically universal usage" in 1961. "Your Book Contract," 35.
5 In this perspective, it is perhaps not very surprising to find a number of Knopf contracts for foreign rights stipulating two gratis copies, to be delivered to the publisher.
6 Authors' Guild, "Your Book Contract," 23.
7 Marcel Duhamel to Michel Hoffman, October 25, 1949. BRH, ED.FR.33.03. Ironically, *False Bounty (Les marrons du feu)* was ultimately published not in the "*Série Noire,*" but by Denoël in their *Oscar* series.
8 See Alan C. Collins to Michel Hoffman, June 26, 1947. BRH, AG.15.02. There were exceptions: in the 1940s the Knopf standard contract provided for a 25% cut for the publisher, while Random House took 10% (The Authors' Guild, "Your Book Contract," 31).
9 See The Authors' Guild, "Your Book Contract," 31.
10 Michel Hoffman to Alan C. Collins, July 17, 1947. BRH, AG.15.02.
11 Michel Hoffman to Alan C. Collins, July 17, 1947. BRH, AG.15.02.
12 My translation. Michel Hoffman to Georges Poupet, September 1, 1947. BRH, ED.FR.38.01. Armand Pierhal was editor of the *Pavillons* series.
13 For more specific figures, see Reynolds, *The Middle Man,* 52, and Strauss, *A Talent for Luck,* 90. Helen Strauss claims to have sold first serial rights to Taylor Caldwell's *The Balance Wheel* to *Woman's Home Companion* for $40,000 in 1950. See also Chandler B. Grannis, ed., *What Happens in Book Publishing* (New York: Columbia University Press, 1957), 231, for an estimate in the late 1950s. Rates for first serial rights extended by *Harper's* and *Atlantic Monthly* ranged from $300 to $4,000 or $5,000, while condensation of books in such magazines as *True, Look, Life,* or *Redbook* went from $2,000 to $15,000 on average. Propositions found in the Hoffman archives, made by *Libération, Paris-Matin, Le Franc-Tireur,* or the small magazine *Cavalcade* between 1945 and 1947 attest to offers ranging from 50,000 to 250,000 francs, approximately $1,000 to $2,000 taking into consideration devaluations (BRH, HOF AG.09.01 and ED.FR.33.03).
14 Michel Hoffman to Alan C. Collins, July 17, 1947. BRH, AG.15.02.
15 See Gertrude Weiner to Michel Hoffman, August 2, 1947. BRH, AG.15.02.
16 See Gertrude Weiner to Michel Hoffman, October 2, 1946. BRH, AG.15.03.
17 Sandler, "Les agents littéraires en France," Volume 2, 111.
18 Gertrude Weiner to Michel Hoffman, October 2, 1946. BRH.
19 Michel Hoffman to Gertrude Weiner, October 7, 1946. BRH.
20 Society of Authors Code of Ethics, 1955.
21 See Betty Ferguson (Curtis Brown) to Fernand Keller, copy to Michel Hoffman, November 7, 1947. BRH, ED.FR.38.01.
22 SAR Code of Ethics, January 26, 1955. SAR Box 1 "By-Laws IV."
23 On the case of Girodias' debt to Henry Miller for the publication of *Sexus,* see Arbitration Decision, February 28, 1955 (BRH, HOF BRH B259). Miller had been represented by Hoffman's attorney, M. Sev.

24 Harold Ober to Nancy Hale, October 14, 1948. Harold Ober & Associates Papers, C0129 Box 46: Folder 5.

25 Peter Jennison, in Dan Lacy, Charles G. Bolté and Peter S. Jennison, eds. *Library Trends*, 11.

26 William M. Childs and David E. McNeill, ed, *American Books Abroad: Toward a National Policy*, (Washington, D.C.: Helen Dwight Reid Educational Foundation, 1986), 56.

27 Peter Jennison, in Dan Lacy, Charles G. Bolté and Peter S. Jennison, eds. *Library Trends*, 12.

28 For 1948, the dollar gap is estimated as follows: the United States held 24 billion dollars' worth of gold, versus 8 billion for the rest of the world. See Julien Brault, "La Banque de France et les transactions internationales de la France des années 1930 aux années 1970," Communication, Mission Historique de la Banque de France Seminar (May 2011), 15. http://www.banque-france.fr/fileadmin/user_upload/banque_de_france/histoire/mission_historique/la-Banque-de-France-et-les-transactions_internationales-de-la-France-des-annees-1930-1970-Julien-Brault.pdf.

29 On this subject, see Léo Levantal and Anselme-Rabinovitch, "Foreign Investments in France and French Exchange Control," *The American Journal of Comparative Law* 3, no. 3 (Summer 1954): 427–428.

30 On the workings of the Office des Changes and the role of the Banque de France, see Brault.

31 In fact Italy established a similar Exchange Office, equally causing trouble for agents dealing with Italian publishers.

32 Gérard Marcy, "Quelques aspects de l'évolution et de la réglementation française du commerce extérieur depuis 1945: contrôle des changes et règlements internationaux," *Revue économique* 9, no. 3 (May 1958): 350.

33 Alan C. Collins to Michel Hoffman, March 15, 1946. BRH, AG.15.03.

34 Michel Hoffman to Alan C. Collins, March 20, 1946. BRH, AG.15.03.

35 Michel Hoffman to Gertrude Weiner, March 23, 1948. BRH, HOF AG.14.02.

36 Michel Hoffman to Nellie Sukerman (Curtis Brown), October 19, 1948. BRH, HOF AG.14.02.

37 Michel Hoffman to Bernice Baumgarten, November 12, 1947. BRH, AG.16.01.

38 SAR Code of Ethics, January 26, 1955, 15.

39 Dionys Mascolo to Michel Hoffman, February 17, 1949. BRH, HOF ED.FR.33.03.

40 Raymond Chandler to Marcel Duhamel, October 9, 1949. BRH, HOF AG.20.01.

41 Michel Hoffman to Alan C. Collins, March 20, 1946. BRH, AG.15.03.

42 Dionys Mascolo to Michel Hoffman, February 17, 1949. BRH, ED.FR.33.03.

43 See BRH, DAI (Demandes d'autorisation d'importation) déposées près l'Office des Changes, BRH C05.

44 Michel Hoffman to Gertrude Weiner, December 28, 1948. BRH, HOF. AG.14.02.

45 Marcy, "Quelques aspects de l'évolution et de la réglementation française du commerce extérieur depuis 1945: contrôle des changes et règlements internationaux," 351.

46 Michel Hoffman to Gertrude Weiner, March 11, 1948. BRH, ED.FR.14.02.

47 Michel Hoffman to Sonia Chapter, December 26, 1945. BRH, HOF AG.09.01.

48 Michel Hoffman to Dionys Mascolo, December 5, 1949. BRH, HOF ED.FR.33.03.
49 On this thorny monetary issue, see Marcy and Chiarella Esposito, "French International Monetary Policies in the 1940s," *French Historical Studies* 17, no. 1 (Spring, 1991): 117–140. Esposito explains how this "maneuver" indeed improved "France's balance of payments toward the dollar area."
50 See Marcy, "Quelques aspects de l'évolution et de la réglementation française du commerce extérieur depuis 1945: contrôle des changes et règlements internationaux," 369–372.
51 See Sandler, vol. 2, interview of Boris Hoffman, 15.
52 Michel Hoffman to Gertrude Weiner, October 5, 1948. BRH, HOF AG.14.02.
53 Gertrude Weiner to Michel Hoffman, September 30, 1947. BRH, HOF AG.15.02.
54 Michel Hoffman to Gertrude Weiner, October 14, 1947. BRH HOF AG.15.02.
55 Harry Maule to Sinclair Lewis, November 21, 1947. Random House Records, 1925–1999. Box 69.

Conclusion

In 1959 the Office des Changes was officially disbanded. Still, the termination was more symbolic than effective and the control of exchange continued until the 1980s. Throughout the 1960s, any leverage that professional organizations and unions might have had to break down the strict regulations was crushed. In spite of these obstacles, the transatlantic book trade continued to expand and required better international protection and regulation, ultimately encompassed by the Universal Copyright Convention (UCC) passed in Geneva in 1952 and ultimately implemented in 1955. It is certainly no coincidence that the four major post-war meetings organized under the sponsorship of United Nations Educational, Scientific, and Cultural Organization (UNESCO) toward the ultimate signing of the convention, were held in Paris—in 1947, 1949, and 1951—and Washington, in 1951. As John Schulman triumphantly put it in November 1952, "It must be kept in mind that the United States is the heart and soul of the Convention. As has been so aptly stated, 'the key to the vitality of the Convention is the United States for our action will chart the course for other nations to follow.'"[1] Several legal experts have pointed out that the Geneva Convention was the result of undisguised concessions to the United States. While amendments to the domestic copyright legislation were a clear deterrent to US membership in Berne, the UCC required virtually no changes except in respect to the US copyright formalities and the manufacturing clause, which were now only applicable to US nationals. The central compromises clearly deferred to US practices and codes: copyright was based on the principle of national treatment, but integrated both the principle of place of first publication, guaranteed by Berne, and the US principle of nationality of authors authors were exempt from copyright formalities, as long as the copyright symbol was affixed on the copies.

In his analysis and commentary of the Convention, John S. Dubin did not conceal its great advantages to the United States. Indeed, he remarked that

> The delegations of other governments strove to the utmost to reach an agreement which all might find acceptable by making concessions towards accommodating their systems to that of the United

States in order to harmonize a minimum number of changes in our domestic legislation. We have sold to the rest of the world our concept of copyright law.[2]

Further evidence of the importance of the United States in the negotiations was provided by the fact that the issue of inclusion of moral rights had been repeatedly voted down, and the principles of the doctrine of *droit d'auteur* were seriously downplayed.[3] For copyright attorneys and presumably for a number of US publishers and agents as well, the text would finally allow the realization of "the long sought goal of a 'Universal republic of letters'."[4] As I have suggested, the "universal republic of letters" was already on its way toward achievement, supported by networks of agents, co-agents, and publishers as early as the 1920s. As far as the circulation of ideas went, Pascale Casanova has underlined that the "republic of letters" had been a reality ever since the last decades of the 19th century. The triumphant tone found in a number of contemporary commentaries clearly links the coming of age of this ideal with US sponsorship and support of the convention. The UCC symbolically heralded a new era in the history of the transatlantic book trade, where the United States would finally become—and be recognized as—a key player, and ultimately take pride of place, from an economic standpoint. Again, as John S. Dubin noted,

> The Convention is of vital importance not only to our economic and financial interests abroad but it is an important part of our foreign policy. We are a great creditor nation and a world economic power not only in the field of tangible properties but also in the intellectual and artistic sphere. Our investments in this latter field are tremendous and through the medium of world commerce, hundreds of millions of dollars are returned annually to this country.[5]

In the midst of the Cold War, the geopolitical impact of the Convention was also emphasized in the contemporary analyses by leading jurors and lawyers. Presented largely as a US achievement, its significance was brought home to the larger American public as an instrument of US cultural diplomacy, vital in the fight against Soviet influence. The absence of the Soviet Union and her satellites was easily interpreted as recognition of the power of the Convention, and, by the same token, of the United States.[6] Unsurprisingly, Secretary of State John Foster Dulles again highlighted the connection, or intersection, between the circulation of books and ideas, with foreign policy, when he urged the Senate to ratify the UCC with these words,

> Participation in the UCC by the United States will not only significantly improve the protection accorded to United States private interests abroad, but will make a substantial contribution to our

general relations with other countries of the free world. Early action by the United States with respect to ratification of the convention will enable the United States to play a leading part in helping to improve international relations in this important field.[7]

The field of American fiction in France was further transformed with the birth of the French *"Livre de poche"* in 1953 and the multiplication of book clubs in the 1950s and 1960s. US agents as well as French co-agents were quick to see the potential earnings in these new ventures. Through Michel Hoffman, the works of John Steinbeck, Marjorie Kinnan Rawlings, Richard Wright, Erskine Caldwell, but also Thomas Merton, Thomas B. Costain, Frank G. Slaughter, Betty MacDonald, and Budd Schulberg found a second life between the covers of the *"Livre de poche."* The series contributed to transforming their bestsellers into long-sellers, with guaranteed printings ranging from 20,000 to over 55,000 copies. The French version of *Reader's Digest* also offered lucrative opportunities for condensations, with guaranteed printings from 100,000 to 120,000.[8] The success of such series and outlets required the drawing up of new contracts and even greater scrutiny paid to the splitting of rights between publisher and proprietor, as well as to the remittance of payments.

Ultimately the passing of the *Code de la propriété intellectuelle* (Intellectual property code) in 1957 helped to professionalize, to some extent, French publishing, as well as to clarify its practices for French authors as well as foreign publishers and agents. Indeed the Code (CPI) represented a long-wished-for synthesis of French copyright legislation that dated back to the Revolution, and aimed to tally French legislation with the recent innovations in international copyright legislation. Most importantly, it codified relations between authors and publishers, focusing on publishing contracts. Probably to the surprise of American publishers and agents, the Code officially defined the publishing contract as a written document, to be signed by the author, and expressly mentioning the rights conceded to the publisher. The mere fact that this essential document required an official definition suggests that variations existed, and implies certain abuses on the part of publishers. As a matter of fact, only in 1977 was a model for a standard contract proposed by the *Syndicat national de l'édition* and the *Société des Gens de Lettres*. Other specifications in the 1957 Code lead us to believe that very possibly French authors in their own country were not as well treated as foreign authors; indeed, the contracts for French rights being drawn up by US or French agents expressly mentioned rights and guarantees that would not be officially codified before 1957, or even before 1992, when the *Code de la propriété intellectuelle* was revised. For instance, the 1992 code made it an obligation for publishers to remit regular royalty statements and to actively pursue the publication of the work under contract. The absence of codification of practices or "ethics code" before 1957 thus partly accounts for the repeated friction points between American publishers and agents on the one hand, and French publishers and co-agents on the other.

By the mid-1980s, works translated from the English language made up 80% of all translations published in France, with works of US origin accounting for 35%; this figure remained stable throughout the 1990s.[9] As the previous chapters show, what we have come to call the "globalization" of the book trade, attested in France by the greater penetration of works originally in the English language, did not begin in the 1960s. A succession of factors thus allowed for the boom in translations to continue after the 1950s; here the local and the global necessarily intersect, as local practices were slowly codified and refined in order to permit a fluid internationalization of the trade. To some extent changes to, and the improvement of, French publishing structures and practices starting in the 1950s were partly due to the impulse of the international book trade, as they compelled nations to harmonize their copyright systems. As agents and co-agents actively participated in the building of the international book trade, we might venture that they too were instrumental in reshaping French local publishing.

In 2010, French sociologist Gisèle Sapiro found in her survey of literary exchanges between New York and Paris that among the first five French houses most responsible for publishing US works in translation in the 1990s, figured Gallimard (first rank), Librairie des Champs Elysées, publishers of "*Le Masque*" series, Presses de la Cité and Albin Michel, all regular correspondents and business partners of Michel Hoffman's in the late 1940s and early 1950s.[10] Agents and co-agents undeniably helped to shape and structure the transatlantic book trade as early as the 1920s, and increasingly in the wake of the Second World War. For sociologists of translation, following Bourdieu's field theory, the transnational field of translation operates on three levels, the cultural, the economic, and the political. I contend that agents work at the crossing of all three; while they might be predominantly economic mediators, they also partake in political and cultural mediations. To all accounts the economic nature of agents' functions is indeed prominent, as the last two chapters attest. In the negotiations of French rights to US works, co-agents were expected to facilitate the circulation of monies, and thus lubricate the chain of transaction. Like US agents abroad, Hoffman acted as broker and banker, forced to comply with French economic and financial policies while aiming to obtain lucrative contracts for both the proprietors and himself. Interestingly, the choice of currency for contracts remains a question to this day in times of financial instability. Some US publishers have simply decided and stipulated that payments should be made in dollars in all cases.[11] Through his negotiations with both parties, Hoffman contributed to determining and assigning an economic value to American works, and often, by the same token, to authors themselves. Although quite often dependent on the terms offered initially by American publishers and on the success and sales of the work within the United States, this economic value might not necessarily reflect that assigned abroad. Furthermore, the adequation between the economic and the literary value of the work might be proportionately at odds, with popular bestsellers sometimes commanding rather high advances.

The period between 1944 and 1955 is especially significant as regards the political dimension of the book trade and of its actors. As we have seen, Hoffman and other co-agents had a central pedagogical mission, as they were made to explain the field of French publishing in terms of political or ideological positions of the imprints, during both the war and the Liberation. In addition to the information on the domestic situation, Hoffman apprised his US partners of the French government's measures concerning French-language publishers in neighboring countries, who had benefitted from the wartime conditions to develop their concerns and compete with Parisian publishers. The possibilities of good match-making thus rested on the co-agents' knowledge of the field at large, and Hoffman was particularly weary of disreputable publishers. Then, Hoffman and fellow agents emulated the essential functions in more general forms of diplomacy (i.e., information gathering, representation, and negotiation). If, according to Jeremy Black, diplomacy is to be understood as the "peaceful management of international relations,"[12] then agents definitely took part in the diplomatic system, both as diplomats of sorts and through their use of classic diplomatic channels. As has been noted, the US Office of War Information provided much-needed help in the transmission and circulation of examination copies or in the supplementing of material resources for the actual publication of volumes in France. As private brokers, agents were also helpers of diplomacy themselves; but whose diplomacy did they serve?

By disseminating French post-war intellectual ideas within the United States through the sale of rights to Camus or Sartre, the Bradley agency can be seen as a mediator in French public diplomacy. In the mid-1940s and early 1950s, Hoffman on the other hand traded mainly in French rights to American books, which suggests that he had become—perhaps unwittingly—a helper to US cultural diplomacy, participating in the distribution of books as "ambassadors" of an American way of life by providing entry into a prized network of publishers, editors, translators, and critics. Hoffman was no doubt aware that in selling serial rights to *Sélection du Reader's Digest*, as the French version was called, he was in fact directly aiding American cultural diplomacy, for the mass-circulation magazine was criticized from early on as the instrument of US cultural "invasion."[13] It is also a well-known fact that the magazine was an instrument of US propaganda operations under the Marshall Plan. Certainly Hoffman worked outside the institutional private-public nexus described by John B. Hench, and many of the titles he negotiated—especially hardboiled crime fiction—fell short of the criteria for "useful" books as determined by the Information Media Guarantee program. Still he would not have established such fruitful connections if he had not, to some extent, shared in some of the culture and values of America.

From this perspective Hoffman did serve as cultural mediator, to the extent that he mediated cultural ideas and values and helped in their adaptation by the French. This is perhaps most particularly evident when we ponder his role as provider of hardboiled detective fiction to two of the most popular crime fiction series, "*Un Mystère*" (Presses de la Cité) and "*Série Noire*" (Gallimard). The latter offers a perfect example of cultural adaptation: on the one hand, the series concentrated the most celebrated US influences of what would develop as the French *roman noir*; on the other hand, although suffused with "Americanisms"—in the identity of the authors, and in the *pastiches* of American novels—the series soon carved out a position for itself as an "icon of French popular culture."[14] Yet in facilitating the so-called invasion of American pulp fiction and the penetration of mass culture through the very importation of a publishing model, Hoffman—along with Duhamel—was probably, in the eyes of many French intellectuals of the time, guilty of desecrating genuine literature and culture, in other terms, high culture. As Thomas Narcejac claimed in his seminal essay on American detective fiction, *La fin d'un bluff: essai sur le roman policier noir américain* (1949), the "*Série noire*" was merely becoming the "cultural equivalent of American fiction factory production," where stories were churned out at the pace of the industrialized work chain."[15]

In a country where anti-Americanism was rampant, where Communist ideas and ideals were prominent, leading many to reject the materialist values for which America came to stand, Hoffman and other agents in France were thorns in the side of French *intellectuels* who viewed American mass culture as noxious and contaminating. It is safe to say that Hoffman, who had fled the Bolshevik regime in the early 1920s and was very active in the networks providing assistance to Soviet dissidents and in passing *zamizdat* copies of Russian texts, could not possibly be suspected of harboring Communist views. Indeed his son has established that the agency was under surveillance in the post-war period.[16] This is not to claim that this would suffice in making Michel Hoffman a blind apologist of the American capitalist way of life. Richard Kuisel forcefully argues in *Seducing the French: the Dilemma of Americanization* (1993) that the threat of an invasion by American culture—viewed both through its "lowering" effect and its strong technical component—fostered a defense of French culture that would ultimately lead to its elevation to the epitome of civilization. For Kuisel, this was a clear sign of the *intellectuels'* and cultural gatekeepers' fear when considering that their positions were coming under attack. Culture could not be equated with

Proust published by the Book-of-the-Month Club; "culture" was, necessarily and quintessentially, *high* culture, unadulterated for the masses.

Is this why American literature remained "Coindreau literature" for so long, to quote Sartre, that eternal gatekeeper? Can this account for the slightly contemptuous categorization of agents and co-agents—along with publishers—merely as commercial mediators? Does this not continue to reflect a strong dichotomy between low and high culture? Quite possibly the weight of Bourdieu's conception of autonomous versus heteronomous poles in the structuring of fields of cultural production has played a role in the preservation of categories such as "letigimate" versus "illegitimate" cultures. Be that as it may, Hoffman was a cultural mediator to the extent that he, like the cultural mediators examined by Pascale Casanova, helped to shape the cultural field of American literature in France, not only by introducing American ideas *in* the texts he helped to translate, but also in the way he presented French publishers with new interrogations and challenges, thereby transforming the field of literary production, in particular through the prism of contractual issues.

As Mary Ann Gillies has shown, early agents in England progressively "insinuated themselves into the fabric of publishing and literary culture, and in the process . . . contributed to a wholesale change in it."[17] Jennifer Sandler concludes from her survey of leading French agents, in very much the same manner; as far as French rights to foreign works are concerned, co-agents in France have now become fixtures in French publishing, albeit unknown to the general public. In the aftermath of the war, agents undeniably participated in the reconstruction of French publishing. Straddling the Atlantic divide, French co-agents mediated between two groups of publishers who had not yet reached the same "maturity," as it were. As a participant on both scenes, pressured by American agents and publishers who were rapidly reorganizing their departments, their filing systems, Michel Hoffman certainly reflected the modernization and rationalization of US publishing to French publishers whose houses remained, for the most part, family businesses. The US—capitalist—model of publishing thus introduced by agents could antagonize or convince. Robert Kuisel has noted how, in the aftermath of the war, French cultural gatekeepers (over)emphasized the "technical" nature of American culture, foregrounding the "Americans' fanatical respect for method, organization, objectivity, science and technology," opposing in a form of "humanistic defense" their own brand of civilization to what they perceived as a menace to French (high) culture.[18] This can be observed in the field of literary production, where many French publishers claimed their attachment to the friendly relations with authors, very much in the way of 19th century gentlemen publishers across the Atlantic, and emphasized their "labor of love." Be that as it may, in the 1950s many French publishers, even those who might disapprove of the "American way," were realizing that something important was "happening in New York City."[19] In fact, Robert Kopp has noted how Gaston Gallimard had realized the economic stakes of publishing, and endeavored to become an *entrepreneur* of letters after two trips to the United States circa 1918. As the famed publisher wrote to author Paul Claudel in 1946,

> In 1919, as I was coming back from America, I understood how necessary it was to give my publishing house a commercial look to distribute the works I so loved. In order to obtain some capital I decided to incorporate. I expanded my office(s), and consequently increased my overheads (. . .) I had to sign contracts with commercial writers (. . .) If I had dedicated myself exclusively to your work, I would not have had the wherewithal to distribute it as it deserved.[20]

While some French cultural gatekeepers may have been irritated by such explicit methods, organization, and rationalization, I contend that the importation of such competences by co-agents precisely helped the advent of a new era for French publishing. The creation and organization of foreign rights departments within the bigger publishing houses in that period may be taken as evidence of a new trend. For Gallimard, Dionys Mascolo was one of the first, following Robert Aron, to handle relations with foreign markets, followed by Michel Mohrt in 1952. Yet it was not before 1960 that Gallimard officially organized its first foreign rights department, to promote their French works on foreign markets.[21] In turn, these specific departments would come to represent a new form of competition for co-agents.

All the same, co-agents' straddling of the cultural divide also allowed them to cope with the pressure exerted by American agents and publishers: being geographically as well as culturally removed from their partners afforded them strategies of resistance. Faced with repeated demands for remittance of statements or payment, they might invoke the infamous French red tape, or French publishers' reluctance to mix finance with art—with or without grounds. Ultimately, the post-war period saw the professionalization of French agents, as evidenced by the organization in 1948 of the first association of literary representatives, which had largely been Michel Hoffman's idea. The creation of this association at that particular time is hardly surprising, considering the various obstacles agents faced, be it from the Office des Changes procedures, or from the French fiscal administration whose understanding of the status of agents varied from one office to the other. The original charter members of the association can certainly be considered as the most important French agents of the time; they included Hoffman, Jenny Bradley, Marie-Louise Bataille, and Marguerite Scialtiel. Organized in a solidly structured and recognized professional association, French agents could probably hope to exert some pressure on the Office des

Changes, as other commercial and professional organizations did. Most significantly, the association was modelled on the New York Society of Authors' Representatives. Hoffman, who initially construed this association as an agents' union, had asked Alan C. Collins to send him the statutes; they were ultimately communicated by Jenny Bradley.[22] Besides the first-hand knowledge of US agents' methods and practices, the influence of the American model of agenting on the French profession as it developed from the mid-1940s onwards is here evidenced. Nevertheless, until very recently the profession remained little known outside publishing, or even recognized fiscally for that matter, partly due to the fact that agents cashed in monies for trading in virtual, intangible goods. As Jennifer Sandler has demonstrated, in the late 1990s agents were still often required to explain their position and the nature of their profession for tax purposes; consequently some were compelled to register under "commercial profession" depending on their annual revenues, while others chose the category of "independent professions," sometimes labelling themselves "editorial counsellors."

In France, authors' representatives, acting as American and British agents do, are few, the most notable being François Samuelson, whose example is repeatedly cited in the press. French publishers remain wary of this profession, especially in its most aggressive "Americanized" form, as epitomized by Andrew "the Jackal" Wylie. Still, they now seem to have reconciled with co-agents, having finally understood the advantages of working with these women—the profession, as in the 1940s, remains largely feminized—and men who will ultimately spare them a lot of administrative hassle, and save them from the "vulgar" task of talking money directly with their transatlantic partners.

Since the death of Jenny S. Bradley in 1983 at the age of 97, the Hoffman agency remains the oldest extant agency in France. Undeniably the early development of close networks with British and American partners—first A.M. Heath, then Curtis Brown, Brandt & Brandt, McIntosh & Otis—and the representation of John Steinbeck, or world rights for Henry Miller, have played an important role in its longevity. In the late 1990s, the agency negotiated an annual average of 200 contracts, and Boris Hoffman assessed that it had sold some 8,000 foreign titles to French publishers since its creation in 1934.[23] It has always been, and remains, a family business: after the death of Michel Hoffman in 1971, his eldest son, Boris, took over the agency. Although he claims to have come unprepared for the task, his command of several foreign languages, his law degree, and his natural warmth, made him one of the most competent, trustworthy, and respected agents in France. He too passed away at the young age of 61, leaving his brother Georges Hoffman at the head the agency. The staff is small: besides Georges Hoffman, there is another agent for the German market, an accountant, a secretary, and a few others. Business is conducted from a cluttered apartment on the Boulevard Saint Germain in Paris, at the very address where the first offices of Sven Nielsen's Presses de la Cité were registered, across the Jardin du Luxembourg. A stone's throw from the historic publishing district—at the heart of Paris.

Notes

1. John Schulman, "A Realistic Treaty," *American Writer*, November 1952, quoted in John S. Dubin, "The Universal Copyright Convention," 118.
2. Dubin, "The Universal Copyright Convention," 118.
3. The Universal Copyright Convention was not retroactive and did not seek to disturb the status quo, in the words of Richard S. MacCarteney, "Toward a Universal Copyright Convention," *Music Library Association* 2, no. 10 (December 1952): 47.
4. Paul J. Sherman, "The Universal Copyright Convention: Its Effect on United States Law," *Columbia Law Review* 55, no. 8 (December 1955): 1137.
5. Dubin, "The Universal Copyright Convention," 119.
6. Ibid., 89.
7. Quoted in Dubin, "The Universal Copyright Convention," 119.
8. See Hoffman account books, BRH, ED.FR.16.05.
9. See Bouvaist, *Pratiques et métiers de l'édition*, 84, and Sapiro, "Les échanges littéraires entre Paris et New York à l'ère de la globalisation." Survey conducted for the Centre européen de sociologie et de sciences politique. April 2010. PDF. http://www.lemotif.fr/fichier/motif_fichier/142/fichier_fichier_etude.paris. new.york.paris.pdf.
10. Sapiro, "Les échanges littéraires entre Paris et New York à l'ère de la globalisation," 35.
11. See interview of Boris Hoffman by Jennifer Sandler, Volume 2, about Random House.
12. Jeremy Black, *A History of Diplomacy*, 12.
13. On the *Sélection du Reader's Digest*, see Brian Angus McKenzie, "Deep Impact: the Cultural Policy of the United States in France, 1948 to 1952," and *Remaking France: Americanization, Public Diplomacy, and the Marshall Plan*.
14. Gorrara, *The Roman noir in Post-War French Culture*, 14.
15. Thomas Narcejac, quoted in Gorrara, *The Roman noir in Post-War French Culture*, 35.
16. Georges Hoffman, interview with the author, February 16, 2014.
17. Gillies, *The Professional Literary Agent in Britain, 1880–1920*, 6.
18. Kuisel, *Seducing the French: The Dilemma of Americanization*, 120.
19. In "Paris capitale éditoriale des étrangers" Jean-Yves Mollier quotes Robert Laffont's claim, circa 1954, that New York had replaced Paris as world capital of letters (386).
20. Gaston Gallimard to Paul Claudel, January 28, 1946, quoted in Kopp, "Regard sur un catalogue de collections," in *Gallimard 1911–2011— Lectures d'un catalogue*, 166.
21. See Sapiro, "A l'international," in *Gallimard, un siècle d'édition, 1911–2011*, 132–134.
22. In November 1947, Hoffman had asked Alan C. Collins to send him the statutes. See Michel Hoffman to Alan C. Collins, November 24, 1947. BRH, AG.15.02. Box 106.
23. Sandler, volume 2, Appendix, 8.

References

Archives

Archives Albin Michel, IMEC.
Archives Hoffman—Bradley. IMEC.
Archives La Table Ronde, IMEC.
Archives Librairie des Champs Elysées—Fonds Hachette, IMEC.
Archives Tallandier, IMEC.
Brandt & Brandt Contract Files, Princeton University.
Charles Scribner's Sons Archive, Foreign Rights—Princeton University.
Curtis Brown, Ltd—Records 1914–2006—Butler Library, Columbia University.
Henry Holt Archives—Princeton University.
Papers of Harold Ober & Associates, Princeton University.
Random House Records, 1925–1999—Butler Library, Columbia University, Correspondence, MS# 1048.
Society of Authors' Representatives Records, 1939–1991, MS# 1173—Butler Library, Columbia University.
The John Day Company, Papers, Princeton University.

Printed Sources

Abel, Richard, Gordon Graham, ed. *Immigrant Publishers: The Impact of Expatriate Publishers in Britain and the United States.* New Brunswick: Transaction Publishers, 2009.
"Agent-auteur-éditeur, un trio qui cherche ses marques," *La lettre de l'Asfored,* Oct-Nov 2006, online, http://www.asfored.org/newsletter.php?nl=35.
"Agents and Authors: Both Sides Are Right." *Coda; Poets and Writers Newsletter 5,* no. 1 (1977): 3–9.
Alfred A. Knopf, Inc. An Inventory of Its Records in the Manuscript Collection at the Harry Ransom Center (online).
Anonymous [One]. "'The Commercialism of Literature' and the Literary Agent." *The Bookman* (October 1906): 134–139.
Assouline, Pierre. *Gaston Gallimard, Un demi-siècle d'édition française.* Paris: Balland, 1984.
Autant-Mathieu, Marie-Christine. "Une rencontre manquée: Boulgakov aux Vieux-Colombier." *Les Cahiers de la Comédie Française* no. 18 (1996): 109–124.

Baneth Jean. "Les paiements internationaux : de la Deuxième Guerre mondiale à la première crise du pétrole." *Revue d'économie financière* "Le financement de l'économie mondiale: l'expérience historique" no. 14 (1990): 133–155.

Barnes, James J. "John Miller: First Transatlantic Publisher's Agent." *Studies in Bibliography* 29 (1976): 373–379.

Barret-Ducrocq, Françoise, ed. *Traduire l'Europe*. Paris: Payot, 1992.

Baruch, Marc-Olivier, ed. *Une poignée de misérables: l'épuration de la société française après la Seconde Guerre mondiale*. Paris: Fayard, 2003.

Baudel, Jules-Marc. "Le droit d'auteur français et le copyright américain: les enjeux." *Revue Française d'Etudes Américaines* no.78 (October 1998): 48–59.

Bayly, Christopher A., Sven Beckert, Matthew Connelly, Isabel Hofmeyr, Wendy Kozol, Patricia Seed. "AHR Conversation: on Transnational History." *The American Historical Review*, 111, no. 5 (December 2006): 1441–1464.

Beal, Shelley Selina. "Theodore Stanton: An American Editor, Syndicator, and Literary Agent in Paris, 1880–1920." Doctoral thesis, University of Toronto, Department of French Studies/Collaborative Program in Book History and Print Culture, 2009.

Benjamin, Curtis G. *U.S. Books Abroad: Neglected Ambassadors*. Washington, D.C.: Library of Congress, 1984.

Berger, Marcel. "Souvenirs d'une agence littéraire (1918–1922)." *Toute l'édition* no. 248 (November 3, 1934): 2.

Bernstein, Martha. "U.S. Cultural Policy in France 1945 to 1958." Doctoral thesis, Université de Montréal, 1998.

Betz, Albrecht, Stefan Martens, ed. *Les Intellectuels et l'Occupation: 1940–1944. Collaborer, partir, résister*. Paris: Editions Autrement, 2004.

Bishop, Wallace Putnam, *The Struggle for International Copyright in the United States*, Ph.D. diss., Boston University, 1959.

Black, Jeremy. *A History of Diplomacy*. London: Reaktion Books, 2010.

Bleton, Paul. "La Frontière médiatique du livre." In *Les Mutations du livre et de l'édition dans le monde du XVIII° siècle à l'an 2000*, edited by Jacques Michon, Jean-Yves Mollier, 453–460. Quebec, Paris: Presses de l'Université de Laval/L'Harmattan, 2001.

Blum, Eleanor. "Paperbound Books in the United States in 1955: A Survey of Content." Doctoral Thesis, PhD in Communications, University of Illinois, 1958.

Bouché, Nicolas. *Intellectual Property Law in France*. The Netherlands: Kluwer Law International, 2011.

Bouché, Nicolas. *Le principe de territorialité de la propriété intellectuelle*. Paris: L'Harmattan, 2002.

Bourdieu, Pierre. "Les conditions sociales de la circulation internationale des idées." *Actes de la recherche en sciences sociales* 145 (December 2002): 3–8.

Bouvaist, Jean-Marie. *Pratiques et métiers de l'édition*. Paris: Editions Promodis/UFR Communication (Paris XIII), 1986.

Brault, Julien. "La Banque de France et les transactions internationales de la France des années 1930 aux années 1970." Communication, Mission Historique de la Banque de France Seminar, May 2011. http://www.banque-france.fr/fileadmin/user_upload/banque_de_france/histoire/mission_historique/la-Banque-de-France-et-les-transactions_internationales-de-la-France-des-annees-1930–1970-Julien-Brault.pdf.

Brier, Evan. *Novel Marketplace: Mass Culture, the Book Trade, and Postwar American Fiction*. Philadelphia: University of Pennsylvania Press, 2009.

Brown, Ellen F., John Wiley. *Margaret Mitchell's Gone with the Wind: A Bestseller's Odyssey from Atlanta to Hollywood*. Plymouth: Taylor Trade, 2011.

Brown, James Oliver. "Literary Agents." *The Writer* (July 1967): 15–17.

Brown, Matthew P. "Book History, Sexy Knowledge, and the Challenge of the New Boredom." *American Literary History* 16, no. 4 (2004): 688–706.

Bruyère, Claire. "Du prestige de l'étranger en littérature." *Histoire(s) de livres—Le livre et l'édition dans le monde anglophone*. Cahiers Charles V 32 (2002): 195–220.

Buisson, E. "Ce que fut, ce qu'est, ce que doit être l'agent littéraire." *Toute l'édition* no. 319 (April 11, 1936): 7.

Casanova, Pascale. "Consécration et accumulation de capital littéraire." *Actes de la recherche en sciences sociales* 144 (September 2002): 7–20.

Casanova, Pascale. *La République mondiale des lettres*. Paris: Seuil, 1999.

Cerisier, Alban, Pascal Fouché, ed. *Gallimard, un siècle d'édition, 1911–2011*. Paris: BNF/Gallimard, 2011.

Charle, Christophe. "Comparaisons et transferts en histoire culturelle de l'Europe. Quelques réflexions à propos de recherches récentes." *Les Cahiers IRICE* "Histoires croisées—Réflexions sur la comparaison internationale en histoire," online. http://irice.univ-paris1.fr/spip.php?article567.

Charle, Christophe. "Le Temps des hommes doubles." *Revue d'Histoire moderne et contemporaine* 39, no. 1 (January-March 1992): 73–85.

Chénetier, Marc. "American Literature in France; Pleasures in Perspective." In *As Others Read Us: International Perspectives on American Literature*, edited by Huck Gutman, 79–95. Amherst: University of Massachusetts Press, 1991.

Childs, William M. and Donald E. McNeil, ed. *American Books Abroad: Toward a National Policy*. Washington, D.C.: Helen Dwight Reid Educational Foundation, 1986.

Cloonan, William and Jean-Philippe Poste. "Literary Agents and the Novel in 1996." *The French Review* 70, no. 6 (May 1997): 796–806.

Coers, Donald V. *John Steinbeck Goes to War: The Moon Is Down as Propaganda*. Tuscaloosa, Al.: University of Alabama Press, 2006.

Coindreau, Maurice-Edgar. "William Faulkner in France." *Yale French Studies* no. 10, "French American Literary Relationships" (1952): 85–91.

Coindreau, Maurice-Edgar [1974]. *Mémoires d'un traducteur. Entretiens avec Christian Giudicelli*. Paris: Gallimard, 1992.

Collins, Alan C. "On Improving the Lot of Authors, Grub Life on 1952's Grub Street." *The Saturday Review* (February 16, 1952): 14; 45–46.

Colvert, James B. "Agent and Author: Ellen Glasgow's Letters to Paul Revere Reynolds." *Studies in Bibliography* 14 (1961): 177–196.

Cooper-Richet, Diana. "La librairie étrangère à Paris au XIXe siècle. Un milieu perméable aux innovations et aux transferts." *Actes de la recherche en sciences sociales. Édition, Éditeurs (1)* 126–127 (March 1999): 60–69.

Cooper-Richet, Diana, Jean-Yves Mollier and Ahmed Silem, ed. *Passeurs culturels dans le monde des médias et de l'édition en Europe (XIXI° et XXI° siècles)*. Lyon: Presses de l'ENSSIB, 2005.

"Cornell Alumni News." vol XXIII, no. 24, March 7, 1921.

Coser, Lewis A. Coser, Charles Kadushin, and Walter W. Powell. *Books: The Culture & Commerce of Publishing*. New York: Basic Books, 1982.

Cossu-Beaumont, Laurence. "Popular Books and the Marketing of African American Best-Sellers." In *Race, Ethnicity and Publishing in America*, edited by Cécile Cottenet, 193–209. Basingstoke: Palgrave Macmillan, 2014.

Curtis Brown, Albert. "Bargaining with Writers." *Harper's Monthly Magazine* 171 (June/November 1935): 26–35.

Curtis Brown, Albert. *Contacts*. New York and London: Harper & Brothers, 1935.

"Curtis Brown Dies; Literary Agent, 78." *The New York Times*, September 24, 1945, 19.

"Curtis Brown, Literary Agent, Is Dead at 78." *The Herald Tribune*, September 24, 1945.

Dambricourt, Isabelle. "L'implantation des traductions américaines en France de 1900 à 1961: le cas de la *Bibliothèque cosmopolite* de Stock." Masters' Thesis, Socio-Cultural History, dir. Jean-Yves Mollier, Université de Versaille-St Quentin en Yvelines, 2001.

Dardis, Tom. *Firebrand: The Life of Horace Liveright*. New York: Random House, 1995.

Darnton, Robert. "What Is the History of Books?" In *The Book History Reader*, edited by David Finkelstein and Alistair MacCleery, 9–26. London: Routledge, 2002.

Darnton, Robert. "What Is the History of Books? Revisited." *Modern Intellectual History* 4, no. 3 (2007): 495–508.

De la Porte, René. "L'édition populaire aux Etats-Unis." *Toute l'édition* no. 362 (March 6, 1937): 8.

Déom, Laurent. "Le roman scout dans les années trente et le chronotope du 'grand jeu'." *Strenæ* 6 (December 20, 2013). Accessed 28 September 2014. http://strenae.revues.org/1072; doi:10.4000/strenae.1072.

Dietzel, Thomas, and Hans-Otto Hügel. *Zeitschriften 1880–1945: Ein Repertorium, Volume 1*. Munchen, New York, Paris: Saur 1988.

Diu, Isabelle and Elisabeth Parinet. *Histoire des Auteurs*. Paris: Perrin, 2013.

Dubin, Joseph S. "The Universal Copyright Convention." *University of California Law Review* 42 (1954): 89–119.

Dubosclard, Alain. *Le livre français aux Etats-Unis 1900–1970*. Paris: L'Harmattan, 2000.

Ely, Stanley E. "Decades of Books: The Curtis Brown Agency." *Poets and Writers Magazine* 24, no. 2 (March/April 1996): 32–41.

Engle, John. "Introduction: Friends and Strangers, Author(s)." *Twentieth Century Literature* 49, no. 1 "American Writers and France" (2003): 1–11.

Erval, François. "Tendances actuelles." *La Gazette des Lettres* 6, no. 4 (January 15, 1951): 20–23.

Espagne, Michel. "Transferts culturels et histoire du livre." *Histoire et civilisation du livre, revue internationale* V (2009): 201–218.

Esposito, Chiarella. "French International Monetary Policies in the 1940s." *French Historical Studies* 17, no. 1 (Spring, 1991): 117–140.

Feather, John. *A History of British Publishing*. 2nd edition. London: Routledge, 2006.

Fine, Richard. "American Authorship and the Ghost of Moral Rights." *Book History* 13 (2010): 218–250.

Finkelstein, David, and Alistair McCleery. *An Introduction to Book History.* New York, London: Routledge, 2005.

Finkelstein, David. *The House of Blackwood: Author-Publisher Relations in the Victorian Era.* University Park: Pennsylvania State University Press, 2002.

Finkelstein, Herman. "The Universal Copyright." *American Journal of Comparative Law* 2, no. 2 (Spring, 1953): 198–204.

Firth, John. "James Pinker to James Joyce, 1915–1920." *Studies in Bibliography* 21 (1968): 205–224.

Ford, Hugh [1975]. *Published in Paris; L'édition américaine et anglaise à Paris 1920–1939.* Paris: IMEC Editions, 1996.

Fouché, Pascal, ed. *Gallimard 1911–2011—Lectures d'un catalogue—Les entretiens de la Fondation des Treilles.* Paris: Gallimard, 2012.

Fouché, Pascal, ed. *L'Edition française depuis 1945.* Paris: Editions du Cercle de la librairie, 1998.

Fouché, Pascal. *L'Edition française sous l'Occupation, 1940–1944.* Volumes I and II. Paris: Bibliothèque de Littérature française contemporaine de l'Université Paris 7, 1987.

Fradkin, Philip L. [2008]. *Wallace Stegner and the American West.* Berkeley and Los Angeles: University of California Press, 2009.

Freedman, Jeffrey. *Material Texts: Books Without Borders in Enlightenment Europe, French Cosmopolitanism and German Literary Markets.* Philadelphia: University of Pennsylvania Press, 2012.

"From Royalties to Options." *Coda. Poets and Writers Newsletter* 10, no. 5 (June/July 1983): 14–17.

Gale, Maggie. *West End Women: Women and the London Stage, 1918–1962.* London: Routledge, 1996.

Gamsa, Mark. "Cultural Translation and the Transnational Circulation of Books." *Journal of World History* 22, no. 3 (2011): 553–575.

Gillies, Mary Ann. *The Professional Literary Agent in Britain, 1880–1920.* Toronto: University of Toronto Press, 2007.

Goldstein, Paul. *International Copyright: Principles, Laws, and Practice.* Oxford: Oxford University Press, 2001.

Golsan, Richard. "From French Anti-Americanism and Americanization to the 'American Enemy'?" In *The Americanization of Europe: Culture, Diplomacy, and anti-Americanism since 1945*, edited by Alexander Stephan, 44–68. New York: Berghan Books, 2006.

Gorrara, Claire. *The Roman noir in Post-War French Culture.* Oxford, New York: Oxford University Press, 2003.

Gouanvic, Jean-Marc. "John Steinbeck et la censure: le cas de *The Moon is Down* traduit en français pendant la Seconde Guerre mondiale." *TTR: Traduction, terminologie, rédaction* 15, no. 2 (2002): 191–202. http://id.erudit.org/iderudit/007484ar. Accessed July 15, 2014.

Gouanvic, Jean-Marc. "Panorama de la traduction-importation de la littérature américaine en France (1820–1960)." *Genèses de Textes—Textgenesen* Volume 3: *Event or Incident/Evénement ou Incident: On the Role of Translation in the Dynamics of Cultural Exchange/Du rôle des traductions dans les processus d'échanges culturels.* Bern: Peter Lang, 2010, 157–176.

Gouanvic, Jean-Marc. *Sociologie de la Traduction. La science-fiction américaine dans l'espace culturel français des années 1950.* Amiens: Artois Presses Université, 1999.

Gousseff, Catherine. *L'Exil russe, la fabrique du réfugié apatride*. Paris: CNRS Editions, 2008.

Grannis, Chandler B. ed. *What Happens in Book Publishing*. New York: Columbia University Press, 1957.

Greenfield, George. *A Smattering of Monsters; A Kind of Memoir*. Columbia, S.C.: Camden House, 1995.

Greenspan, Ezra. *George Palmer Putnam, Representative American Publisher*. Philadelphia: State University of Pennsylvania Press, 2000.

Groves, Jeffrey. "Courtesy of the Trade." In *A History of the Book in America, Volume 3, The Industrial Book, 1840–1880*, edited by Scott E. Casper and Janice Radway, 139–147. Chapel Hill: University of North Carolina Press, 2007.

Gross, Gerald. ed. *Publishers on Publishing*. London: Secker & Warburg, 1962.

Hanrahan, John Keith. Comp. *The Literary Market Place. A Directory for Publishers, Broadcasters and Advertisers*. New York: R.R. Bowker, 1940–1955.

Heilbron, Johan. "Echanges culturels transnationaux et mondialisation: quelques réflexions." *Regards sociologiques* 22 (2001): 141–154.

Heilbron, Johan. "Le système mondial des traductions." Translated by Anaïs Bokobza. In *Les contradictions de la globalisation éditoriale*, edited by Gisèle Sapiro, 253–274. Paris: Nouveau monde éditions, 2009.

Hemmungs Wirten, Eva. "A Diplomatic *Salto Morale*: Translation Trouble in Berne, 1884–1886." *Book History* 14 (2011): 88–109.

Hench, John B. *Books as Weapons: Propaganda, Publishing, and the Battle for Global Markets in the Era of World War II*. Cornell: Cornell University Press, 2010.

Hepburn, James. *The Author's Empty Purse and the Rise of the Literary Agent*. Oxford: Oxford University Press, 1968.

Hill, Murray. "Murray Hill Views Literary Agents." *The Bookman* (November 1921): 234–240.

"Histoire des editions Stock." http://www.editions-stock.fr/sites/default/files/admin/historique_complet_a_telecharger.pdf, accessed July 1, 2014.

Hoffman, Georges. "Agent littéraire." In *Dictionnaire encyclopédique du livre*, edited by Pascal Fouché et al., 39–40. Paris: Éditions du Cercle de la librairie, 2002.

Holman, Valerie. "The Impact of War: British publishers and French publications 1940–1944." *Publishing History* 48 (2000): 41–65.

Holt, Henry. "The Commercialization of Literature." *Atlantic Monthly* 96, no. 5 (November 1905): 577–599.

Howsam, Leslie. "What Is the Historiography of Books? Recent Studies in Authorship, Publishing, and Reading in Modern Britain and North America." *Historical Journal* 51, no. 4 (December 2008): 1089–1101.

Index Translationum, 1932–1960.

Iriye, Akira. *Global and Transnational History: The Past, Present, and Future*. Basingstoke: Palgrave Macmillan, 2013.

Irr, Caren. *Pink Pirates. Contemporary American Writers and Copyright*. Iowa City: University of Iowa Press, 2010.

Interview of Georges Borchardt by Jolgie Ferrari-Adler, September/October 2009, accessed June 27, 2014. http://www.pw.org/content/agents_editors_qampa_agent_georges_borchardt.

James, Marion. "The United States and the Movement for Universal Copyright, 1945–52." *Library Quarterly* 25, no. 1 (1955): 219–234.

Jaszi, Peter and Martha Woodmansee. "Copyright in Transition." In *A History of the Book in America, vol. 4, Print in Motion: The Expansion of Publishing and Reading in the United States, 1880–1940*, edited by Carl F. Kaestle and Janice Radway, 90–101. Chapel Hill: University of North Carolina Press, 2009.

Jeanpierre, Laurent. "'Modernisme' américain et espace littéraire français : réseaux et raisons d'un rendez-vous différé." In *L'espace culturel transnational*, edited by Anna Boschetti, 385–426. Paris: Nouveau monde éditions, 2010.

Jenn, Ronald. "From American Frontier to European Borders," *Book History* 9 (2006): 235–254.

Johnson, Malcolm. "The Foreign Distribution of American Publications." *Library Quarterly* 24, no. 1 (1954): 114–123.

Johnston, Robert H. *New Mecca, New Babylon: Paris and the Russian Exiles, 1920–1945*. Montreal: McGill-Queen's University Press, 1988.

Jordan, John O. and Robert L. Patten, ed. [1995] *Literature in the Marketplace: Nineteenth-Century British Publishing & Reading Practices*. Cambridge: Cambridge University Press, 2003.

Joseph, Michael. "The Literary Agent." *The Bookman* (September 1925): 34–39.

Joste, Juliette. "L'Agent littéraire en France—réalités et perspectives." Unpublished report for MOTiF (June 2010). http://www.lemotif.fr/fichier/motif_fichier/161/fichier_fichier_l.agent.litta.raire.en.france.pdf.

Juratic, Sabine. "Commerce et marchés du livre, vus de Paris, à l'époque moderne." In *50 ans d'histoire du livre: 1958–2008*, edited by Dominique Varry, 44–61. Lyon: Presses de l'ENSSIB, 2014.

Kahane, Jack. *Memoirs of a Booklegger*. Newmarket, ON.: The Obolus Press, 2010.

Kammen, Michael. *American Culture, American Tastes; Social Change and the 20th Century*. New York: Basic Books, 1999.

Kaplan, Fred. *Gore Vidal, A Biography*. London: Bloomsbury Publishing, 2000.

Karl, Frederick R. "Conrad and Pinker: Some Aspects of the Correspondence." *Journal of Modern Literature* 5, no. 1 (February 1976): 59–78.

Kennedy, Liam, and Scott Lucas. "Enduring Freedom: Public Diplomacy and U.S. Foreign Policy." *American Quarterly* 57, no. 23 (June 2005): 309–333.

Kennedy, Richard S. ed. *Beyond Love and Loyalty. The Letters of Thomas Wolfe and Elizabeth Nowell*. Chapel Hill and London: University of North Carolina Press, 1983.

Kuisel, Richard. *Seducing the French: The Dilemma of Americanization*. Berkeley: University of California Press, 1993.

La Pie-Grièche. "Il nous est né des traducteurs nouvelle manière, mais il faut encore s'entendre." *Toute l'édition* no. 361 (February 7, 1937): 3.

Lacy, Dan. "The Overseas Book Program of the United States Government." *Library Quarterly* 24, no. 1 (1954: January/October): 178–191.

Lacy, Dan. "The Role of American Books Abroad." *Foreign Affairs* 34, no. 3 (1956): 405–417.

Lacy, Dan, Charles G. Bolté and Peter S. Jennison, eds. *Library Trends* 5, no. 1 "American Books Abroad" (July 1956).

Lahire, Bernard. *Franz Kafka. Eléments pour une théorie de la création littéraire*. Paris: La Découverte, 2010.

Larocque, Edward Tinker. "Our Books Abroad." *Books Abroad* 22, no. 1 (Winter 1948): 11–13.

Latour, Bruno. *Reassembling the Social: An Introduction to Actor-Network-Theory*. Oxford: Oxford University Press, 2005.

Letourneux, Matthieu. "Supports, réseaux, définitions—logiques sérielles et cohérences discursives dans les collections populaires pour la jeunesse de l'entre-deux guerres." *Strenæ* 6 (December 20, 2013)/ Accessed 28 September, 2014. http://strenae.revues.org/1065; doi:10.4000/strenae.1065.

"Leurs traductions préférées." *La Gazette des Lettres* 6, no. 4 (January 15, 1951): 28–29.

Levantal, Léo and L. Anselme-Rabinovitch. "Foreign Investments in France and French Exchange Control." *American Journal of Comparative Law* 3, no. 3 (Summer 1954): 427–428.

Levin, Harry. "Some European Views of Contemporary American Literature." *American Quarterly* 1, no. 3 (Autumn 1949): 264–279.

Levine, Lawrence. *Highbrow/Lowbrow: The Emergence of Cultural Hierarchy in America*. Cambridge, Mass.: Harvard University Press, 1988.

Lhomeau, Franck. "Le roman noir à l'américaine." *Temps Noir* no. 4 (2000): 4–33.

Lhomeau, Franck. "Le véritable lancement de la Série Noire." *Temps Noir* no. 4 (2000): 50–127.

Loué, Thomas. "Le Congrès international des éditeurs 1896–1938—Autour d'une forme de sociabilité professionnelle internationale." In *Les Mutations du livre et de l'édition dans le monde du XVIII° siècle à l'an 2000*, edited by Jacques Michon and Jean-Yves Mollier, 531–543. Quebec, Paris: Presses de l'Université de Laval/L'Harmattan, 2001.

Lourie, Samuel Anatole. "The Trading with the Enemy Act." *Michigan Law Review* 42, no. 2 (October 1943): 205–234.

Luey, Beth. "The Organization of the Book Publishing Industry." In *A History of the Book in America, vol 5: The Enduring Book, Print Culture in Postwar America*, edited by David Paul Nord, Joan Shelley Rubin, and Michael Schudson, 29–54. Chapel Hill: University of North Carolina Press, 2009.

Luey, Beth. *Expanding the American Mind: Books and the Popularization of Knowledge*. Amherst: University of Massachusetts Press, 2010.

Lynes, Carlos, Jr. "The 'Nouvelle Revue Française' and American Literature, 1909–1940." *The French Review* 19, no. 3 (January 1946): 159–167.

MacCarteney, Richard S. "Toward a Universal Copyright Convention." *Music Library Association* 2, no. 10 (December 1952): 46–48.

Malraux, André. "A Preface for Faulkner's *Sanctuary*." *Yale French Studies*, no. 10, "French-American Literary Relationships" (1952): 92–94.

Marcy, Gérard. "Quelques aspects de l'évolution et de la réglementation française du commerce extérieur depuis 1945: contrôle des changes et règlements internationaux." *Revue économique* 9, no. 3 (May 1958): 348–384.

Martin, Henri-Jean, Roger Chartier, Jean-Pierre Vivet, ed. *Histoire de l'édition française, Tome IV: Le livre concurrencé, 1900–1950*. Paris: Promodis, 1986.

Mathy, Jean-Philippe. *Extrême-Occident: French Intellectuals and America*. Chicago: University of Chicago Press, 1993.

McDonald, Peter D. *British Literary Culture and Publishing Practice, 1880–1914*. Cambridge: Cambridge University Press, 1997.

McGill, Meredith. *American Literature and the Culture of Reprinting*. Philadelphia: University of Pennsylvania Press, 2007.

McGill, Meredith. "Copyright." In *A History of the Book in America, vol. 3, The Industrial Book, 1840–1880*, edited by Scott E. Casper and Janice Radway, 158–178. Chapel Hill: University of North Carolina Press, 2007.

McKenzie, Brian Angus. "Deep Impact: the Cultural Policy of the United States in France, 1948 to 1952." Doctoral Dissertation, History, State University of New York at Stony Brook, 2000.

McKenzie, Brian Angus. *Remaking France: Americanization, Public Diplomacy, and the Marshall Plan*. Oxford: Berghahnbooks, 2005.

McNamara, Jack Donald. "Literary Agent A.D. Peters and Evelyn Waugh, 1928–1966: Quantitative Judgments Don't Apply." Doctoral Thesis, University of Texas at Austin, 1983.

Mendershausen, Horst. "Foreign Aid with and without Dollar Shortage." *Review of Economics and Statistics* 33, no. 1 (February 1951): 38–48.

Michon, Jacques and Jean-Yves Mollier. *Les Mutations du livre et de l'édition dans le monde du XVIII° siècle à l'an 2000*. Quebec, Paris: Presses de l'Université de Laval/L'Harmattan, 2001.

Miller, Laura J. and David Paul Nord. "Reading the Data on Books, Newspapers and Magazines, A Statistical Appendix." In *A History of the Book in America, vol 5: The Enduring Book, Print Culture in Postwar America*, edited by David Paul Nord, Joan Shelley Rubin, and Michael Schudson, 503–518. Chapel Hill: University of North Carolina Press, 2009.

Mollier, Jean-Yves. "L'édition française dans la tourmente de la Seconde Guerre mondiale." *Vingtième Siècle. Revue d'histoire* 4, no. 112 (2011): 127–138.

Mollier, Jean-Yves. *Édition, presse et pouvoir en France au XXe siècle*. Paris: Fayard, 2008.

Mollier, Jean-Yves. "Paris capitale éditoriale des mondes étrangers." In *Le Paris des étrangers depuis 1945*, edited by Antoine Marès, Pierre Milza, 373–394. Paris: Publications de la Sorbonne, 1994.

Moretti, Franco. *Atlas of the European Novel, 1800–1900*. London, New York: Verso, 1998.

Moretti, Franco. *Graphs, Maps, Trees: Abstract Models for a Literary History*. London, New York: Verso, 2005.

Murat, Laure. *Passage de l'Odéon, Sylvia Beach, Adrienne Monnier et la vie littéraire à Paris dans l'entre-deux guerres*. Paris: Gallimard, 2003.

Nadeau, Maurice. "Une littérature d'urgence." *La Gazette des Lettres* 6, no. 4 (January 15, 1951): 17–20.

Neyfakh, Leon. "Glamour, Amour: A Grande Dame of Publishing Looks Back." *The New York Observer* online (February 26, 2008) [accessed April 8, 2009].

Nicoll, William Robertson. "The Literary Agent." *The Bookman* (May 1895): 249–251.

Nimmer, David. "Nation, Duration, Violation, Harmonization: an International Copyright Proposal for the United States." *Law and Contemporary Problems* 55, no. 2 (1992): 211–239.

Ninkovich, Frank A. *The Diplomacy of Ideas: U.S. Foreign Policy and Cultural Relations, 1938–1950*. Cambridge: Cambridge University Press, 1981.

Nord, David Paul, Joan Shelley Rubin, and Michael Schudson, ed. *A History of the Book in America, Vol. 5: The Enduring Book, Print Culture in Postwar America*. Chapel Hill: University of North Carolina Press, 2009.

O'Brien, Justin. "American Books and French Readers." *College English* 1, no. 6 (March 1940): 480–487.

Ogborn, Miles and Charles W.J. Withers. *Geographies of the Book*. London: Ashgate, 2010.

Olivero, Isabelle. "The Paperback Revolution in France, 1850–1950." In *The Culture of the Publisher's Series, Vol. 1, Authors, Publishers and the Shaping of Taste*, edited by John Spiers, 72–87. Basingstoke: Palgrave Macmillan, 2011.

Olivero, Isabelle. *L'invention de la collection*. Paris: IMEC Editions; Editions de la Maison des Sciences de l'Homme, 1999.

Page, Walter Hines. [1905] *A Publisher's Confession*. Garden City and New York: Doubleday, Page & Company, 1923.

Parfait, Claire. "Un succès américain en France: *La Case de l'Oncle Tom*." *E-rea* 7, no. 2 (2010). Accessed 20 June 2014. http://erea.revues.org/981; doi:10.4000/erea.981.

Parinet, Elisabeth. *Une histoire de l'édition à l'époque contemporaine, XIX°–XX° siècle*. Paris: Seuil, 2004.

Perrot, Michelle. "Qu'est-ce qu'un métier de femme?" In *Les femmes ou les silences de l'histoire*, 201–207. Paris: Flammarion, 1998.

Peterson, Wallace C. "Planning and Economic Progress in France." *World Politics* 9, no. 3 (April, 1957): 351–382.

Peyre, Henri. "American Literature through French Eyes." *Virginia Quarterly Review* 23, no. 3 (1947): 421–438.

Pierrat, Emmanuel [2000]. *Le droit d'auteur et l'édition*. Paris: Editions du Cercle de la Librairie, 2005.

Pierrat, Emmanuel. *Le droit du livre*. Paris: Editions du Cercle de la Librairie, 2005.

Poulain, Martine [2008]. *Livres pillés, lectures surveillées. Une histoire des bibliothèques françaises sous l'Occupation*. Paris: Gallimard, 2013.

"Propriété Littéraire et artistique—Traductions." *Bibliographie de la France, Journal Général & Officiel de la Librairie* 2, no. 40 (October 4, 1935): 203.

"Quelle sûreté donne le chèque barré?" *Bibliographie de la France* 2, no. 22 (May 27, 1932): 159.

Radway, Janice. *A Feeling for Books; The Book-of-the-Month Club, Literary Taste, and Middle Class Desire*. Chapel Hill: University of North Carolina Press, 1997.

Raeff, Marc. *Russia Abroad. A Cultural History of the Russian Emigration, 1919–1939*. Oxford, New York: Oxford University Press, 1990.

Raven, James. "Selling Books Across Europe, c. 1450–1800: An Overview." *Publishing History* 34 (January 1, 1993): 5–19.

Rectanus, Mark W. *Literary Series in the Federal Republic of Germany from 1960 to 1980*. Wiesbaden: Otto Harrassowitz, 1984.

Reynolds, Paul R. "The Literary Agent; His Function, Life, and Power." *Saturday Review* (October 8, 1966): 113–114.

Reynolds, Paul R., Jr. *The Middle Man*. New York: William Morrow & Co., 1971.

Reynolds, Paul R. "Should Every Writer Have an Agent?" *Saturday Review* (January 9, 1965): 69–75.

Rice, Howard C. "Seeing Ourselves as the French See Us." *The French Review* 21, no. 6 (May 1948): 432–441.

Richards, Pamela Spence. *Scientific Information in Wartime. The Allied-German Rivalry, 1939–1945*. Westport, Ct.: Greenwood Press, 1994.

Richter, Noë. "La lecture publique de 1940 à 1945." In *La vie culturelle sous Vichy*, edited by Jean-Pierre Rioux, 117–135. Paris: Editions Complexe, 1990.

Rioux, Jean-Pierre, ed. *La vie culturelle sous Vichy*. Paris: Editions Complexe, 1990.

Roger, Philippe. *The American Enemy: The History of French Anti-Americanism*. Translated by Sharon Bowman. Chicago: University of Chicago Press, 2005.

Rolls, Alistair, "An Uncertain Space: (Dis-)Locating the Frenchness of French and Australian Detective Fiction." In *Mostly French: French (in) Detective Fiction, Modern French Identities*, vol. 88, Oxford: Peter Lang, 2009, 19–51.

Rubin, Joan Shelley. *The Making of Middlebrow Culture*. Chapel Hill: University of North Carolina Press, 1992.

Samuels, Edward. *The Illustrated Story of Copyright*. New York: St Martin's Griffin, 2002.

Sandler, Jennifer. "Les agents littéraires en France." Master's Thesis, Socio-Cultural History. Under the supervision of Jean-Yves Mollier, Université de Versailles-St Quentin en Yvelines, France, 2001.

Sapiro, Gisèle. "A l'international." In *Gallimard, un siècle d'édition, 1911–2011*, edited by Alban Cerisier and Pascal Fouché, 124–147. Paris: BNF/Gallimard, 2011.

Sapiro, Gisèle, ed. *Les contradictions de la globalisation éditoriale*. Paris: Nouveau Monde éditions, 2009.

Sapiro, Gisèle. "Les échanges littéraires entre Paris et New York à l'ère de la globalisation." Survey conducted for the Centre européen de sociologie et de sciences politique. April 2010. PDF. http://www.lemotif.fr/fichier/motif_fichier/142/fichier_fichier_etude.paris.new.york.paris.pdf.

Sapiro, Gisèle, ed. *Translatio; Le marché de la traduction en France à l'heure de la mondialisation*. Paris: CNRS Editions, 2008.

Sapiro, Gisèle. *La guerre des écrivains, 1940–1953*. Paris: Fayard, 1999.

Sartre, Jean-Paul. "American Novelists in French Eyes." *Atlantic Monthly* 78, no. 2 (August 1946): 114–118.

Saunders, Max [1996]. *Ford Madox Ford: A Dual Life: Volume II: The After-War World*. Oxford: Oxford University Press, 2012.

Schweitzer, Sylvie. *Les Femmes on toujours travaillé. Une histoire du travail des femmes aux XIX° et XX7 siècles*. Paris: Odile Jacob, 2002.

Serry, Hervé. "Constituer un catalogue littéraire. La place des traductions dans l'histoire des éditions du Seuil." *Actes de la Recherche en Sciences Sociales*, no. 144 (2002): 70–79.

Sherman, Paul J. "The Universal Copyright Convention: Its Effect on United States Law." *Columbia Law Review* 55, no. 8 (December 1955): 1137–1175.

Simonin, Anne. *Les Editions de Minuit, 1942–1955: le devoir d'insoumission*. Paris: IMEC Editions, 1994.

Smithies, A. "European Unification and the Dollar Problem." *Quarterly Journal of Economics* 64, no. 2 (May 1950): 159–182.

Smulyan, Susan. *Popular Ideologies: Mass Culture at Mid-century*. Philadelphia: University of Pennsylvania Press, 2007.

Snaije, Olivia. "French Literary Agents Stage a Quiet Revolution." http://publishingperspectives.com/2009/12/french-literary-agents-stage-a-quiet-revolution/ December 15, 2009, accessed May 22, 2014.

Spaulding, Martha. "'Martini-Age Victorian'." *Atlantic Monthly* May 2004. Online.

Strauss, Helen. *A Talent for Luck, An Autobiography*. New York: Random House, 1979.

Sussman, Jody. "United States Information Service libraries." Occasional Paper, University of Illinois Graduate School of Library Science, no. 111 (December 1973).

Tadié, Benoît. "Essor du récit criminel transatlantique: esquisse d'un champ de recherche" *Transatlantica* 1 (June 19, 2012), accessed 26 October 2014. http://transatlantica.revues.org/5785.

Tebbel, John. *A History of Book Publishing in the United States, Vol IV: The Great Change, 1940–1980*. New York: R.R. Bowker, 1981.

Tebbel, John. *Between Covers, the Rise and Transformation of American Book Publishing*. New York, Oxford: Oxford University Press, 1987.

The Authors' Guild. "Your Book Contract—A Guide for the Use of Members of the Authors' Guild in the Negotiation of Contracts with Book Publishers," 1961.

"The Editor Parenthesizes." *Books Abroad* 19, no. 1 (1945): 98–99.

"The Ill Wind That Blew Good to Swiss Publishers." *Books Abroad*, 19, no. 4 (1945): 357–358.

"The Publishing Situation in France." *Books Abroad* 19, no. 4 (1945): 356–357.

The Writers' and Artists' Year-Book, 1912–1964.

Trédant, Paul. "Gangsters de l'édition—leur activité aux Etats-Unis." *Toute l'édition*, no. 264 (February 23, 1935): 4.

Varry, Dominique, ed. *50 ans d'histoire du livre: 1958–2008*. Lyon: Presses de l'ENSSIB, 2014.

Venuti, Lawrence. *The Scandals of Translation, Towards an Ethics of Difference*. London: Routledge, 1998.

Vergez-Chaignon, Bénédicte. *Histoire de l'épuration*. Paris: Larousse, 2010.

Weber, Ronald. *Hired Pens: Professional Writers in America's Golden Age of Print*. Athens: Ohio University Press, 1997.

West, James L. *American Authors and the Literary Marketplace since 1900*. Philadelphia: University of Pennsylvania Press, 1988.

West, James L. "The Chace Act and Anglo-American Literary Relations." *Studies in Bibliography* 45 (1992): 303–311.

West, James L. "The Expansion of the National Book Trade System." In *A History of the Book in America, vol. 4, Print in Motion: The Expansion of Publishing and Reading in the United States, 1880–1940*, edited by Carl F. Kaestle and Janice Radway, 78–89. Chapel Hill: University of North Carolina Press, 2009.

Who's Who in Literature? edited by Mark Meredith, Liverpool: The Literary Year Books Press, 1927.

Wilfert-Portal, Blaise. "Cosmopolis et l'Homme invisible." *Actes de la Recherche en Sciences Sociales* no. 144 "Traductions: les échanges littéraires internationaux" (September 2002): 33–46.

Wilfert-Portal, Blaise. "La place de la littérature étrangère dans le champ littéraire français autour de 1900." *Histoire & mesure* XXIII, no. 2 (December 1, 2011). Accessed 17 June 2014. http://histoiremesure.revues.org/3613.

Wincor, Richard. *Literary Rights Contracts*. New York: Harcourt Brace, 1979.

Winship, Michael. "The Rise of a National Book Trade System in the United States." In *A History of the Book in America, vol. 4, Print in Motion: The Expansion of Publishing and Reading in the United States, 1880–1940*, edited by Carl F. Kaestle and Janice Radway, 56–77. Chapel Hill: University of North Carolina Press, 2009.

Winship, Michael. "The Transatlantic Book Trade and Anglo-American Culture in the Nineteenth Century." In *Reciprocal Influences. Literary Production, Distribution and Consumption in America*, edited by Steven Kind and Susan S. Williams, 98–122. Columbus: Ohio State University Press, 1999.

Wolf, Michaela, and Alexandra Fukari, ed. *Constructing a Sociology of Translation*. Amsterdam: John Benjamins Publishing Company, 2007.

Index

For Product Safety Concerns and Information please contact our EU
representative GPSR@taylorandfrancis.com
Taylor & Francis Verlag GmbH, Kaufingerstraße 24, 80331 München, Germany